The Powers of Distance

❖

The Powers of Distance

COSMOPOLITANISM AND
THE CULTIVATION OF DETACHMENT

✤

AMANDA ANDERSON

PRINCETON UNIVERSITY PRESS

PRINCETON AND OXFORD

Copyright © 2001 by Princeton University Press
Published by Princeton University Press, 41 William Street,
Princeton, New Jersey 08540
In the United Kingdom: Princeton University Press,
3 Market Place, Woodstock, Oxfordshire OX20 1SY
All Rights Reserved

Library of Congress Cataloging in Publication Data
Anderson, Amanda
The powers of distance : cosmopolitanism and the
cultivation of detachment / Amanda Anderson.
p.   cm.
Includes bibliographical references and index.
ISBN 0-691-07496-8 (acid-free paper) —
ISBN 0-691-07497-6 (pbk. : acid-free paper)
1. English literature—19th century—History and criticism.
2. Literature and society—Great Britain—History—
19th century.   3. Alienation (Social psychology) in
literature.   4. Postmodernism (Literature)—Great Britain.
5. Modernism (Literature)—Great Britain.
6. Difference (Psychology) in literature.   7. Internationalism
in literature.   8. Irony in literature.   I. Title.

This book has been composed in Caledonia

Printed on acid-free paper: ∞

www.pup.princeton.edu

Printed in the United States of America

1   3   5   7   9   10   8   6   4   2

1   3   5   7   9   10   8   6   4   2
(Pbk.)

For Allen, Jackson, and Emily

❖ Contents ❖

❖ Acknowledgments ❖

This book has benefited immeasurably from the responses of colleagues and friends, many of whom read significant portions of the manuscript. I thank James Eli Adams, Phil Barrish, Nina Baym, Michael Bérubé, Patrick Brantlinger, James Buzard, Julie Carlson, Cathy Caruth, Jerry Christensen, Barry Faulk, Peter Garrett, Dilip Goankar, Giles Gunn, Danny Hack, Simon Joyce, Deidre Lynch, Alan Lui, Bill Maxwell, Andrew Miller, Carol Neely, Melissa Orlie, Don Pease, Adela Pinch, Yopie Prins, Harry Shaw, David Thomas, and Joe Valente. I am especially grateful to Bruce Robbins and George Levine, both of whom carefully read the entire manuscript as well as several related essays. I cannot possibly repay my debt to my deeply cherished friend Jeff Nunokawa, whose rigorous readings of these chapters have been a major contribution to my thinking. Among close and dear friends I am also lucky to count Janet Lyon, who has helped me with this project in numerous ways, not least through the example of her own work; Carine Melkom-Mardorossian, whose indefatigable ability to converse on all things has been a constant source of inspiration; and Jean Rhodes, whose keenness, wit, and superior companionship kept me going on many a windswept afternoon in Champaign, Illinois.

I also thank my new colleagues at Johns Hopkins for their engaged and challenging responses to early materials, and for making Hopkins such a stimulating place to work: Sharon Cameron, Bill Connolly, Frances Ferguson, Michael Fried, Jonathan Goldberg, Neil Hertz, Ruth Leys, Walter Michaels, Michael Moon, Steve Nichols, Ron Paulson, John Plotz, Robert Reid-Pharr, Sasha Torres, Irene Tucker, and Judith Walkowitz. I am particularly grateful to Sharon Cameron for her careful reading of an earlier version of the chapter on Arnold.

This project was supported in its early stages by the William and Flora Hewlitt Foundation and the University of Illinois Research Board; a leave from the English Department of Johns Hopkins University enabled me to complete the manuscript. I am also grateful to my editor, Mary Murrell, for her persistent interest in the project and for her judgment and speediness. I also thank audiences at the following universities, where portions were presented: Indiana University, Dartmouth College, the University of Texas at Austin, Florida State University, SUNY-Buffalo, the University of Michigan, Harvard University, UC Santa Barbara, and Emory University.

A previous version of chapter 4 appeared as "George Eliot and the Jewish Question," *The Yale Journal of Criticism* 10 (1997): 39–61; the first section of chapter 1 is excerpted from "The Temptations of Aggrandized Agency: Feminist Histories and the Horizon of Modernity," *Victorian Studies* 43 (2000): 43–65.

Without the support of my family, this book would not have been possible. For their love and companionship, I thank Sara Anderson, Helen Anderson, Howard Goodfriend, Philip and Patricia Anderson, Warren and Alice Hance, Lindsay Kosnik, and Chris Kosnik. My deepest thanks to my immediate family: to Allen Hance, my cherished companion and closest critic; to our amazing son, Jackson, conversationalist *extraordinaire*; and to our darling new daughter, Emily, all sweetness and determination.

Baltimore, Maryland

The Powers of Distance

Forms of Detachment

In an 1856 *Westminster Review* article entitled "The Natural History of German Life," George Eliot considers the ethnographical studies of Wilhelm Riehl, a German scholar committed to the comprehensive analysis of the history and character of social classes and ethnic groups in his home country. Eliot has great admiration for Riehl and uses the occasion to formulate the principles and methodologies that should inform any properly historical social science and any authentic realism in art. In large measure, Eliot pursues this aim indirectly, through a critique of those cultural representations—scholarly, scientific, parliamentary, or aesthetic—that bespeak a detached or distanced relation to social life. For Eliot, such detachment results variously in distortion, idealization, or moral insensitivity. Riehl's ethnography, by contrast, serves as a crucial antidote to abstract or speculative forms of knowledge. Eliot sees in Riehl an ideal participant-observer whose conclusions are appropriately derived from "gradually amassed observations" accrued through "immediate intercourse with the people." Devoted to inductive method, shorn of prejudice, Riehl is, "first of all, a pedestrian, and only in the second place a political author."[1]

Ranging over a wide array of topics and cultural spheres, Eliot's essay serves as an illuminating example of what I argue is a prevalent Victorian preoccupation with distinctly modern practices of detachment, a preoccupation characterized by ambivalence and uncertainty about what the significance and consequences of such practices might be. Indeed, despite its initial strong critique of distance and abstraction, Eliot's essay overall manifests both subtlety and ambiguity when considering the purpose and consequences of cultivated distance, whether it be conceived in scientific, philosophical, or aesthetic terms. Throughout the piece Eliot repeatedly distinguishes among the specific qualities of detachment that attend different modern practices, endorsing some, criticizing others. For example, while Goethe's assiduous antiphilistinism negates all parochial points of view and thereby "helps us to rise to a lofty point of observation, so that we may see

---

[1] George Eliot, "The Natural History of German Life," in *Selected Essays, Poems and Other Writings*, ed. A. S. Byatt and Nicholas Warren (Harmondsworth: Penguin, 1990), 127. Subsequent page number references will be cited parenthetically in the text.

things in their relative proportions," distanced viewpoints elsewhere permit only broad outlines that obscure the crucial realities of lived experience (138). This opposition between desirable and undesirable forms of detachment, I contend, exemplifies a more general tendency within Victorian cultural debate. An ideal of critical distance, itself deriving from the project of Enlightenment, lies behind many Victorian aesthetic and intellectual projects, including the emergent human sciences and allied projects of social reform; various ideals of cosmopolitanism and disinterestedness; literary forms such as omniscient realism and dramatic monologue; and the prevalent project of *Bildung*, or the self-reflexive cultivation of character, which animated much of Victorian ethics and aesthetics, from John Stuart Mill to Matthew Arnold and beyond. Yet at the same time many Victorians were wary of certain distancing effects of modernity, including the overvaluing and misapplication of scientific method as well as the forms of alienation and rootlessness that accompanied modern disenchantment, industrialization, and the globalization of commerce. As a result, many writers displayed a complex ambivalence toward the powers of modern distance, one that is legible, for example, in the opposing symbolism attaching to representative figures across the literature of the period. The dandy, the Jew, and the fallen woman, for example, respectively focused anxieties about ironic distance, rootlessness, and heightened exile, while the doctor, the writer, and the professional tended to represent the distinct promises of modernity: progressive knowledge, full comprehension of the social totality, and the possibilities of transformative self-understanding.

The Powers of Distance focuses on a core of writers and texts whose own landscapes of ambivalence reflect some of the culture's most deeply felt concerns about the promises and challenges of modernity. All of the writers that I consider—George Eliot, John Stuart Mill, Charlotte Brontë, Charles Dickens, Matthew Arnold, and Oscar Wilde—explore in a sustained way what it means to cultivate a distanced relation toward one's self, one's community, or those objects that one chooses to study or represent. While each writer manifests unique ways of conceptualizing detachment, and of distinguishing among its different forms, a series of recurrent questions animate Victorian writings about the distanced or impartial view. There are procedural and educational questions about how ideal forms of detachment might best be cultivated; there are philosophical questions about whether such procedures produce reliable forms of knowledge or valuable forms of art; there are psychological and cultural questions about whether individuals are even capable of transcending their interests, their pasts, and their racial heritage; and there are moral and political questions about whether forms of cultivated detachment uniformly promote the well-being or overall progress of individuals, communities, or nations.

In demarcating the cultivation of distance as a distinctive topos within Victorian culture, this study aims to enlarge and reframe current understandings of aesthetic and intellectual practice in nineteenth-century Britain. In large measure it seeks to do so simply by reconstructing the ways in which individual writers actively configured the series of questions I enumerate above. But there is also a polemical thrust to this book. Despite the ostensible neutrality in my repeated references to the self-division or ambivalence that characterizes Victorian thought on detachment, one of the central aims of this study is to take seriously the specific ways in which individual Victorians constructed their ideals, to consider not only the limits but also the distinctive virtues of their conceptions of enabling detachment. This approach goes against the grain of much recent work in literary and cultural studies, which follows the critique of Enlightenment in its insistence that cultural ideals of rationality or critical distance are inevitably erected as the exclusive province of elite groups. It is certainly the case, as my analyses will confirm, that valorized forms of detachment within Victorian culture are often allotted to those empowered by virtue of their gender, their race, their nationality, or their social position. What the philosopher Thomas Nagel memorably dubbed "the view from nowhere" is always actually a view from somewhere, a somewhere determined not only by the social and cultural identity of the author but also by historical and cultural horizons more broadly construed.[2] Yet to call a practice of detachment situated is not quite the same thing as adopting a prevailing attitude of suspicion or dismissal toward it. Thus while I expose hierarchies and exclusions when they occur—and to the extent that they are visible to me—I resist those modes of analysis that too uniformly or precipitously discredit the very attempt to elaborate an ideal of critical distance. The phrase "the powers of distance" is therefore meant to register not only and not even predominantly those forms of domination, control, or management that we associate with specific modern forces such as instrumental reason or institutional surveillance: it is also meant to acknowledge the considerable gains achieved by the denaturalizing attitude toward norms and conventions that marks the project of the Enlightenment and its legacy. While I believe that detachment takes many different forms, and produces many different effects—beneficial, harmful, and indifferent—I defend the progressive potentiality of those modern

[2] Thomas Nagel, *The View from Nowhere* (New York: Oxford University Press, 1986).

practices that aim to objectify facets of human existence so as to better understand, criticize, and at times transform them. In defending detachment, however, I do not mean to suggest that absolute objectivity can be achieved, or that one ever fully or finally inhabits any given practice of detachment. When I refer to the cultivation of detachment, I am referring to the *aspiration* to a distanced view. Such aspirations take many different forms and are often envisioned as complex and ongoing self-critical practices. Indeed, many of the writers I examine conceived their ideals in terms of a dialectic between detachment and engagement, between a cultivated distance and a newly informed partiality.

As I have indicated, the promises and dangers of distance were cast not only in terms of their effects on impersonal intellectual, aesthetic, or political goals—they were understood as practices having an intimate and profound bearing on moral character. This may be the facet of Victorian detachment that is most foreign to our current ways of framing questions of identity, critique, and practice. Indeed, insofar as nineteenth-century judgments about distance were suffused with moral rhetoric, it was the result of a recurrent struggle to set characterological dimensions of detachment in some kind of legible relation to more impersonal practices of cultivated distance. This aim is at the heart of the Arnoldian conception of culture, for example, which yokes practices of disinterestedness to the cultivation of character, both drawing on and transforming the tradition of *Bildung*. But it takes negative forms as well, as for example when Dickens worries that the adoption of totalizing views, a practice integral to the project of omniscience, can prompt habits of suspicion that damage character. These characterological cultural formations can be seen as another version of the "moralized objectivities" that historian of science Lorraine Daston demonstrates as inherent to scientific development in the nineteenth century, although the forms of detachment in the realm of aesthetics and the human sciences do not typically subscribe to the ethos of extreme restraint and self-effacement that Daston finds in the natural sciences.[3] A persistent conjoining of ethical and methodological questions, however, marks speculation across the disparate

---

[3] See Lorraine Daston, "The Moral Economy of Science," *Osiris* 10 (1995): 3–24; Lorraine Daston and Peter Galison, "The Image of Objectivity," *Representations* 40 (1992): 81–128; and Lorraine Daston, "Objectivity and the Escape from Perspective," *Social Studies of Science* 22 (1992): 597–618. For a prominent twentieth-century instance of an approach that calls for the integration of ethos and method in social science, see Max Weber, "Science as a Vocation," in *From Max Weber: Essays in Sociology*, ed. H. H. Gerth and C. Wright Mills (New York: Oxford University Press, 1946), 129–56.

intellectual fields of science, social science, and art. George Levine's recent and forthcoming work on epistemology's dependency on narrative and its "moral urgencies" eloquently speaks to this broader nineteenth-century pattern, a pattern that informs my own analyses.[4]

As a key motif of the study, the issue of moral character lies behind my frequent privileging of the term *detachment* over any other broad rubric that might denote distance, objectivity, and dislocation. *Detachment* is meant to encompass not only science, critical reason, disinterestedness, and realism, but also a set of practices of the self, ranging from stoicism to cosmopolitanism to dandyism. While the choice of a single term to cover such disparate practices inevitably results in some unavoidable moments of compromised precision, I am convinced that the disadvantages are offset by the term's capacity to demonstrate the asserted connection, both within single writers and in the culture at large, between the personal and the impersonal, between character and intellectual practice, between ascesis and aesthetics. Flexibility of reference is also required precisely because the blurring of potentially discrete forms, terms, and concepts characterizes Victorian attempts to assert interrelations between moral and intellectual practices.

Victorian forms of detachment have been underexplored in recent criticism, for reasons very specific to our own current disciplinary conditions. To put the case most generally, and most tendentiously, an incoherence about detachment shadows much of contemporary debate in literary and cultural studies, with discernible effects on the study of historical cultural formations. On the one hand, pointed critiques of detachment have been generated across a broad spectrum of theories that influence current criticism. For example, within much materialist, feminist, poststructuralist, and identity-based criticism, claims to objectivity or reflective reason are seen as illusory, pretentious, hierarchical, and even violent; set against such claims, either implicitly or explicitly, are the opposing ideals of avowed situatedness, embodiedness, particularity, and contingency. On the other hand, within some of these same bodies of criticism, detachment simultaneously and often surreptitiously operates as the negative freedom that permits critique, exposure, irony, or parody. The situation is especially acute within feminist theory, where aestheticist or constructionist tendencies vie with longstanding critiques of those conceptions of disembodied or detached subjectivity that seem to deny or exclude the body, the feminine, and the particular. On the one hand, that is, the feminist project routinely takes a dim and distanced

---

[4] George Levine, "The Narrative of Scientific Epistemology," *Narrative* 5 (1997): 227–51; and George Levine, *Dying to Know: Scientific Epistemology and Narrative in Nineteenth-Century England* (Chicago: University of Chicago Press, forthcoming).

view of cultural representations of femininity, rigorously demystifying their ideological force and exposing them as mere constructs; on the other hand, however, the feminist project often seems to understand women to have a more immediate and authentic relation to experience and the body, and it does so in part by casting aspersions on "masculine" stances of objectivity or detachment.[5]

I take up the conditions of contemporary theory more fully later in the introduction and return to them throughout the study, but the incoherence I identify here has a crucial effect on historical studies that I want to isolate at the outset. Insofar as critiques of detachment have been directed toward Victorian ideals of science, objectivity, or reason, they remain extrinsic approaches fundamentally uninterested in exploring the ways in which Victorians themselves grappled with the issue of detachment.[6] A hermeneutics of suspicion considers investments in critical distance as self-damning, interpreting them as masked forms of power rather than as emergent practices that might themselves be the subject of ongoing critique. (This type of distinction will be key, for example, in chapter 4's rejection of many recent readings of *Daniel Deronda*.)[7] Even when they incorporate a compensatory insistence on moments of negative freedom or critical subversion, these hermeneutics still do not adequately address the question of how precisely the Victorians conceptualized critique. *The Powers of Distance* tries to present alternatives to such interpretive tendencies, and I explore a particularly salient set of methodological impasses in the following chapter, when I examine

---

[5] For a symptomatic attempt to finesse this dual relation to detachment through an argument that women hold an "eccentric" position that places them both within and without the culture, see Teresa de Lauretis, *Technologies of Gender: Essays on Theory, Film, and Fiction* (Bloomington: Indiana University Press, 1987).

[6] For an example of such an approach applied to Eliot, see Daniel Cottom, *Social Figures: George Eliot, Social History, and Literary Representation* (Minneapolis: University of Minnesota Press, 1987). For an example of such an approach applied to omniscience in Dickens, see D. A. Miller, *The Novel and the Police* (Berkeley: University of California Press, 1988). For discussion of such approaches applied to Arnold, see chapter 4 of this study. For feminist critiques of scientific objectivity, including specific discussion of the nineteenth century, see Mary Jacobus, Evelyn Fox Keller, and Sally Shuttleworth, eds., *Body/Politics: Women and the Discourses of Science* (New York: Routledge, 1990).

[7] For an eloquent critique of the hermeneutics of suspicion as it has informed much recent work in literary studies, see Eve Kosofsky Sedgwick, "Paranoid Reading and Reparative Reading; or, You're So Paranoid, You Probably Think This Introduction Is about You," in *Novel Gazing: Queer Readings in Fiction*, ed. Eve Kosofsky Sedgwick (Durham: Duke University Press, 1997), 1–37.

feminist approaches to Victorian culture. For the moment I want simply to point out that the prevailing approaches to detachment flatten out the past, ultimately forestalling any real analysis of the ways in which Victorian authors themselves actively and even obsessively engaged questions about critical detachment, questions that lie at the heart of their struggle with the conditions of modernity. Studies that bracket or simplify the question of detachment at the theoretical or methodological levels fail to examine this important dimension of the culture.

Victorian Perspectives

The cultivation of distance informed many intellectual and aesthetic practices in the Victorian era, including ethnography, sociology, and novelistic discourse, to name some of the most prominent. By way of introduction, I will explore the approach to detachment in two Victorian polymaths, George Eliot and John Stuart Mill, both of whom were closely involved in debates over the development of various sciences of the human. Eliot is particularly salient here, insofar as her famous essay on Riehl relates the project of the novel to new ethnographic and protosociological methods. Her essay is structured by a series of distinctions that will recur throughout this study, between situated and "objective" knowledge, between science and letters, between false abstraction and the cultivation of self-reflexivity. It begins with a vivid juxtaposition meant to illuminate the limits of those forms of knowledge that are not authorized by direct experience. Remarking that "it is an interesting branch of psychological observation to note the images that are habitually associated with abstract or collective terms," Eliot contrasts the images that the word *railways* might evoke in a person "not highly locomotive" with those of a person who "had successively the experience of a 'navvy', an engineer, a traveller, a railway director and shareholder, and a landed proprietor in treaty with a railway company" (107). While the former would imagine only a series of truncated images deriving from limited experience (a standard train schedule, the station near home, a known stretch of rail), it is probable, according to Eliot, that the range of images presented to the latter "would include all the essential facts in the existence and relations of the *thing*" (107; Eliot's emphasis).

One key distinction that Eliot derives from her example is that between truly comprehensive knowledge and baseless generalities. Multiple forms of experience produce a thorough knowledge based on an aggregate of perspectives and interests, but limited knowledge allows, and even prompts, immodest conclusions and complacent views from nowhere:

> Now it is possible for the first-mentioned personage to entertain very expanded views as to the multiplication of railways in the abstract, and their ultimate function in civilization. He may talk of a vast network of railways stretching over the globe, of future 'lines' in Madagascar, and elegant refreshment-rooms in the Sandwich Islands, with none the less glibness because his distinct conceptions on the subject do not extend beyond his one station and his indefinite length of tram-road. But it is evident that if we want a railway to be made, or its affairs to be managed, this man of wide views and narrow observation will not serve our purpose. (107–8)

The ironic view taken here of sweeping or distant views is reiterated in various ways throughout the essay. Generally, Eliot manifests skepticism about any abstract theory that remains unchecked by lived experience and direct knowledge. Direct acquaintance is most needed in the representation of social life, where abstractions, distortions, and idealizations plague both theory and art. Eliot acerbically faults "the splendid conquests of modern generalization," chief among which is the subsumption of dense social life to "economical science" and "algebraic equations" (111, 112). In a related argument, she asserts that most artistic representations of working people remain in thrall to "the influence of idyllic literature," bearing no relation to a "real knowledge of the People" (109, 112). By way of example, Eliot claims that it is only when haymakers are seen from a distance that they appear jocund, or happy, or that the scene itself appears "smiling" (109). "Approach nearer, and you will certainly find that haymaking time is a time for joking, especially if there are women among the labourers; but the coarse laugh that bursts out every now and then, and expresses the triumphant taunt, is as far as possible from your conception of idyllic merriment" (109).

In contrasting the distortions of distance with a reliable understanding based on situated observation and informed experience, Eliot's critique of social knowledge focuses on inadequacies not simply of method or principle but also, and fundamentally, of stance. Eliot is interested in exposing the falsehoods that issue from acts of distancing, but she is equally interested in examining the psychological and social attitudes that accompany such detached and objectifying relations to the social world. In this, Eliot shares with many of her contemporaries a preoccupation with the distinctly moral dimensions or consequences of modern detachment. From a larger social standpoint, detachment will promote social policies insufficiently attuned to the precise conditions and needs of social groups, insofar as there is a commonality between the "thin" generalizations prompted by narrow experience and the overzealous application of abstract science to human life. But for Eliot acts of distancing produce a more primary effect, which is psychological: the underdevelopment of the moral faculties, particularly the faculty of sympathy. Only the close observation of situated subjects activates the sympathies of the scholar who studies them, and only forms of representation that duplicate that close observation activate the sympathies of the reader. For Eliot, this problem is related to the problem of idealization in realist art, which she likewise construes as a function of distance and deficient experience. Idyllic portrayals of the working class derail the authentic project of art, which is precisely to prompt the development of our moral faculties and the enlargement of our experience: "The greatest benefit we owe to the artist, whether painter, poet, or novelist, is the extension of our sympathies. . . . Art is the nearest thing to life; it is a mode of amplifying experience and extending our contact with our fellow-men beyond the bounds of our personal lot" (110).

According to Lorraine Daston, during the nineteenth century meticulous procedures of close scientific observation formed part of complex moral economies; what has appeared to some later commentators as a bid for strict amoral neutrality was actually a developed and disciplined practice conceived in the most stern of moral terms: as duty, restraint, and self-command; as suppression of the personal, idiosyncratic, or local in favor of the communicable, the sharable, and the universal. For Daston, there is no way to separate those forms of objectivity that emerged in the nineteenth century from their moral self-conception, so fully interwoven and co-implicating are they. The ultimate moral ideal underlying the nineteenth-century scientific development of aperspectival and mechanical objectivity was sociability: by making appeal in the one case to a "featureless observer," which combats all idiosyncrasies or particular characteristics of individuals, and in the other to a mode of measurement that would expunge all tendencies to judge or interpret, the findings of science would become fully transmissible to any member of the international scientific collectivity. Active, vigilant self-suppression was fundamental to these procedures, which paradoxically required stringent personal practices on the part of individual scientists so as to efface all individuality. And scientists in part defined their vigilant practices of self-suppression against what they perceived as the indulgent individualism of the artist: "L'art, c'est moi; la science, c'est nous," in the words of Claude Bernard.[8]

[8] Quoted in Daston, "The Moral Economy of Science," 22.

Daston's research on the history of scientific objectivity can be usefully contrasted to Eliot's essay on the scientific or idealizing treatment of human life. On the one hand, Eliot's views are informed by the same deep integration of ethos and method. Intellectual methods, whether employed by art or by social science, are seen to reflect and produce distinctive ethical effects, at both the individual and the societal level. By Daston's account aperspectival objectivity produces forms of impartiality that will transcend barriers to communicability and advance collective knowledge; by Eliot's account sympathetic observation will likewise produce a form of understanding that is at once reliable and ethical. Of course, Eliot differs from Daston's nineteenth-century scientists in her concern with the effects that scientific method may have on the study of those objects that constitute the domain of the social sciences and their allied arts, namely, human beings and their multiple forms of life. While Daston and Peter Galison observe that "the history of various forms of objectivity might be told as how, why, and when various forms of subjectivity came to seen as dangerously subjective," Eliot insists that the moral story is not complete unless we carefully examine how, why, and when various forms of *objectivity* came to be seen as dangerously *objective*.[9] Daston shows how the rigorous cultivation of objectivity in the natural sciences was linked to individual moral ascesis as well as a larger ideal of sociability; Eliot shows how the stance of detached analysis undermines the individual's moral character and responsiveness, and also produces false forms of knowledge. The ideal of participant observation in Riehl is then presented by Eliot as a solution to both the moral and epistemological consequences of this dangerous detachment.

But it is crucial to realize that Eliot mounts her criticism not simply to promote Riehl's participant-observation, but also to sharpen her own contrasting ideals of critical distance. For despite her endorsement of situated knowledges, and despite her critique of abstract economic theory and statistics, Eliot both relies on and makes direct appeal to specific forms of distanced understanding. Her opening example illustrating the importance of lived experience secures its authority through appeal to "an interesting branch of psychological observation," thereby rendering experience itself an object of scientific study. An act of distancing is also implicit in the ideal of pedestrian observation, which brings a sharpened critical distance to its humble travels. And, not insignificantly, Eliot's withering irony throughout the essay works persistently to place her objects of critique at a proper distance. Beyond this, Eliot appeals to the wide and the long view in her con-

[9] Daston and Galison, "The Image of Objectivity," 82.

ception of natural history, which studies the evolution of social life in its multifarious forms. This viewpoint is something more than the aggregate of perspectives that combine to produce a full range of experience in the case of the railways example. While "wide views" are baseless if spun out of "narrow observation," they are requisite to a comprehensive understanding of social life, especially if one is to honor the particular phase of development that the peasant or worker inhabits, or to map the ethnicities and classes that constitute any national entity. Natural history in fact requires practitioners of "sufficient moral and intellectual breadth" (112).

The conditions of modernity, moreover, require certain practices of reflection able to repair the dislocations wrought by nontraditional or defamiliarizing forms of life. Eliot's thinking here manifests a complex web of philosophical and political investments. Much of Eliot's discussion of the peasant and working classes is driven by conservativism, insofar as it cautions against the untimely application of abstract revolutionary theory to groups of people who are not advanced enough to adopt its formulas. When speaking of the German peasant's devotion to custom, Eliot in fact argues that the peasant is not ready for the institutional historical changes—codified governance and the rule of law—that have enveloped him: "He finds himself in a new element before an apparatus for breathing in it is developed in him" (122). But modernity's disruptions of smooth organic development can also be overcome, in the case of cultivated individuals, by ennobling practices of reflection, as becomes evident in Eliot's comparison of England with Europe:

> The nature of European men has its roots intertwined with the past, and can only be developed by allowing those roots to remain undisturbed while the process of development is going on, until that perfect ripeness of the seed which carries with it a life independent of the root. This vital connexion with the past is much more vividly felt on the Continent than in England, where we have to recall it by an effort of memory and reflection. (128–29)

This line of argument functions in large measure to discredit revolutionary movements on the Continent while at the same time articulating an ideal of reflection fully dissociated from revolutionary critique, as negative and dislocating conditions of modernity create the possibility for practices of reflection that enrich the individual precisely by spanning historical and cultural distances. For even as Eliot loosely associates peasant life with vital connection to the past and town life with an overly cultivated tendency toward disconnection and abstraction, the act of recollection is conceived as a valuable one, and the peasant's entrenchment in custom carries a negative valence precisely insofar as it is unreasoning, blind, and lacking in self-consciousness. This valuing of a higher-order self-consciousness is also manifest in Eliot's critique of philistinism, a critique that directly precedes her praise of Goethe's "lofty point of observation":

> [T]he *Philister* is the personification of the spirit which judges everything from a lower point of view than the subject demands—which judges the affairs of the parish from the egotistic or purely personal point of view—which judges the affairs of the nation from the parochial point of view, and does not hesitate to measure the merits of the universe from the human point of view. (137)

In other words, Eliot's critique of abstraction and valuing of rootedness ambiguously coexists with a certain promotion of cultivated detachment, which is placed in the service of a broader historical consciousness and an ever-widening aspiration toward cosmopolitanism. Even as the opportunities of modernity result from its negative conditions, they produce a positive result and a positive recognition of the very distance that otherwise issues in a mood of lament.

Such ambiguity is not so much outright contradiction as the impulse to assert distinctions of value. Modernity must be managed, in Eliot's view, so as to curtail its excesses and fulfill its most progressive potential. This orientation produces subtle dialectical thinking, yet there are some distinctly conservative, even reactionary, dimensions to it. Eliot is drawn, like other members of her culture, to manage her own ambivalence by mapping her distinctions onto differences of class, race, and gender; her own anxieties about the irretrievability of traditions, for example, are countered by assertions that peasants or women are natural preservers of tradition. Speaking of a Slavonic race that lives among the Germans and experiences German customs and forms of government as "antagonistic to their national exclusiveness," Eliot writes, "but the *wives* and *mothers* here, as elsewhere, are a conservative influence, and the habits temporarily laid aside in the outer world are recovered by the fireside" (115). Even as Eliot promotes a reflective relation to tradition more generally, she suggests that the conservative role played by hearth and home is a healthful one, enabling "recovery." The women's stabilizing powers counter the effects of dislocation here, as elsewhere in Eliot they will serve to steady a more self-conscious embrace of modern opportunities by the heroic masculine subject.

Eliot also makes more direct, and more tenable, distinctions between specific intellectual and aesthetic practices. For example, she contends that a comprehensive social science must aspire to encompass and apply the principles and methodology of the life sciences (understood here as descriptive rather than explanatory disciplines) rather than stopping short at models derived from the more abstract and predictive sciences:

> [S]ocial science, while it has departments which in their fundamental generality correspond to mathematics and physics, namely, those grand and simple generalizations which trace out the inevitable march of the human race as a whole, and, as a ramification of these, the laws of economical science, has also, in the departments of government and jurisprudence, which embrace the conditions of social life in all their complexity, what may be called its Biology, carrying us on to innumerable special phenomena which outlie the sphere of science, and belong to Natural History. (130)

Somewhat differently, art for Eliot is capable of supplementing abstract forms of knowledge by promoting a self-overcoming that enables attention to others, and thereby lays the ground for moral evolution: "Appeals founded on generalizations and statistics require a sympathy ready-made, a moral sentiment already in activity; but a picture of human life such as a great artist can give, surprises even the trivial and the selfish into that attention to what is apart from themselves, which may be called the raw material of moral sentiment" (110).

In her reflections on the proper way to observe social bodies, Eliot participates in a more pervasive cultural concern with the nature, meaning, and effects of the various sciences of the human. Her endorsement of Riehl's procedure of pedestrian observation, coupled with her calls for disinterestedness and sympathy, is an example of what Christopher Herbert has identified as the conflicted postures of ethnographic subjectivity, which begin to appear in the nineteenth century and continue to inform the development of anthropology in the twentieth century.[10] Such conflicted postures attempt to mediate between sympathetic immersion and detached analysis and judgment. One early and remarkably self-aware Victorian instance of such an ethnographic approach is Harriet Martineau's prescient sociological treatise on travel writing, *How to Observe Manners and Morals* (1838). In this text, as Herbert has demonstrated, Martineau espouses an ethnographic method that privileges sympathetic understanding and eschews prejudice yet simultaneously makes appeal to a universal moral principle of charity so as both to ground the principle of sympathy and to evade the potential imperative to sympathize with cruel or violent customs.

---

[10] Christopher Herbert, *Culture and Anomie: Ethnographic Imagination in the Nineteenth Century* (Chicago: University of Chicago Press, 1991).

For Eliot, the project of ethnography is closely linked to the project of the novel, both in its ethico-methodological ideals and in its need to define itself against negative forms of detachment. The close connection between these two ways of making sense of one's own culture is evident in Herbert's book, which explores novelistic versions of ethnography; it has been explored even more extensively in James Buzard's recent work on the novel as a form of proto-anthropology.[11] Yet while ethnography serves as a central cultural site for such conflicted approaches to detachment, it is, as the broad reach of Eliot's essay shows us, only one arena where the powers of distance become a site of intense moral, intellectual, and psychological interrogation. John Stuart Mill is another Victorian whose thinking exhibits a subtle and multi-faceted approach to modern detachment. It is useful to contrast his thinking to Eliot's by way of general introduction, insofar as his investments in the fields of ethics and political philosophy prompt a defense of impartiality and neutrality, yet his apprehensions about liberalism's limits bring into play a similar impulse to counter the deracinating effects of modernity.

Mill's elaboration of an ideal of impartiality appears in key passages in *On Liberty* and *Utilitarianism*. In a famous passage from the latter essay, Mill defends his theory against those who claim that utilitarianism, by virtue of its embrace of eudaemonism, privileges selfish interests above all others:

> I must again repeat, what the assailants of utilitarianism seldom have the justice to acknowledge, that the happiness which forms the utilitarian standard of what is right in conduct, is not the agent's own happiness, but that of all concerned. As between his own happiness and that of others, utilitarianism requires him to be as strictly impartial as a disinterested and benevolent spectator.[12]

An impartiality tinged with sympathy is for Mill not only an ethical but also an intellectual ideal. In *On Liberty* and in "Bentham," for example, Mill construes the search for truth as a process utterly dependent on the capacity to comprehend and consider opposing points of view. Bentham's thought

---

[11] James Buzard, *"Anywhere's Nowhere": Fictions of Autoethnography in the United Kingdom* (Princeton: Princeton University Press, forthcoming); James Buzard, "Translation and Tourism: Scott's *Waverley* and the Rendering of Culture," *The Yale Journal of Criticism* 8 (1995): 31–59; James Buzard, "'Anywhere's Nowhere': Bleak House as Autoethnography," *The Yale Journal of Criticism* 12 (1999): 7–39.

[12] John Stuart Mill, "Utilitarianism," in John Stuart Mill and Jeremy Bentham, *Utilitarianism and Other Essays*, ed. Alan Ryan (Harmondsworth: Penguin, 1987), 288. Subsequent page number references will be made parenthetically in the text.

was limited, his truth could only be incomplete and partial, not because he erred within the terms of his own stringent method, but because he "failed in deriving light from other minds," a capacity that for Mill is fundamentally linked to sympathy and imagination.[13]

By and large, Mill privileges the capacity to achieve distance from one's own perspective and interests, conceiving the movement toward truth as the result of a continuously enacted impartiality on the part of the individual. This approach involves, however, a complex dialectic of detachment and engagement: ethical and epistemological progress is achieved through the flexible agency of sympathetic understanding. In this Mill's thought shares similarities with the method of *Verstehen* elaborated by Dilthey and the ideal of value-neutrality elaborated by Weber. There is in fact a striking progression of ideas about interests and passions in *On Liberty*. When discussing the ideal of public debate, Mill insists that ideas only remain alive when they constitute a form of "living belief"; doctrines that no longer inspire the active and articulate devotion of their adherents devolve into dead dogma, contributing to a situation that vitiates the intellectual and moral condition of society. In order for individuals properly to develop their own ideas and convictions, Mill argues, they must fully consider a range of opposing arguments. This position is similar to the critique of Bentham. But he stresses here that the process of considering counterarguments should not be simply an intellectual or pedagogical exercise. Opposing views must, as Mill puts it, be brought "into real contact with [one's] own mind," and this can only occur if one "[hears] them from persons who actually believe them."[14] If one fails to develop one's ideas in this manner, then one does not genuinely "possess" the truth:

> Ninety-nine in a hundred of what are called educated men are in this condition; even of those who can argue fluently for their opinions. Their conclusion may be true, but it might be false for anything they know: they have never thrown themselves into the mental position of those who think differently from them, and considered what such persons may have to say; and consequently they do not, in any proper sense of the word, know the doctrine which they themselves profess. (42–3)

[13] John Stuart Mill, "Bentham," in Mill and Bentham, *Utilitarianism and Other Essays*, 146. Subsequent page number references will be made parenthetically in the text.

[14] John Stuart Mill, "On Liberty," in *On Liberty and Other Essays*, ed. John Gray (Oxford: Oxford University Press, 1991), 42. Subsequent page number references will be made parenthetically in the text.

The effect of such a situation is detrimental to the understanding, and in this passage truth does not exist—or exist in any way that matters—apart from the process by which it is understood and developed. Mill is also addressing here what for him is a related question of character. While the thrust of this particular discussion has to do with the detrimental effect that uncritically formed belief has on the cause of truth, it also speaks to the moral and intellectual damage to individuals who acquire their beliefs in this inadequate manner. Thus while Mill disparages beliefs that issue out of mere interest or inflamed passion and insists on the impartial consideration of opposing beliefs, his concept of character lends moral dimension to what could appear to be a lifeless, detached, or mechanical process. In the same manner, in *Utilitarianism* spectatorship is given a moral dimension—benevolence— and impartiality becomes something that allows an improving process. Or, as Mill puts it later in *On Liberty* when returning to the importance of vital debate, "it is not on the impassioned partisan, it is on the calmer and more disinterested bystander, that this collision of opinions works its salutary effect" (58).

It is of course above all the categories of character and virtue that are foregrounded in Mill's immanent critique of the utilitarianism of Jeremy Bentham. Mill believed in and wanted to preserve the eudaemonistic principle underlying utilitarianism, the claim that human beings are motivated above all to pursue happiness, to increase their pleasure and decrease their pain. But he felt that Bentham's narrow formulation of self-interest failed to give this principle its proper scope and thereby prompted justifiable criticisms that utilitarianism held a reductive and ultimately dishonorable view of human nature. Mill faulted Bentham for failing to consider the fact that honor, integrity, and the cultivation of character can (and should) be key elements motivating the pursuit of happiness. For Mill, the only Benthamite concept that comes even close to such motives is "love of reputation," yet this motive is fatally limited in its subordination of honor to a more narrowly construed self-interest. Beyond this fundamental critique of Benthamism, Mill also asserts that "the cultivation of an ideal nobleness of will and conduct" should prevail over any other standard of happiness with which it comes into conflict (130). Indeed, if it does prevail, Mill asserts, then a higher standard of happiness will necessarily be advanced.

The significance of Mill's appeal to an impartiality conceived in characterological terms is that, like other elements in his thought, it brings a potentially value-neutral liberal pluralism, and a potentially thin version of procedural disinterestedness, within the orbit of a substantial conception of the good. In so doing, it counters what for Mill was a threatening aspect of the modernity whose political principles he otherwise did so much to advance. For while Mill's concern about the impact of mass society on political vitality is frequently emphasized, it is important to recognize that Mill was also deeply concerned with the attenuation of attachments and the loss of whole ways of life, even as he promoted the autonomous authorization of belief and personal liberties. In discussing, in the essay on Coleridge, the conditions of permanence required for any form of political society, Mill partly resolves this tension by asserting that it is possible to feel loyalty and attachment to the democratic principles of "individual freedom and political and social equality."[15] He in fact sees democracy as the form of political attachment most likely to prevail in modern times. But significantly, Mill adds a further and related condition of permanence that retroactively seems to imply that attachment to freedom does not constitute a sufficiently binding element for modern polities. Much closer in character to nationalism, what Mill describes as "a strong and active principle of cohesion among the members of the same community or state" involves feelings of common interest, sympathy, and a sense of "oneness" with one's fellow people (195). Mill directly dissociates this notion from "nationality in any vulgar sense of the term," yet it is clear that he believes that a traditional sense of community must provide ballast to the principles of liberalism and a counterforce to the centrifugal energy of *Gesellschaft* (195).

For Mill, national cohesion and individual character provide the counterweight to those consequences of cultivated detachment that most worry him: the atomizing effects of individualism and the impersonal, value-neutral tendencies of impartiality. Nonvulgar attachment and cultivated virtue are asserted in face of the fear that his own age is one of mere "transition," debilitatingly given over to critique and disaffiliation. So deeply felt is this historical condition, and its attendant dangers, that Mill at times will seem seriously to compromise his own liberalism. Looking forward in the *Autobiography* to a future "which shall unite the best qualities of the critical with the best qualities of the organic periods," Mill imagines a world in which thought is free but beliefs are "deeply engraven on the feelings by early education and general unanimity of sentiment."[16] In a similar vein, Mill sometimes reconceives the arduous, dialogical search for truth as a larger historical dialectic whereby opposing truths are gradually brought

[15] John Stuart Mill, "Coleridge," in Mill and Bentham, *Utilitarianism and Other Essays*, 194. Subsequent page number references will be made parenthetically in the text.

[16] John Stuart Mill, *Autobiography*, ed. Jack Stillinger (Boston: Houghton Mifflin, 1969), 100.

into harmony with one another. But to a significant degree Mill seeks to redress the dangers of detachment through appeal to the cultivated practices of individuals, thereby locating the correction of modernity's excesses in the refinement of its own processes of ongoing reflexivity. Here what cushions the negative critique of tradition or custom is an imagined process whereby the newly defamiliarizing principle of happiness will become, paradoxically, actively habitual. For Mill, it is not enough simply to demonstrate the truth or cogency of the fundamental doctrines of utilitarianism or liberalism—they must become a way of life. Securing a way of life requires education, training, and forms of self-cultivation. These are, in their most noble forms, a set of willed practices that become habitual. In this manner, Mill imagines a re-embedding of those principles first brought to light through a rigorous examination and distantiation of embedded custom.

Eliot and Mill are two thinkers who, despite their apprehensions, emphasize the potentialities of modern powers of distance, even when those powers are linked to negative conditions of modernity: dislocation, alienation, estrangement. There are significant differences in their thinking, however. Eliot is in many instances a more conservative thinker, one who places reflective practices in the service of retrieving tradition. By contrast, Mill wants to give modern practices the force of tradition, and he tries to imagine ways in which this might be done. Both thinkers, however, share the view that the historical condition of modernity brings with it challenges, dangers, and opportunities. And in their promotion of positive ideals of cosmopolitan and self-critical practice, Mill and Eliot can be contrasted to Victorian writers whose dominant impulse is to elevate modes of life and work that recover a lost, prereflective unity. Such alternate routes are evident in John Ruskin's appeal to the Gothic stoneworker's unity of thought and action; in William Morris's attempt to reunite art and labor through an ideal of craft; or in Thomas Carlyle's invocation of a dawning spiritual affirmation that would replace the pathological modern condition of heightened self-consciousness. In these writers, and across many Victorian appeals to medieval traditions, modern detachment is largely construed in negative terms: as debilitating alienation from organic forms of life; as a sickly privileging of rationality over creativity and spirituality; and as the baleful psychological effect of increasing materialism.

In the chapters that follow, I explore the Victorian topos of detachment by means of five exemplary instances. Each chapter focuses on a defined cultural problematic or issue and draws out the response to that issue by a single author. The methodology is selective rather than exhaustive, aiming not to produce a detailed historical narrative but rather to comprehend the character of five significant and considered responses to modern practices of detachment, in a manner similar to the one I have adopted in discussing Eliot and Mill. Chapter 1 begins with a reconsideration of the relation between Victorian ideals of detachment and ideologies of gender. I contend that recent feminist cultural analysis of the Victorian period has failed adequately to describe the multiple ways in which Victorians conceived of feminine critical consciousness. Even in their most sophisticated Foucauldian and Bourdieuvean forms, feminist approaches construe Victorian mythologies of femininity too narrowly, restricting their focus to the diffusive power of "the angel in the house," and then assimilating her force or influence to forms of modern power that operate unreflectively through human subjects. While feminist paradigms have contributed significantly to our understanding of the ways that cultures assign the capacity for detachment exclusively to male subjects, they have been less successful in identifying distinctive forms of feminine detachment, or in moving beyond a negative conception of detachment as the violent and illusory denial of one's location in the world and one's physical being. I bring these issues to bear upon an analysis of Charlotte Brontë's *Villette*, a novel that can be read as a complex rumination on practices of feminine detachment, from the surveillance of Mme. Beck, to the impersonality of Mrs. Bretton, to the cool observations and thwarted stoicism of the narrator, Lucy Snowe.

The three chapters that follow concentrate on a series of authors whose understanding of detachment is intricately related to ideas about nationalism and cosmopolitanism. These chapters challenge the assumption that nationalistic or imperialistic ideologies persistently prevail in the work of nineteenth-century writers, establishing the pertinence of cosmopolitan ideals to any full consideration of Victorian understandings of race, nation, and empire. While cosmopolitanism can in certain key instances be shown to support nationalism and imperialism, and while its own elitist and narrowly European forms must be acknowledged, it still often gives voice, within the Victorian context, to a reflective interrogation of cultural norms. As I argue in chapter 2, Dickens's *Little Dorrit* in fact goes some way toward advancing a radical cosmopolitanism over and against European conceptions of the cultivated traveler and the Grand Tour, even as it seems to hold up modest affirmation of duty and communities of manageable scale as its informing ideals.

Dickens's ambivalent relation to radical critique stems from his sense that the practice of omniscience, as a suspicious and detached view required for mapping hierarchies of power, threatens to corrode moral character even as it produces the illuminations of critical insight. His attribution of a psychological moral dimension to larger intellectual and aesthetic practices is thus a negative version, as I suggested earlier, of Matthew Arnold's own vexed espousal of disinterestedness as a vocation. Chapter 3 reconsiders Arnold's famous critical ideal, paying heed to an underrecognized aspect of Arnold's encounter with modernity. Across his proliferation of forms of detachment—from scientific objectivity to cosmopolitanism to disinterestedness—Arnold consistently attempts to conceive of detachment as morally ennobling, and to argue that achievements of impersonality rely on the most finely tuned of historical, social, and personal conditions. While Arnold's ideal of detachment is neither particularly progressive nor even plausible, I argue for the importance of this reading of Arnold to any genealogy of Victorian detachment, especially insofar as the ideal of enacted impersonality places Arnold in a closer relation to Pater and Wilde, challenges the idea that he espouses an abstract universalism, and provides an altered context for considering the contemporary vogue of Foucault's aesthetics of existence.

George Eliot's contribution to Victorian thinking about cultivated detachment is manifest across her fiction and critical prose, but it achieves its fullest expression in her last completed novel, *Daniel Deronda*. In chapter 4, I argue that Daniel's postconventional cultivation of partiality and ethnic affiliation gives voice to a reconstructed cosmopolitan nationalism rather than, as is often argued, a flight from modernity into organic traditionalism. In the process, I place Eliot's novel within the tradition of English and Continental thinking on the Jewish Question, which obsessively considers questions of affiliation and disaffiliation, tradition and modernity, belonging and detachment. Foregrounding Deronda's reflective and gradual embrace of an openended Jewish identity, Eliot's novel refuses the prevailing tendency to associate the Jew with static traditionalism on the one hand, and hypermodern rootlessness, or radical detachment, on the other. At the same time, however, the novel's portrayal of Daniel's mother, who dwells in self-imposed exile from the project of cultivated partiality that defines the hero's life mission, reveals Eliot's inability to embrace the possibility that one might actively and productively choose a persistent detachment from tradition or cultural affiliation. It is no accident, moreover, that Eliot remains most vexed by a feminine form of radical rootlessness, insofar as ideal womanhood for her underwrites the bonds of family, community, and nation that form the object of reflexive processes of affiliation and endorsement.

Chapter 5 concludes the study with a discussion of Oscar Wilde, the most prominent representative of the late-Victorian celebration of irony, dandyism, and aestheticism—precisely those forms of detachment that promoted the greatest degree of wariness and suspicion among earlier Victorians. Interestingly, to the extent that detachment is a focus in contemporary literary scholarship on the nineteenth century, it has been primarily within the sphere of late-Victorian culture, and above all within queer analyses of the Aesthetic movement, and of Oscar Wilde in particular, who is singled out for his artful denaturalization of social norms and accepted truths. To a significant extent, this focus on Wilde and Aestheticism is driven by the privileging of ironic over other modes of detachment in contemporary queer and postmodern theory. My own approach to Wilde places him in closer alignment with the ambivalence of his predecessors, largely through a reconsideration of the tension between melodrama and irony in the society comedies. By focusing on the role of the epigram and punctuated moments of heroic dandyism, I argue that Wilde repeatedly grappled with the ethical limits of cultivated detachment, despite his many programmatic utterances to the contrary. As in the case of Eliot, Wilde's deeper investments are most legible in his portrayal of detached—in this case, dandified—women. This reading of Wilde serves as an occasion both to criticize the overvaluing of irony in postmodern criticism and to break down what I consider to be a debilitating and untenable opposition between ironic detachment and normative critical theory.

THEORETICAL CONSIDERATIONS

What I earlier identified as an incoherence on the subject of detachment in contemporary theory could be viewed more charitably as a continuation of the very struggle over terms and ideals that characterizes the Victorian encounter with modernity. Just as the Victorians played various forms of detachment against one another, casting some as progressive and ennobling, and others as dangerous and corrupting, so too, one might argue, do contemporary thinkers elevate certain practices of critique over others, seeking to dissociate their own cultivation of distance from traditional (and tainted) forms of reason, objectivity, or disinterestedness. To an extent, it is necessary to acknowledge and describe this persistent formal feature in the intellectual history of detachment, yet we need not adopt a position of neutrality simply because there is a history of divided approaches to this cultural topos. In considering the multiple roles that detachment plays in current literary and cultural studies, I will argue against current denigration of explicit ideals of critical distance, with a view to clarifying my own guiding assumptions throughout the study, as well as the theoretical convictions that motivated a reconsideration of forms of cultivated distance in the Victorian era. It is my view that both Victorian and contemporary thinkers generate false oppositions and exclusions in their consideration of differing modes and practices of detachment, and that the results in both instances are truncated forms of theory.

The critiques of detachment most prevalent in our discipline take two distinct forms. In the first place, detachment is criticized as an illusory ideal. This claim orients feminist, postmodern, and pragmatist arguments that scientific objectivity and critical rationality are forms of knowledge that fundamentally deny their own situatedness. The postmodernist and pragmatist share the antifoundationalist position that no individual or community can denude itself of its defining practices, interests, and norms, all of which are historically variable. Postmodern and poststructuralist thinkers also stress the fact that such practices and norms can never be understood apart from those forms of power and hierarchy that structure them. In this view, associated preeminently with Foucault's influential work on knowledge and discipline, what counts as truth is not only situated, but inseparable from power, and hence never disinterested, pure, or objective. Similarly, many feminists assert the importance of the embodied nature of our existence, arguing that intellectual ideals of objectivity and rationality seek to deny the physical world, both its limits and its distinctive forms of experience and insight.[17]

In the second place, detachment is criticized as a form of power that disavows its own violence and exclusivity. This critique obviously overlaps to some degree with the first critique, insofar as detachment's inseparable relation to power is one reason why it must be exposed as an illusory ideal.

[17] The literature on these topics is extensive. Examples of the pragmatist position include Barbara Herrnstein Smith, *Contingencies of Value: Alternative Perspectives for Critical Theory* (Cambridge: Harvard University Press, 1988); Stanley Fish, *Is There a Text in This Class? The Authority of Interpretive Communities* (Cambridge: Harvard University Press, 1980); Richard Rorty, *Consequences of Pragmatism: Essays, 1972–1980* (Minneapolis: University of Minnesota Press, 1982). For examples and reconsiderations of the feminist position, see Alison Jaggar, *Feminist Politics and Human Nature* (Totowa, N.J.: Rowman and Allenheld, 1983); Susan Bordo, *The Flight to Objectivity: Essays on Cartesianism and Culture* (Albany: State University of New York Press, 1987); Linda Alcoff and Elizabeth Potter, eds., *Feminist Epistemologies* (New York: Routledge, 1993); Louise M. Antony and Charlotte Witt, *A Mind of One's Own: Feminist Essays on Reason and Objectivity* (Boulder: Westview Press, 1993). Also see Michel Foucault, *Power/Knowledge: Selected Interviews and Other Writings, 1972–1977* (New York: Pantheon, 1980); Jean-François Lyotard, *The Postmodern Condition: A Report on Knowledge*, trans. Geoff Bennington and Brian Massumi (Minneapolis: University of Minnesota Press, 1988).

Versions of this argument appear across many bodies of criticism and theory. Feminist histories of science have asserted an intimate relation between the celebration of male rationality and the denigration of nature and femininity.[18] Feminist studies of modernist aesthetics have shown that practices of detachment, denaturalization, and self-transformation are frequently gendered male and sharply counterposed to images of femininity as mired in nature or custom.[19] Critiques of Enlightenment rationality and the emergent public sphere have argued that the prerogatives of critical reason and open debate were assigned exclusively to the bourgeois European masculine subject and hence entailed acts of violence and exclusion against women, the lower class, and non-European races.[20] Foucauldian analyses of disciplinary power assert not only that forms of ostensibly impartial knowledge were used to codify and control, but also that subjective experiences of autonomy and critical distance are generated via a subtle ruse of modern power, which renders subjects docile by creating illusions of freedom at the heart of interior mental life.[21]

Over and against these critiques, by no means exhaustive, we may place opposing defenses of detachment. The most prominent and sustained of these appears in the work of Jürgen Habermas, whose insistence that Enlightenment is not a tainted but rather an unfinished project has provided the foil against which many critiques of detachment have been waged. Habermas's critical theory focuses on the emancipatory potential of communicative rationality and the critically transformative effects made possible by

---

[18] L. J. Jordanova, *Sexual Visions: Images of Gender in Science and Medicine Between the Eighteenth and Twentieth Centuries* (Madison: University of Wisconsin Press, 1989); Sandra Harding, *The Science Question in Feminism* (Ithaca: Cornell University Press, 1986); Evelyn Fox Keller, *Reflections on Gender and Science* (New Haven: Yale University Press, 1984).

[19] Rita Felski, *The Gender of Modernity* (Cambridge: Harvard University Press, 1995); Elaine Showalter, *Sexual Anarchy: Gender and Culture at the Fin de Siècle* (New York: Viking, 1990); Andreas Huyssen, *After the Great Divide: Modernism, Mass Culture, and Postmodernism* (Bloomington: Indiana University Press, 1986); Charles Bernheimer, *Figures of Ill-Repute: Representing Prostitution in Nineteenth-Century France* (Cambridge: Harvard University Press, 1989).

[20] Nancy Fraser, *Justice Interruptus: Critical Reflections on the "Postsocialist" Condition* (New York: Routledge, 1997); Carole Pateman, *The Disorder of Women: Democracy, Feminism, and Political Theory* (Stanford: Stanford University Press, 1989); Craig Calhoun, ed., *Habermas and the Public Sphere* (Cambridge: MIT Press, 1992).

[21] D. A. Miller, *The Novel and the Police* (Berkeley: University of California Press, 1988).

the postconventional interrogation of cultural norms. Against those who have conflated power and knowledge, Habermas has sought to differentiate (in Kantian fashion) the particular irreducible forms of reason operative in the cognitive, technical, practical, and aesthetic registers. He has used this framework as a basis for a critique of the subject-centered philosophical tradition as well as the normatively underdeveloped aspects of contemporary theory. His more recent work on European politics and the history of the nation-state has further privileged the cultivation of detachment in its promotion of commitment to democratic procedures over and above any ethnic conception of nationality, and in its endorsement of postnational and cosmopolitan institutions.[22]

But there are other defenders of detachment apart from Habermas and the proponents of communicative ethics. Queer theory strongly valorizes certain forms of detachment in its radical anti-essentialism, in its paradoxical conception of communities of disidentification, and in its political investment in parody and other subversive practices of denaturalization.[23] As I stated earlier, this aspect of queer theory is illustrative of a more pervasive contemporary tendency to endorse ironic modes of expression and critique while simultaneously viewing critical reason as illusory and dangerous, not to mention embarrassingly earnest. In debate with the critical theorist Seyla Benhabib, for example, Judith Butler strongly cautions against any investment in the concept of philosophical distance: "The lure of a transcendental guarantee, the promise of philosophy to 'correct existence,' in the sense that Nietzsche ironically imagined, is one which seduces us away from the lived difficulty of political life."[24] Here the necessary contingency and situatedness of political life is invoked; yet elsewhere it is precisely the acts of parodic distancing that illuminate and subvert defining matrices of power.

As I suggested previously, such shifting perspectives may be said to share the attitude of ambivalence that I have identified in Victorian culture. As in the case of Wilde, and in accordance with strong currents in modernist and

---

[22] Jürgen Habermas, *The Philosophical Discourse of Modernity*, trans. Frederick Lawrence (Cambridge: MIT Press, 1987); *The Inclusion of the Other: Studies in Political Theory*, ed. Ciaran Cronin and Pablo De Greiff (Cambridge: MIT Press, 1998).

[23] Judith Butler, *Gender Trouble: Feminism and the Subversion of Identity* (New York: Routledge, 1990); Diana Fuss, ed., *Inside/Out: Lesbian Theories, Gay Theories* (New York: Routledge, 1991); Michael Warner, ed., *Fear of a Queer Planet: Queer Politics and Social Theory* (Minneapolis: University of Minnesota Press, 1993).

[24] Judith Butler, "For a Careful Reading," in Seyla Benhabib et al., *Feminist Contentions: A Philosophical Exchange*, with an introduction by Linda Nicholson (New York: Routledge, 1995), 131.

postmodernist thought, the emphases are simply reversed, as irony and radical disaffiliation are elevated over the now disparaged ideals of disinterestedness, objectivity, and reason. This double gesture characterizes many intellectual positions that espouse the radical critique of cultural norms while simultaneously asserting that traditional forms of critical detachment propel the most pernicious forms of modern power. From this perspective, nontraditional, indirect, or inherently restless modes of critique—irony, performance, negative freedom—become the favored forms of detachment.

At the same time, those contemporary theorists who defend Enlightenment ideals display forms of ambivalence that are similar to the delicate maneuvers evident in the thinking of Victorians such as Eliot and Mill. Benhabib, for example, attempts to balance a universalist defense of critical reason with an insistence on the necessarily situated nature of all identity. Her project is informed by Habermas but also by Hegel, whose entire project is underwritten, arguably, by the dialectic of estrangement and refamiliarization. On the one hand, Benhabib privileges a theoretical practice of critical detachment. Over and against those postmodernists, pragmatists, and communitarians who suggest that our activities as critics are always determined by the norms of our communities, Benhabib argues that social criticism needs philosophy, "precisely because the narratives of our cultures are so conflictual and irreconcilable that, even when one appeals to them, a certain ordering of one's normative priorities and a clarification of those principles in the name of which one speaks is unavoidable."[25] In extreme instances, cultural conditions might even require the social critic to become an exile, to radically separate him- or herself from the reified customs and practices of a corrupt society. In this conception, then, some form of disidentification (as a radicalization of postconventionality) structures social criticism itself and may lead in rare instances to actual or virtual separation from a particular society.

On the other hand, at other moments in her work, Benhabib seems to assume that by challenging "constitutive attachments," by promoting oneself as wilfully detached, one risks either returning to a false neutrality or toppling the whole edifice of communicative ethics through a postmodern celebration of negative freedom. The fact that exile is conceived as an extraordinary recourse that must be undertaken in the name of revitalization indicates that Benhabib harbors a deep uneasiness about the impact that radical critical detachment may have on the social, moral, and psychological

[25] Seyla Benhabib, "Feminism and Postmodernism," in Benhabib et al., *Feminist Contentions*, 27.

stability of individuals and communities. Benhabib thus emphasizes a reflective but affirmative relation to cultural identity: her liberalism carries with it the same underlying investment in attachment and cohesion that appeared in Mill, just as she shares with Eliot a dual commitment to situated and detached knowledges.

Illuminating in this regard is Habermas's debate in the seventies with Hans-Georg Gadamer, which turned precisely on how best to conceive and describe those practices that attempt to reflect critically upon traditions and norms.[26] The terms of this exchange have receded somewhat, having been eclipsed by the antinomies of the Habermas-Foucault debate, but they are fundamental to an analysis of Victorian detachment, particularly insofar as the concept of tradition plays such a prominent role in nineteenth-century thought. Essentially, Habermas faults Gadamer's hermeneutic method for its overprivileging of a conservative relation to tradition. In its idea of interpretation as an internal dialogue with tradition, as a form of participation in tradition, Gadamer's hermeneutics does not promote the forms of radical distancing that are requisite to ideology critique. For Habermas, tradition can be adequately comprehended only through an objectivating framework that grasps the systemic dimensions of power and labor. Although Gadamer stresses practices of reflection, he does not acknowledge that tradition is "profoundly transformed as a result of scientific reflection." Or, as Habermas more vividly asserts, in the cultivation of distanced views, "the dogmatism of life-praxis is shaken."[27]

Gadamer responds by claiming that Habermas posits too sharp a distinction between tradition and reflection. Just as all forms of judgment involve

[26] Recent discussions of the Habermasian position on communicative rationality and the value of postconventional critique have tended almost uniformly to contrast his thinking with Foucault's work on disciplinary regimes of modern life, as they relate to institutions, knowledges, and the formation of subjectivity. The main issue in such discussions, viewed from the Foucauldian perspective, becomes whether it is possible to construe communicative rationality as ever operating in isolation from relations of power. Leaving aside for a moment whether it is fair to accuse Habermas of neglecting the dimension of power in his conceptions of communicative rationality, the debate in this form does not encourage any sustained engagement with the practices of self-reflection that Habermas describes, because such practices of reflection must always be viewed through the Foucauldian lens as mystified by their practitioners and serving the ends of power. To compare Habermas's debate with Gadamer to his debate with Foucault is to see a curious reversal of roles, insofar as Habermas faults Gadamer for an inattention to questions of power.

[27] Jürgen Habermas, *On the Logic of the Social Sciences*, trans. Shierry Weber Nicholsen and Jerry A. Stark (Cambridge: MIT Press, 1988), 168.

prejudgments determined by our inescapable horizon of linguistically and socially formed understanding, so too are all practices of reflection historically contingent and context-dependent. Reflection never breaks free from context or from the embeddedness of social and historical life. Hence in a crucial sense it is always continuous with tradition. Gadamer likewise insists that it is not he who promotes a stark antinomy in his privileging of authority over its dissolution, or tradition over reflection, but rather Habermas who unduly isolates detachment from tradition as the signal mark of critical achievement:

> What is at issue is merely whether reflection always dissolves substantial relations or whether it can also *consciously* accept them. . . . That tradition as such should be and remain the only ground of validity of prejudgments—a view that Habermas attributes to me—flies directly in the face of my thesis that authority rests on knowledge. Having attained maturity, one can—but need not!—accept from insight what he adhered to out of obedience.[28]

As we shall see, in *Daniel Deronda* George Eliot reconciles modernity and tradition by elevating such informed consent into what verges on a prescriptive ideal, defined against the denigrated mode of theatrical self-fashioning that exemplifies Leonora Halm-Eberstein's rejection of constraining Jewish patriarchy. Such fears of radical detachment as inform Eliot's novel also give rise to Dickens's anxieties about the moral effects of cultivated suspicion and Arnold's attempts to generate an ideal of detachment that can counter the amorality of restless irony.

The source of the dispute between Habermas and Gadamer is whether self-reflexivity is ultimately or always in the service of transformative critique: Gadamer makes a strong bid for the value of reflective endorsement of tradition, while Habermas emphasizes the liberatory dislocation involved in acts of critical distancing. Neither thinker in this debate is particularly concerned with aesthetic practices of detachment, such as this study will consider when it explores the self-fashioning of Deronda's mother or the Wildean dandy. What the Habermas-Gadamer debate discloses, however, is a phenomenon that is confirmed by more comprehensive analysis of the nineteenth- and twentieth-century debates on detachment: critical reflec-

---

[28] Quoted in Thomas McCarthy, *The Critical Theory of Jürgen Habermas* (Cambridge: MIT Press, 1978), 189. Also see Hans-Georg Gadamer, "On the Scope and Function of Hermeneutical Reflection," in *Philosophical Hermeneutics*, trans. David E. Linge (Berkeley: University of California Press, 1976), 18–43.

tion or postconventional critique can take a plurality of forms, including a reflective return to tradition or primary affiliations, a committed devotion to systemic analysis and wholesale social transformation, or a persistent attitude of rebellion or irony.

Against attempts to elevate particular forms of detachment over others, *The Powers of Distance* endorses a pluralism when it comes to evaluating how practices of reflection might express themselves. By such a standard, a reflective return to the various cultural identities that define one can be just as critically aware as persistent detachment. At the same time, however, the pluralism I endorse is a critical pluralism, not a relativistic one. This means that, in a manner similar to the liberal privileging of the right over the good, my analyses seek to advance self-consciously pluralistic conceptions of detachment over hierarchical, exclusive, or insufficiently self-critical ones. I place the highest value on forms of detachment that remain self-consciously informed by a postconventional and ongoing interrogation of cultural norms and systems of power, and I am critical of attempts to disassociate certain forms of detachment from what are viewed as the "contaminations" of rational critique. As Pierre Bourdieu trenchantly observes, one can only criticize false or distorted versions of objectivity by refining one's methods of self-reflexive, detached critique: "the most effective reflection is one that consists in objectifying the subject of objectification."[29] At the same time, however, I am critical of those defenders of modern rationality who discredit forms of detachment that are seen as "light," aestheticized, or amoral. In many instances, such allegedly negative or nonproductive forms of detachment are associated with subordinate gender, sexual, ethnic, and class positions. Such invidious distinctions, whether between forms or practitioners of detachment, require rigorous critique. This standard of evaluation is applied not only to those who defend the tradition of rational critique, but also to those who elevate ironic forms over serious norms.

My conception of detachment shares affinities with contemporary uses of the term *cosmopolitanism*, even as it takes Victorian understandings of the latter as one object of study. Many of those who espouse the new cosmopolitanism define it as the capacious inclusion of multiple forms of affiliation, disaffiliation, and reaffiliation, simultaneously insisting on the need for informing principles of self-reflexivity, critique, and common humanity. Like the term *detachment* in my usage, cosmopolitanism is a broad concept, comprising intellectual, aesthetic, and ethical elements. In a manner that seems

[29] Pierre Bourdieu, *Pascalian Meditations*, trans. Richard Nice (Stanford: Stanford University Press, 2000), 10.

to shadow the Victorians, moreover, current understandings of cosmopolitanism assert an integral relation between ethical stance and intellectual practice. As Bruce Robbins writes, cosmopolitanism involves an intellectual dedication to "planetary expansiveness of subject matter" while simultaneously according primary value to concrete intercultural exchange: it is "an impulse to knowledge that is shared with others, a striving to transcend partiality that is itself partial."[30] Like the nineteenth-century tendency to fuse method and ethos, cosmopolitanism is the expression of the need above all to enact or embody universalism, to transform it into a characterological achievement. Lastly, like the term *cosmopolitanism*, the term *detachment* in this study moves between descriptive and prescriptive senses, on the one hand describing a range of practices and conditions, and on the other endorsing an ideal.

Despite these affinities, I favor *detachment* as an umbrella term which, in my usage, can refer not only to the more strictly cultural and internationalist practices found under the rubric of cosmopolitanism, but also to those systemic or objectifying critiques of power that characterize social science or critical theory, two key foci of the study.[31] Since I particularly want to defend the progressive potentialities of systemic critique, I needed a term that could clearly denote such practices. This term also allows me to consider with more precision when and how Victorian ideals of detachment do and do not extend beyond a narrowly characterological emphasis to embrace forms of experience that are intersubjective or collective. The term *cosmopolitanism*, which is itself divided between individualist and intersubjective elements, often blurs this distinction by compounding it. That is, while cosmopolitanism places a value on reciprocal and transformative encounters between strangers variously construed, it simultaneously has strongly indi-

[30] Bruce Robbins, *Secular Vocations: Intellectuals, Professionalism, Culture* (London: Verso, 1993), 181, 194. For examples of the new cosmopolitanisms, see Pheng Cheah and Bruce Robbins, eds., *Cosmopolitics: Thinking and Feeling Beyond the Nation* (Minneapolis: University of Minnesota Press, 1998).

[31] It is for this reason, for example, that Pheng Cheah has argued for the introduction of the more critical concept of the *cosmopolitical*; a similar Marxist discomfort with the limits of bourgeois cosmopolitanism motivates Tim Brennan's Gramscian critique of cosmopolitanism; and indeed, Robbins's more recent work has turned to a focus on the term *internationalism*, with an increased privileging of the politics over the ethics of globalization. See Pheng Cheah, "Introduction Part II: The Cosmopolitical—Today," in *Cosmopolitics*, ed. Cheah and Robbins, 20–41; Tim Brennan, *At Home in the World: Cosmopolitanism Now* (Cambridge: Harvard University Press, 1997); Bruce Robbins, *Feeling Global: Internationalism in Distress* (New York: New York University Press, 1999).

vidualist elements, in its advocacy of detachment from shared identities, its emphasis on affiliation as voluntary, and its appeal to self-cultivation. But although I conceive of *detachment* as both broader in reference and more supple analytically than *cosmopolitanism*, it remains the case that key moments in the book were inspired by contemporary debates over the latter term, as I shall make clear at the beginning of chapter 2, and throughout the analyses of Dickens, Arnold, and Eliot.

This study is devoted to the elaboration of what must necessarily remain a precarious and merely regulative ideal. Current critiques of detachment cannot comprehend the topic in this form, often reflecting instead a frustrated idealism as well as an unproductive tendency to assume that endorsements of reflective detachment necessarily also project a substantial and full-fledged claim about the nature of human identity. The frustrated idealism is evident in an immediate and unwarranted assumption that any and all practices of cultivated distance claim a kind of pure or absolute objectivity for themselves. Countering with the view that no such objectivity exists, critics show themselves unable to imagine critical distance as a temporary vantage, unstable achievement, or regulative ideal: it's all or nothing. A similar attitude is evident in the corollary assumption that all defenses of detachment entail an essential claim about identity or consciousness, one that denies or disavows the embodied and situated character of human existence. In *Sources of the Self*, Charles Taylor acknowledges that many Enlightenment understandings of reason involved "reading the stance of disengagement, whereby we objectify facets of our own being, into the ontology of the subject." Yet, as Taylor points out, one can identify and critique particular ontologies of the subject without abandoning the ideals of "self-responsible reason and freedom": "These ideals can and do have their validity (however limited by others); we can still recognize the development of this power (within proper bounds) as an important achievement of modernity, even when we cast off this invalid anthropology."[32] In other words, practices of detachment do not define the sum and total or the *telos* of human practices or experiences, and they cannot be understood apart from their historical forms. In calling disengagement a "stance," Taylor suggests that it is one practice among others, and this is a view I share, though I happen to believe it is a vitally important practice, in part because, in its most appealing and promising form, it represents an aspiration more than a certainty, one con-

[32] Charles Taylor, *Sources of the Self: The Making of Modern Identity* (Cambridge: Harvard University Press, 1989), 514.

nected to the ongoing achievement of many social and political goods, including knowledge of social conditions and ills, and practices of deliberative democracy and cosmopolitanism.

The idea that cultivated detachment is an ongoing aspiration and incomplete achievement appears entirely lost to view from certain pragmatist perspectives, which do not acknowledge that practices of detachment might be distinguished in any way from practice in general. In an ostensibly offhand remark at the conclusion of his essay "Critical Self-Consciousness, or Can We Know What We're Doing?" Stanley Fish attempts to fold in the rather startling point that, despite his assertions that critical self-consciousness does not even exist, its "appeal . . . will survive any argument I make against it."[33] He attributes this to the nature of convictions, which one always experiences as universally true: "even though the self-reflective clarity of critical consciousness cannot be achieved, the experience of having achieved it is inseparable from the experience of conviction" (467). Fish thus brings in a universal psychology to account for the awkward fact that his own reflections are not prompting any significant transformation in the convictions of others. But what he fails to address is his initial comment, that the *appeal*, not the sure experience, of critical self-consciousness would remain. The cultivation of detachment involves an attempt to transcend partiality, interests, and context: it is an aspiration toward universality and objectivity. The norms through which that aspiration finds expression may be situated, the aspiration may always be articulated through historically available forms, but as an aspiration it cannot be reduced to a simple form of illusion, or a mere psychological mechanism. There are practitioners of detachment who are as certain of their achievement as Fish is of his argument, but there are also practitioners of detachment who are ambivalent, hesitant, uneasy, and sometimes quite thoughtfully engaged in a complex process of self-interrogation and social critique. It is to the fuller understanding of their work that the following chapters are committed.

---

[33] Stanley Fish, "Critical Self-Consciousness, or Can We Know What We're Doing?" in *Doing What Comes Naturally: Change, Rhetoric, and the Practice of Theory in Literary and Legal Studies* (Durham: Duke University Press, 1989), 465. Subsequent page number references will be cited parenthetically in the text.

CHAPTER ONE

Gender, Modernity, and Detachment

DOMESTIC IDEALS AND THE CASE OF CHARLOTTE BRONTË'S *VILLETTE*

In his 1864 lecture "Of Queens' Gardens," John Ruskin delivers the following remark about the ideal education of woman: "All such knowledge should be given her as may enable her to understand, and even to aid, the work of men: and yet it should be given, not as knowledge,—not as if it were, or could be, for her an object to know; but only to feel, and to judge."[1] This quotation exemplifies the centrality of gender divisions to many Victorian understandings of the roles that different intellectual and aesthetic practices should play in modern life. Ruskin's deep investment in woman as the guardian of sympathy and moral judgment is accompanied by a need to protect her from what he perceives as the alienating practices of objective knowledge, abstract reasoning, and heightened self-consciousness. In a rather bizarre elaboration, Ruskin goes on to envision the woman as one whose moral imagination will ideally transform and see beyond any text of history written by a man:

> It is of little consequence how many positions of cities she knows, or how many dates of events, or names of celebrated persons—it is not the object of education to turn the woman into a dictionary; but it is deeply necessary that she should be taught to enter with her whole personality into the history she reads; to picture the passages of it vitally in her own bright imagination; to apprehend, with her fine instincts, the pathetic circumstances and dramatic relations, which the historian too often only eclipses by his reasoning, and disconnects by his arrangement: it is for her to trace the hidden equities of divine reward, and catch sight, through the darkness, of the fateful threads of woven fire that connect error with its retribution. (88)

[1] John Ruskin, "Of Queens' Gardens," in *Sesame and Lilies*, ed. Robert Kilburn Root (New York: Henry Holt, 1901), 87. Subsequent page number references will be cited parenthetically in the text.

Typically adduced as the classic instance of the Victorian separate spheres doctrine, in which women are guardians of the private, emotional life and men withstand the demands of active, public life, Ruskin's lecture moves well beyond such simple oppositions when it elaborates a form of feminine moral potency reliant not only upon sympathetic imagination but also upon a distinctly critical judgment allied to religious insight. In doing so, it reveals the internal complexity and multifaceted character of the Victorian understanding of ideal femininity, which on the one hand emphasized selflessness and sympathetic communing, and on the other allotted to women far-reaching forms of guardianship and influence, which in turn depended on cultivated practices of moral discernment, impersonal judgment, and even self-crafting.

Such tensions between selflessness and influence, and sympathy and judgment, are intimately related to the larger cultural concern with practices of detachment that I described in the introduction. I begin in this opening chapter with the particular thematic of gender because I believe that representations of femininity in the Victorian period prominently play out the promises and dangers of cultivated distance, in ways that have not been sufficiently recognized in the scholarly literature and that might help to shed light on some of the seemingly least conventional portrayals of women and gender in the culture, many of which I explore in subsequent chapters. I also begin here because a critical analysis of influential feminist scholarship on Victorian conceptions of gender will provide me the opportunity to secure more fully the key theoretical and methodological claims governing the study as a whole, ones that will inform the subsequent chapters' treatment of race and nationalism.

The crucial point to stress at the outset is that it would be misleading to assume or to insist that women are simply excluded from those forms of detachment seen as intellectually or morally heroic in the culture. In this sense the developed feminist critique of objectivity or impersonality as indicatively masculine cannot do justice to the materials at hand. As we see above, although Ruskin wants women to be denied a scientific stance toward objects of study, he at the same time insists that their emotional knowledge extend to a form of active moral judgment. The strange asymmetry in his argument—where knowledge is opposed not simply to feeling but also to judgment—reveals a dual movement in the culture at large. On the one hand, there was a tendency to restrict women to more immediate or traditional forms of life and knowledge, thereby guarding them and the culture more generally against a too vertiginous embrace of modernity and its

defamiliarizing perspectives. On the other hand, insofar as forms of cultivated distance were associated with moral progress, they were actively inte-
grated into the model of feminine influence. Indeed, modern practices of
detachment began to exert pressure upon, and transform, the domestic ideal
as traditionally conceived, especially via the elaboration of ideals of impersonal motherhood and female authorship.

This chapter will begin by exploring in some detail the theoretical contours of recent feminist scholarship in Victorian literary and cultural studies.
I will then move to the consideration of a case study, Charlotte Brontë's
Villette, a novel that serves as a powerful and wide-ranging example of the
Victorian literature of detachment, with particular pertinence to the gender
dimensions of the topic. I argue that Brontë's novel constitutes both an analysis and a phenomenology of detachment in its use of the framework of
cosmopolitan comparison to register a range of practices that rely upon cultivated distance, including professional disinterestedness, surveillance, impersonal motherhood, aesthetic observation, and stoicism.

FEMINISM AND THE POWERED SUBJECT

In her influential essay, "Gender: A Useful Category of Historical Analysis,"
Joan Wallach Scott advanced the notion that feminist history ideally aspires
not only to uncover women in history, but to argue for the primacy of gender
to the symbolic formations of culture and the political arrangements shaping
social life.[2] Such an agenda has been dramatically evident in theoretically
minded feminist scholarship on the Victorian and modern periods, which
has positioned women and cultural forms of femininity as vital structuring
agents in the ideological advent of modernity. A prime example of this approach would be Nancy Armstrong's *Desire and Domestic Fiction: A Political History of the Novel*, which provocatively asserts, "the modern individual is first and foremost a female."[3] A Foucauldian understanding of the
advent of modern power, and its development throughout the eighteenth
and nineteenth centuries, underwrites Armstrong's bold claim, even as her
work also aligns itself with the tradition of cultural materialism.[4] Armstrong's

[2] Joan Wallach Scott, "Gender: A Useful Category of Historical Analysis," in *Gender and the Politics of History* (New York: Columbia University Press, 1988), 28–50.

[3] Nancy Armstrong, *Desire and Domestic Fiction: A Political History of the Novel*
(New York: Oxford University Press, 1987), 66. Subsequent page number references
will be cited parenthetically in the text.

[4] For a helpful analysis of the way these paradigms inform Armstrong's study, see

book, as well as Mary Poovey's roughly contemporaneous *Uneven Develop-ments: The Ideological Construction of Gender in Mid-Victorian England*, locates gender, and more specifically the construction of ideal middle-class femininity, at the heart of the ideological formation of the modern bourgeois subject and its articulation in literary and social narratives.[5] Similarly, Eliza-beth Langland's *Nobody's Angels: Middle-Class Women and Domestic Ideol-ogy in Victorian Culture* assigns to women the primary task of consolidating and regulating cultural capital, a key form of bourgeois hegemonic power.[6]

In laying claim to forms of feminine power, and to the primacy of gender within modern ideologies, these critics nonetheless display a certain dis-comfort with the question of just how critically reflective modern women subjects might be presumed to be. On the one hand, feminine agency is imagined as continuous with unreflective forms of power that are simply transmitted by culturally embedded subjects. Yet on the other hand, strange exceptions occur, wherein certain historical subjects are exempted from net-works of power and consequently accorded an aggrandized form of agency marked by both critical detachment and political potency. I read this recur-ring formation as a peculiar hybrid product resulting from the interplay of forces among contemporary theoretical commitments, the specific history of feminist scholarship, and the peculiarities of Victorian gender ideology. As we shall see, this particular rhetorical pattern within literary feminist studies is an instance of the underdeveloped and often contradictory approach to detachment within contemporary theory, but in this case certain key ele-ments within Victorian gender ideology compound the problem, insofar as they help to reinforce the oddly nonreflective agency that has been attrib-uted to the Victorian middle-class ideal.

The critical formations that appear in Armstrong's and Poovey's texts are governed, from one perspective, by the trope of metalepsis, the transforma-tion of an effect into a cause. For within historicist-theoretical feminism of the late 1980s, the lure of a constructionist victimology was repudiated and to a large extent replaced by a conception of women as instrumental agents of those forms of power that were potentially seen to determine her.

Judith Newton, "History as Usual?: Feminism and the 'New Historicism,'" *Cultural Critique* 9 (1988): 87–121.

[5] Mary Poovey, *Uneven Developments: The Ideological Work of Gender in Mid-Victorian England* (Chicago: University of Chicago Press, 1988). Subsequent page number references will be cited parenthetically in the text.

[6] Elizabeth Langland, *Nobody's Angels: Middle-Class Women and Domestic Ideol-ogy in Victorian Culture* (Ithaca: Cornell University Press, 1995). Subsequent page number references will be cited parenthetically in the text.

Poovey's and Armstrong's studies would be two versions of this formation. Vigorously debunking the understanding of women as mere objects of power, and insisting on the unacknowledged centrality of gender to the rise of modern bourgeois and disciplinary institutions, both scholars grant to middle-class women a form of influence coextensive with the practices of power that their studies always at least implicitly critique. Middle-class women become the paradoxically potent agents of a power that effectively speaks through them.[7]

The description of women as instruments of modern power may at first glance seem better to describe Armstrong than Poovey, since Poovey's principal claim is that the feminine domestic ideal serves simply as symbolic anchor to Victorian ideological reproduction across many registers. Her textual analyses in *Uneven Developments* repeatedly establish what she at one point calls the "epistemological centrality of woman's self-consistency to the oppositional structure of Victorian ideas" (9). An emphasis on the symbolic function of gender, that is, need not involve the claim that women serve as primary instruments of power. Nonetheless, on the level of social practices, Poovey's idealized middle-class wife unmistakably serves as the crucial conduit for the forms of power that secure modern identity. In Poovey's reading of Charles Dickens's *David Copperfield*, for example, the feminine domestic ideal consolidates masculine identity and guides the narrative of individual fulfillment that underwrites bourgeois ideology:

> Because her domestic authority—indeed, her self-realization—depended on her ability to regulate her own desire, the faithful woman as wife anchored her husband's desire along with her own, giving it an object as she gave him a home. In this model, self-regulation was a particularly valuable and valued form of labor, for it domesticated man's (sexual) desire in the private sphere without curtailing his ambition in the economy. (115)

[7] I don't mean to suggest that alternatives to victimology in feminist history only began to occur with the publication of these studies in the late 1980s. In the 1970s, the reconsiderations of women's place within history by cultural feminists was accompanied by assertions of women's influence on history, and by conceptualizations of women's forms of community and solidarity. Indeed, some feminists have insisted that work in women's history in the 1970s was cognizant of the issues of power and agency that are often attributed to poststructuralism, new historicism, and Foucault. See Catherine Hall, *White, Male, and Middle-Class: Explorations in Feminism and History* (Cambridge: Polity Press, 1992), 14–15. My discussion of the trope of metalepsis here has to do with feminist historiographical developments within established poststructuralist and new historicist horizons.

Poovey's analysis here is consonant with Armstrong's insistence on the centrality of the female subject, and of feminine forms of power and surveillance, to the development and consolidation of bourgeois identity.

This manner of establishing the vital significance of gender within the history of power is shared as well by Langland's *Nobody's Angels*. Drawing on the sociology of Pierre Bourdieu, Langland argues that Victorian middle-class women were defined by the broadly social and public task of regulating cultural capital. Rather than simply playing a key role in the making of modern privatized selfhood, the domestic woman enforced elaborate distinctions of class that subtly demarcated and defined an emergent middle class. Langland insists that there was a more complex model of feminine management than either Armstrong or Poovey identifies: women performed the crucial work of establishing and maintaining social hierarchy; they did not merely represent privatized virtue or self-regulating interiority. Yet despite this difference, there is an underlying continuity of approach here: Langland may support a different vision of how social practices articulate relations of power, but her inscription of femininity into the narrative of modernity is similar. As in the case of Poovey and Armstrong, the middle-class woman is the principal instrument of a power that is instantiated in her fundamental practices yet falls below the level of conscious strategy. An adept manager and social tactician, the middle-class woman nonetheless cannot be said to reflect critically upon the power that she represents. Neither victim nor plotter, she yet remains entirely continuous with the modern form of power that she promulgates. She is powerful but not critical, profoundly effective but not self-reflective. As Langland puts it, in a passage elaborating Bourdieu's conception of *habitus*, "Whereas genteel women oriented themselves toward specific goals of class hegemony, their actions were rarely the product of conscious deliberation and calculation, rather the result of an unconscious disposition (inscribed even in the body through speech and bearing) to act in certain ways" (10).

In focusing on the middle-class woman, these theorists clearly wish to bring to the fore a submerged chapter in the rise of the middle class and of modern disciplinary power. They considerably complicate the traditional materialist feminist insight that middle-class women are empowered by their class and disempowered by their gender, arguing that the convergence of class and gender ideology produced a distinctive subject-position that served to secure bourgeois hegemony. In this respect gender becomes the site of power's enactment, not the occasion for oppression. Indeed, given the particular set of ambitions and anxieties guiding these projects, one can see

why the middle-class woman would become the privileged site of interrogation. First, such an approach gives to women, and to the ideology of gender,
a central role in modernization and class consolidation: this may seem more
empowering, ultimately, than recovering submerged voices within radical or
working-class culture, which appear doomed to a certain marginality to this
main story.[8] Second, it also serves to acknowledge middle-class complicity
in practices of power, thereby answering to prominent charges in the late
1970s and early 1980s that middle-class women were blindly projecting
their particular experience as a universal one for all women. The analyses of
the distinctive power of middle-class women within the larger society over-
comes this blindness, as have more recent studies of the ways in which the
Victorian ideology of femininity supported the larger project of Empire.[9]

[8] There is, however, an important body of feminist scholarship treating the place
of women in working-class culture and working-class radical politics. See ibid., 124–
50. See also Dorothy Thompson, "Women and Nineteenth-Century Radical Politics:
A Lost Dimension," in *The Rights and Wrongs of Women*, ed. Juliet Mitchell and Ann
Oakley (Harmondsworth: Penguin, 1976), 112–38. Barbara Taylor, *Eve and the New
Jerusalem: Socialism and Feminism in the Nineteenth Century* (London: Virago,
1983). There is a tendency to emphasize particularism, resistance, and the materiality
of labor in analyses of working-class women, insofar as they cannot be assimilated to
dramatic hegemonic or modernizing processes in the way that middle-class women
can. For a book that both manifests and ruminates powerfully on these tendencies,
see Carolyn Kay Steedman, *Landscape for a Good Woman: A Story of Two Lives*
(New Brunswick: Rutgers University Press, 1987). For an instance of this tendency
within one of the studies I am discussing, see the analysis of Hannah Cullwick in
Langland, *Nobody's Angels*, 209–21. For an interesting study of solidarity and community within a subculture of working-class prostitutes, see Judith R. Walkowitz,
Prostitution and Victorian Society: Women, Class, and the State (Cambridge: Cambridge University Press, 1980).

[9] See Raina Lewis, *Gendering Orientalism: Race, Femininity, and Representation*
(New York: Routledge, 1996); Jenny Sharpe, *Allegories of Empire: The Figure of the
Woman in the Colonial Text* (Minneapolis: University of Minnesota Press, 1993);
Deirdre David, *Rule Britannia: Women, Empire, and Victorian Writing* (Ithaca: Cornell University Press, 1995); Jennifer Brody, *Impossible Purities: Blackness, Femininity, and Victorian Culture* (Durham: Duke University Press, 1998). In some measure,
these studies can be seen to employ the paradigm under discussion, whereby women
become the conduits for modern imperial power, which is linked to the disciplinary
project of subject formation within the domestic sphere (in both the familial and the
national sense). Deirdre David's *Rule Britannia* in particular stresses how the conception of women's moral influence played into imperial ideas, especially in light of
the symbolic importance of the queen. But the work on gender and imperialism in
the Victorian period has a distinctive theoretical legacy, and in some significant ways
these studies do not fit the paradigm I identify in works focusing more narrowly on
national class culture. Influenced by the postcolonial theories of Gayatri Spivak and

In general terms, the highlighting of middle-class women's histories and interests, and the insistence that these interests are linked to the interests of bourgeois and imperial hegemony, has enabled feminist scholars to reframe their acknowledgment of women's power within a legitimating hermeneutics of suspicion. One might be tempted, in a further turning of the screw of suspicion, to read the scholarly disavowal of deliberate calculation by the domestic woman as an attempt to diminish her responsibility, to hold to the inspiration of her profound efficacy without having to construct her as a malign oppressor. Without dismissing such a reading, I would also like to suggest that we may here be encountering a moment in which an entrenched understanding of Victorian gender ideology matches the interpretive exigencies of the present moment. For as in the traditional nineteenth-century representation of feminine virtue, which ideally had many desirable social and moral ramifications, which ideally diffused itself through many capillaries, certain contemporary images of feminine power project a form of agency that, while far-reaching in its effects, has no real capacity for the detached examination and critique of its aims and motives. The Victorian domestic angel was often described as making her presence and influence felt without any element of deliberation, calculation, or even self-awareness. This ideological formation conforms uncannily to the current "reconstruction" of domestic power as, to adapt a formulation of Foucault's, "both intentional and nonsubjective."[10]

Interestingly, however, this feminist theorization of gender and power, which combines a nuanced social constructionism with a distinctive enlargement of feminine efficacy, typically exhibits points of symptomatic strain. Indeed, in tension with the understanding of feminine power that

---

Homi Bhabba, these analyses of gender and imperialism tend to focus on the ways in which white middle-class women consolidated their sense of self against an excluded racialized, native other. Such accounts position themselves primarily against liberal feminist approaches that try to celebrate women's autonomy or finding of voice, arguing that liberal projects involve the exclusion of others. They are not so much interested in repudiating victimology, then, as in repudiating problematic claims to agency. Similarly, these studies often highlight the conflicted nature of women's relation to imperial ideology, tracing a complex psychic interplay between complicity and critique, as well as the ways in which women are positioned allegorically in relation to the imperial project. In their intrasubjective focus, in their relentlessly negative critique of the liberal feminist model, and in their focus on internal textual oscillations, they do not prosecute the claim of women as central agents of modern power in the way that the metaleptical models do.

[10] Michel Foucault, *The History of Sexuality: An Introduction*, vol. 1, trans. Robert Hurley (New York: Random House, 1978), 94.

undergirds their central arguments, there frequently appear within these accounts one or two privileged and anomalous figures who are granted deeper insight into the workings of power, and who seem not simply to instantiate modern power but to manipulate if not inaugurate it. These are the exceptional and aggrandized figures I invoked at the outset of the chapter. I have in mind here, for example, Armstrong's treatment of the Brontës, who hold the dubious honor of "[establishing] a tradition of reading that would universalize modern desire in order to implant it within every individual as the very thing that makes him or her human" (202). Another instance would be Poovey's treatment of Florence Nightingale, portrayed as deftly deploying different elements of Victorian ideology so as to secure the professionalization of nursing. Generally, a certain higher-order reflexivity is often at least implicitly granted to *authors* of realist texts whose *characters* represent unself-conscious modes of power—such would be the case not only with Armstrong's treatment of the Brontës but also with Langland's approach to Elizabeth Gaskell and Margaret Oliphant. That is, whereas Gaskell's and Oliphant's characters might be said to be the embedded but also blinkered tacticians that Langland wants to retrieve from history, the authors are granted a larger understanding of the philosophical and social beliefs undergirding the identification of such practices. As Langland baldly puts it at one moment, Gaskell "represents reality as a construction" (120). Indeed, Langland explicitly assimilates Gaskell to the position of the privileged theorist with insight into the ruses of power: "[Gaskell's] narrative procedures suggest we should heed Michel Foucault, who recognizes behind 'minute material detail' the presence of 'alien strategies' of power and knowledge" (114). Margaret Oliphant is presented as an even more impressive poststructuralist avant la lettre, with full awareness of the free play of signification and the performative identities that her heroines less reflectively inhabit (165–66).

Similarly striking, and perhaps most dramatic among the examples, is the manner in which Mary Poovey's Florence Nightingale becomes endowed with an uncanny ability to understand and manipulate the whole of Victorian ideology. Not simply a woman who serves as a conduit for power, or whose influence draws on the larger forces that work through her, Florence Nightingale appears at a crucial point in Poovey's analysis actually to take a read on the current ideological formation and then selectively deploy its variables to open up a space for professional nursing in the Crimean War. I quote at some length to give the full flavor of Poovey's analysis, which begins by showing how Nightingale stressed the potency inherent in the domestic ideal:

If Nightingale's exploitation of the militancy inherent in the domestic ideal helped authorize the supremacy of nursing, it also aligned her vision of the nurse with another enterprise gaining momentum at midcentury. To appreciate the connection between these two campaigns, it is helpful to cast Nightingale's project in terms only slightly more militaristic than the ones she provided. If we view her campaign for nursing as an imperialistic program, we can see that it had two related fronts. The first was the "domestic" front within medicine; in this battle, Nightingale's opponents were medical men; her object was to carve out an autonomous—and ultimately superior—realm for female nursing. The second front was the "foreign" front of class; in this skirmish, her enemies were the "dirt, drink, diet, damp, draughts, drains" that made lower-class homes unsanitary; her object here was to bring the poor and their environment under the salutary sway of their middle-class betters. *Nightingale's strategy was to foreground the second campaign, which was a project shared by middle-class men, to mask the subversive character of the first, domestic campaign, which decidedly was not.* But the rhetoric in which this strategy was accomplished made Nightingale's vision of nursing particularly amenable to appropriation by English politicians and imperialists, who had their own foreign front to conquer. (188–89; my emphasis)

One might welcome this kind of analysis as giving back what the *David Copperfield* analysis seemed to preclude: the capacity for reflexive critique of the ideologies encountered by the situated historical subject. This positive explanation could of course equally be applied to Langland's descriptions of Gaskell and Oliphant. But one might also question why the representation is taken so far: indeed, what is interesting here is that Nightingale becomes almost indistinguishable from Poovey herself, in the same manner that Gaskell and Oliphant become ersatz Langlands. While Nightingale clearly is an actor in a complex cultural field, she also manifests a capacity to survey from above, like a battle commander planning out tactics on a scale model. One might immediately wonder, upon reading this description, whether Nightingale may be not strategically foregrounding the "second campaign" but rather simply inhabiting it as ideology. That is, her "strategy" may have been effective but nonintentional. Why, one is led to ask, *does* Poovey want to ascribe such superagency to Nightingale?

It answers a need, I suggest, to get beyond the models of agency and power that affect the metaleptic formations analyzed earlier, in which "empowered" subjects simply exercise or transmit modern disciplinary power. Here, at least, however fantastically, the woman uses power formations to

advance women's entry into professional practices, practices that are not re-
ducible to disciplinary power but share *some* of its aims and effects. Through
figures such as Nightingale, the critics awkwardly displace an anxiety in
their own self-conceptions, awarding the valorized individual a detached
understanding of the very ideological formations that they otherwise imply
operate unreflectively *through* historical subjects. On one level these critics
are skeptical that any such detachment is possible, yet at another level they
rely on such detachment for the promulgation of their critical social theories.
This problematic gets symptomatically displayed in strangely aggrandized
portraits of historically situated subjects, which sit uneasily next to the other
figurations of women as unreflexively coextensive with forms of power.

The forms of detachment, critique, and transformative intervention that I
have been examining have all been associated with individuals presented as
extraordinary by the critic or historian of culture: this certainly might be
adduced as a reason for the overstatements that I perhaps uncharitably call
"aggrandized agency." It is inevitable that feminists would want to bring
heroic or otherwise prominent women within the annals of history, and
some celebration of their historical influence is surely in order. But I want
to hold to the significance of the distinction I have been drawing. It is precisely because agency and critical reflection are insufficiently or confusedly
theorized that such exaggerated representations occur. They can escape notice because they approximate conventions in hagiographic recovery work,
or, alternately, the marriage of auteur-theory and constructionism in much
recent poststructuralist theory, where manipulative detachment by otherwise constrained subjects rather capriciously appears. The particularly
strong claims about the subject-constituting effects of modern power or cultural capital virtually invite symptomatic excesses in the work of critics simultaneously committed to the critical and transformative potential of feminist and materialist traditions.[11]

The inconsistent approaches to agency within feminist criticism are determined by a complex interplay among contemporary theoretical formations,
feminist conventions, and the idiosyncratic contours of Victorian gender
ideology. Occluded in these approaches, most importantly for my present

---

[11] This particular rhetorical pattern within feminist literary studies may be contrasted to feminist work within the discipline of history, which tends to promote a
more situated conception of agency that in very different ways evades the question
of detachment. For an extended analysis and comparison, see Amanda Anderson,
"The Temptations of Aggrandized Agency: Feminist Histories and the Horizon of
Modernity," *Victorian Studies* 43 (2000): 43–65.

purposes, are the ways in which gendered conceptions of consciousness in the nineteenth century reflect pervasive Victorian preoccupations with modern practices of detachment. Within the horizon of Victorian modernity, the domestic ideal often acted as the symbolic guarantor of the project of reflective affiliation or cultivated detachment that marked the privileged masculine subject. When the projects of self-authorization opened up by the loss of traditional forms of belief seemed also to threaten cherished forms of organic connection—to family, community, or nation—then conceptions of nonreflective femininity could be adduced as consolation or support. If women somehow naturally or intuitively preserved tradition, men could be actively modern without experiencing vertiginous rootlessness. And indeed, it was not simply ideal femininity that played out these preoccupations: negative or excessive versions of modernity were often figured as feminine impurity. The fallen woman, for example, symbolized acute forms of modern alienation, as someone both buffeted by impersonal forces and condemned to nonliberatory modes of consciousness, doomed to perpetual self-objectification.[12] Recent work on Victorian masculinity has demonstrated, moreover, how precarious were practices of masculine ascesis, itself a cultivated relation to self-development haunted by fears of compromised autonomy.[13] Any adequate understanding of gender and detachment in the Victorian period must acknowledge these cultural formations in their complexity, as well as the many active challenges and emergent forces that were pressuring and at times transforming them. To isolate simply one internal complexity that is lost to view in the analyses I have been critiquing: at the same time that women novelists themselves often could not fully escape less enlightened economies of gender, they were themselves participating in the larger project of the novel as a practice of critical detachment through the mode of realism, which aspired to a systemic representation of social life.[14]

[12] As I have argued elsewhere. See Amanda Anderson, *Tainted Souls and Painted Faces: The Rhetoric of Fallenness in Victorian Culture* (Ithaca: Cornell University Press, 1993).

[13] See James Eli Adams, *Dandies and Desert Saints: Styles of Victorian Manhood* (Ithaca: Cornell University Press, 1995).

[14] For an analysis keenly attuned to the tension between observer and observed within women's writing (fictional and nonliterary works of social investigation), see Deborah Epstein Nord, *Walking the Victorian Streets: Women, Representation, and the City* (Ithaca: Cornell University Press, 1995). Feminist narratologists are also more alert to this kind of informing tension: see, for example, Susan Sniader Lanser, *Fictions of Authority: Women Writers and Narrative Voice* (Ithaca: Cornell University Press, 1992).

By disclosing these gendered aspects of Victorian configurations of detachment, we can better understand some complicated variations on the usual patterns. One key aspect of Victorian ideology brought to light by my discussion of *Villette*, for example, is the tension that results when forms of feminine impersonality—in this case, new "professional" conceptions of motherhood and cultivated practices of aesthetic observation—vie with investments in nonreflective femininity. Many of British literary culture's most "perverse" representations of feminine critical consciousness could profit from such revisionist analysis. I have in mind figures such as Rosa Dartle in *David Copperfield*, Edith Dombey in *Dombey and Son*, and Marian Halcombe in *The Woman in White*; two further examples, Miss Wade in *Little Dorrit* and Leonora Halm-Eberstein in *Daniel Deronda*, will be discussed in later chapters. These are just a few characters who profoundly exceed the standard typologies of Victorian gender ideology, as well as its theoretical recapitulations. Many of them do so by instantiating available practices of self-reflection, from cosmopolitan and travel-writing traditions, vanguard aesthetics, omniscient realism, the social sciences, and from models of professional authority ranging from medicine to motherhood. Certainly much significant work has recently been done establishing women's roles as public actors, travelers, professionals, and observers, even within some of the studies I have been discussing.[15] My analysis complements that work but also seeks to reframe it by considering women's practices of detachment in light of the broader cultural preoccupation with modern powers of distance, rather than seeing them primarily as a challenge to conventional gender roles or an extension of transpersonal forms of power.

BRONTË'S *VILLETTE*: A DETACHMENT OF ONE'S OWN

To illuminate more immediately the broader set of claims I advance above, I turn now to Charlotte Brontë's *Villette*, a mid-Victorian novel that quite self-consciously takes up questions of detachment in its foregrounding of different modes of observation, alienation, and cultivated emotional distance. Central to the first-person narrative of the self-describedly cool Lucy

---

[15] See Nord, *Walking the Victorian Streets*; Barbara Leah Harman, *The Feminine Political Novel in Victorian England* (Charlottesville: University Press of Virginia, 1998); Monica F. Cohen, *Professional Domesticity in the Victorian Novel: Women, Work, and Home* (Cambridge: Cambridge University Press, 1998).

Snowe is an ongoing interrogation of prescribed gender roles, cultural norms, and institutional practices, particularly those shaping the family, the school, the church, and the arts. Beginning with both the formative experiences of homelessness and estrangement during her youth in England and the international standpoint introduced by the subsequent change of venue to the "cosmopolitan city" of Villette (Brussels), the novel explores multiple forms of detachment, associated with a range of psychological states, cultural prescriptions, institutional practices, and intellectual and aesthetic modes.[16]

What Brontë's novel establishes, above all, is the importance of taking forms of detachment into consideration when dealing with the gender ideology of the Victorian period. As many feminist readings of the novel have pointed out, *Villette* presents a world in which women are routinely subjected to various forms of scopic and modern disciplinary power. Yet it also establishes the ways in which cultivated observation and distance were seen as constitutive not only of emergent professional and aesthetic practices, but also of femininity and maternity themselves. Indeed, given its seemingly expansive conception of women's agency and social power, *Villette* could be seen as the perfect case study for the feminist claims that I analyzed in the first half of the chapter. But a close consideration of Brontë's novel ultimately reveals the shortcomings of those projects, even as it illuminates the basis of their appeal.

Villette provides a complex map of detachment in its portrayal of masculine professional disinterestedness (Dr. John/Graham Bretton), maternal impersonality (Mrs. Bretton), feminine polish (Polly), institutional and familial surveillance (Mme. Beck), aggressive scrutiny (M. Paul), and self-effacing observation (Lucy Snowe). In a sense the novel is an extended record of Lucy's refusal of the limited and sometimes even damaging forms of detachment that manifest themselves around her, even as she aims, with uneven results, to claim a detachment she can call her own. Her life narrative thus registers with some sensitivity the ways in which prevalent conventions and practices made it almost impossible for Victorians to imagine a positive, and disinterestedly critical, conception of feminine detachment. If one focuses on the opposing characters of Mrs. Bretton and Mme. Beck, for example, one is faced with equally unattractive options: a kind but oblivious impersonality or a power of surveillance tainted by self-interest. The narrator's apprehension of these forms of detachment and the traps they pose,

---

[16] Charlotte Brontë, *Villette* (Harmondsworth: Penguin, 1979), 145. Subsequent page number references to this edition will be made parenthetically in the text.

however, itself constitutes a species of critical reflection, though, as we shall see, it remains an intractably elusive one.

Ultimately, Brontë's novel gives us a more richly conceived, and historically nuanced, understanding of feminine agency than we saw operating in the feminist analyses that appealed to unreflective forms of power, on the one hand, and aggrandized agents, on the other. Indeed, it does so precisely by acknowledging and demystifying the force of these figures. Moreover, insofar as the novel uses the first-person narration of Lucy Snowe to stage a reflective engagement with questions of detachment, *Villette* discourages an interpretive strategy that relies upon an unacknowledged distinction between knowing authors and constructed characters, as in the criticism of Langland and Armstrong, where Victorian authors like Gaskell, Oliphant, and the Brontës were accorded a level of critical insight into subject-constituting forms of power that were on another level denied to the characters within the novel, and to the historical forms of consciousness that were being "read off" of those very characters.

Fundamental to the novel's thematics of detachment is a pervasive ambivalence on Lucy's part about her own marginal status, an ambivalence that stems from Lucy's personal history, her critical perspective on prevailing gender norms, and her vexed relation to the very modes of surveillance and withdrawal that define her status as an artist and social critic. In psychological terms, and partly because of her own obtrusively unspecified history of personal loss, Lucy persistently seeks to mute her own affect and sustain a stoic tranquillity and calm. She reacts to those who intrude their powers of scrutiny upon her by attempting to shield or distance herself, wary of the perpetual threat of failed intimacy and the acute potential of misrecognition. Insofar as her self-imposed therapeutic project masks a frustrated ideal of reciprocal and unguarded intimacy, Lucy's embrace of it remains awkward. In more broadly social and institutional terms, however, Lucy's cultivation of detachment traces to her critique of contemporary gender roles, not simply as a defense against the narrowly romantic aspirations allotted to women, or the constraining sequence of roles that typically mark "la vie d'une femme," but also as a complex mirroring, and aesthetic appropriation, of the forms of surveillance, impersonality, and neutrality that marked Victorian discourses of femininity and professionalism.

Individual characters within the novel represent different enactments of social roles and forms of institutional power, against or by means of which Lucy attempts to define herself. Indeed, given the sense of the uncanny pervading the novel, these characters have the air of shadow selves haunting the narrator.[17] As many critics have noticed, one character whose own practices of power seem especially to haunt Lucy's imagination is Mme. Beck, the schoolmistress who employs Lucy at the pensionnat in Villette.[18] From one perspective, Mme. Beck can be easily assimilated to a Foucauldian feminist model that recognizes the middle-class woman not as a figure relegated to a narrowly conceived domestic and emotional sphere, but rather as an agent of modern disciplinary power and its broad familial and institutional processes of surveillance and regimentation.[19] Yet it is crucial to note that Lucy portrays the power of Mme. Beck, both mother and school director, as negative and as culturally alien, associating Mme. Beck's management practices with Jesuitical Catholicism and dubious "continental" practices that fail to promote genuine moral awareness and growth. Missing from the world as Mme. Beck construes and constructs it is any hallowed sense of privacy or

[17] See Sandra M. Gilbert and Susan Gubar, *The Madwoman in the Attic: The Woman Writer and the Nineteenth-Century Literary Imagination* (New Haven: Yale University Press, 1979), 399–440, for an interpretation of the novel based on reading the many women characters as doubles for Lucy. Also see Janice M. Carlisle, "The Face in the Mirror: *Villette* and the Conventions of Autobiography," *ELH* 46 (1979): 262–89.

[18] For discussions of Mme. Beck as a double for Lucy, see Gilbert and Gubar, *The Madwoman in the Attic*, 408–9; Joseph Allan Boone, *Libidinal Currents: Sexuality and the Shaping of Modernism* (Chicago: University of Chicago Press, 1998), 42–43; Joseph Litvak, "Charlotte Brontë and the Scene of Instruction: Authority and Subversion in *Villette*," *Nineteenth-Century Literature* 42 (1988): 473–75; Nina Auerbach, *Communities of Women: An Idea in Fiction* (Cambridge: Harvard University Press, 1978), 103.

[19] For a discussion of how easily this novel can be made to fit a Foucauldian paradigm, see Boone, *Libidinal Currents*, 37–45. Boone focuses on the surveillance enacted by M. Paul, Mme. Beck, and the institution of the Catholic Church; he does not focus particularly on Mme. Beck as a figure for a specifically feminine form of disciplinary power. Insofar as Mme. Beck's form of power is primarily institutional, many critics dissociate her from the family and from femininity, stressing Lucy's perception of her as masculine (e.g., in comparing her to Napoleon) and as suited to masculine political arenas. But the fact that home and school are conflated for Mme. Beck would also invite a reading that assimilated feminine domestic power to the larger project of modern disciplinary institutions. Of course the novel cannot be seen as endorsing such a model of power, even if it might be said to recognize it: Lucy's insistence on Mme. Beck's inadequate mothering introduces a strongly critical perspective on the idea of a feminine power comprising family and state. For this reason, it makes sense to read this novel, as Nina Auerbach has done, as wishing to create a strict division between the state and the family. See Auerbach, *Communities of Women*, 97–113.

interiority, either personal or familial. Just as her home is continuous with the institution of the school that she directs, so too her maternal activities are indistinguishable from her pedagogical ones: both are marked by secrecy, surveillance, and absence of affect.

Mme. Beck represents a power that is continuous both with forms of control associated with the state and its several agencies and with what in the English imagination of the novel should remain as a protected sphere of the family and the private affections.[20] Indeed, far from being the conduit for an efficacious power of subject-formation, as English middle-class femininity was in the studies by Poovey and Armstrong, Mme. Beck is the representative of a fundamentally amoral and external system that Lucy sees as doomed to fail insofar as it cannot speak to the soul of its subjects. Thus despite her admiration for Mme. Beck, Lucy rejects her observational practice as a form of influence that is both immoral and ineffective. Mme. Beck applies the same "hollow system" to her own transgressive eldest child, the unbridled Desirée, as she does to her students and teachers. When Desirée steals items from her mother, her mother simply steals them back. "Never once, I believe, did [Mme. Beck] tell her faithfully of her faults, explain the evil of such habits, and show the results which must thence ensue. Surveillance must work the whole cure. It failed of course" (158).

Mme. Beck displays no emotion and no sympathy, though she practices a rational benevolence at the level of society, giving generously to classes of people but acting distantly toward those around her. We are told, moreover, that "interest was the master-key of madame's nature" (136), that no appeal to feeling could ever sway her in any case where she stood personally to lose or gain. In her pursuance of power based on cloaked omniscience, Mme. Beck thus represents the cultivation of systemic observation in the service of interest and power. In this sense she operates as a negative version of the practice of discreet observation that informs this novel's project of first-person narration; she is also defined against the disinterested observation symbolized by Dr. Graham Bretton, the English medical doctor, as well as the mild, drowsy maternalism of Mrs. Bretton, Lucy's godmother.

[20] In its representation of the power structure of Mme. Beck's pensionnat and the larger world of Villette, this novel largely conflates state, church, and school, though certainly the Belgian culture was at this time undergoing marked contests of power between Catholics and liberals. The only hint we get of such larger political divisions within the country is when we read that most of M. Paul's colleagues were freethinkers and not dutiful Catholics. Otherwise the novel largely imagines a sort of pervasive power that comprises empire, church, and school (particularly in the iconography of the fête).

Despite Lucy's seemingly firm judgments about Mme. Beck's practices, however, the attempt to draw distinctions between Mme. Beck and those, including Lucy, who represent English forms of femininity and professional expertise is a highly precarious venture, as many critics of the novel have remarked.[21] First, it is often difficult to draw clear lines between the forms of institutional power exercised within the Catholic world of Villette and those that define the constraining conventions of English culture. Lucy may perceive Mme. Beck and Catholicism as clear antagonists to her principles and freedom, but the Brettons and Britain do not function consistently as clear counterexamples. At the same time, a simple deconstruction of the novel's oppositions between England and the continent also fails to disclose the complex cultural and intercultural drama at play. It will not do, that is, simply to say that Lucy and the other English characters themselves inhabit or engage forms of power that are analogous to, or just as constraining as, the forms of power that the narrator projects as "continental." For what is centrally at stake here is the narrator's attempt to lay claim to certain practices of detachment, while at the same time carefully assessing and responding to other forms which she rejects or from which she seeks to establish distance. *Villette* displays a keen awareness that very fine, and potentially collapsible, distinctions may be separating different forms of detachment. Some of those distinctions are associated with differences of culture, gender, and religion, but the admission of a near equivalence of many of the English and continental practices results in an uncertain position, one that can sometimes only be indicated by negative critique of both cultures, a move of what might be called radical detachment that itself produces great psychological strain on the narrator. This is a delicate project, and the power of the novel resides largely in its exacting phenomenology of the difficulties involved in any attempt to achieve affective or cognitive mastery over this process.

It has been argued that Lucy herself is complicit with the constraining ideology of femininity that characterizes the English world of the novel.[22] But the narrative actually manifests an oscillation between two different modes of response. On the one hand, Lucy generates critiques of institutions and prevailing cultural conventions based on a set of seemingly stable ideals.

[21] See Rosemary Clark-Beattie, "Fables of Rebellion: Anti-Catholicism and the Structure of *Villette*," *ELH* 53 (1986): 821–47; Ruth Bernard Yeazell, *Fictions of Modesty: Women and Courtship in the English Novel* (Chicago: University of Chicago Press, 1991), 169–93. Also see Gilbert and Gubar, *The Madwoman in the Attic*; Boone, *Libidinal Currents*; Litvak, "Charlotte Brontë and the Scene of Instruction"; Auerbach, *Communities of Women*.

[22] See Clark-Beattie, "Fables of Rebellion," and Yeazell, *Fictions of Modesty*.

The world as represented by Villette—Catholicism, surveillance, absolut-ism—is criticized from the standpoint of English ideals—Protestant inward-ness, disinterested knowledge, and personal liberty. Supplementing these basic ideals is a belief in the broader moral ideal of inner growth rather than external conformity, and a promotion of feminine modesty and maternal solicitude. On the other hand, Lucy experiences difficulty in affirming the English ideals, especially when they are considered in isolation from the continental practices they oppose.[23] The disinterestedness of Dr. John, the deindividualizing effects of Polly's modesty, and the impersonality of Mrs. Bretton all produce an ambivalent response in Lucy, both insofar as they are experienced as forms of oppression and because her own practices of with-drawn observation seem inevitably to mimic them as much as they mimic the interested surveillance of Mme. Beck. The consequent narrative ten-sion, and in particular the famous elusiveness of the narrator, are less com-plicity in English conventions of femininity than a countermove of pure negation that leaves Lucy, to adapt one of her own self-descriptions, a "placeless person" (103). This placelessness is a symptom of her attempt to find a detachment that she can call her own.

For this reason, it does not fully make sense to read this novel, as many have done, as the narrative of Lucy's hard-earned bid for independence.[24] To do so is to occlude the thematics of detachment and to foreground instead an opposition between control and autonomy, where autonomy involves a capacity to achieve integration and stand against the forms of power that otherwise constrain and condition the individual. Such an approach not only fails adequately to acknowledge Lucy's reflective refusals, but also cannot

[23] Despite her emphasis on Lucy's debilitating investment in English conventions of femininity, Clarke-Beattie also brilliantly demonstrates this strange economy in the text, whereby the English standards that fuel the critique of Catholicism and Villette themselves become structures of oppression when considered in isolation. I take issue, however, with Clark-Beattie's tendency to reduce Lucy's practices of detachment entirely to coded feminine behavior. See Clark-Beattie, "Fables of Rebellion."

[24] A version of this argument appears, as Karen Lawrence points out, in those readings that claim that Lucy's growth can be measured by her increasing willing-ness and ability to abandon her position as observer and play a central role in her own life. See Karen Lawrence, "The Cypher: Disclosure and Reticence in *Villette*," *Nine-teenth-Century Literature* 42 (1988): 448–50. As Lawrence points out, such readings fail to register Lucy's active desire to remain overlooked and to exploit and cultivate her observer status. Lawrence cites as instances of such readings Gilbert and Gubar, *The Madwoman in the Attic*, and Brenda R. Silver, "The Reflecting Reader in *Vil-lette*," in *The Voyage In: Fictions of Female Development*, ed. Elizabeth Abel et al. (Hanover: University Press of New England, 1983), 90–111.

distinctly formulate the manner in which she also attempts to endorse and lay claim to positive practices of detachment—moral, institutional, and aesthetic. Only by recognizing the text's dual impulses toward radical placelessness and cultivated detachment can we make sense of Brontë's complex approach to Victorian gender ideology, an approach that cannot be accommodated by either the feminist analyses I discussed earlier or those liberal feminist interpretations of *Villette* that presuppose autonomy as the basis for Lucy's self-fulfillment.

As a narrator and a participant-observer of her shifting situation, Lucy cultivates a distinctly critical distance. Not simply looking back over her life and describing it to us, Lucy seems always already to have constituted herself as an onlooker of her own existence. In her capacity as such, she makes a series of judgments about those individuals and practices with which she comes in contact. She is thus at once both critically reflective and constrained by circumstance, and hence she herself certainly fits neither the model of unreflective feminine power nor the model of the aggrandized agent. Her capacities for detached analysis and judgment do not translate into extravagant power, as for example in the case of Poovey's Nightingale. Rather, Lucy herself subjects the ambitious form of power represented by Mme. Beck to subtle scrutiny, playing out an attraction to a more potent agency and control than she herself is capable of attaining, or pretends to own, while on the other hand insisting on its moral flaws and ultimate inefficacy: Lucy, that is, refuses to aggrandize what projects itself as a kind of omnipotence based on omniscience.[25] Lucy is contemptuous of Mme. Beck's system of surveillance because it operates extrinsically, failing to prompt or inspire any genuine moral growth or self-understanding. It both employs and promotes artificiality, deception, and indirection. A fundamentally limited form of power, it mistakes evidence for knowledge, and knowledge for control. At the same time, Lucy acknowledges Mme. Beck's power as a talent for administration that would immediately be recognized as virtuosity in fields that place strategic interests above any moral principle:

> I say again, madame was a very great and a very capable woman. That school offered for her powers too limited a sphere; she ought to have swayed a nation: she should have been the leader of a turbulent legislative

[25] The rejection of omniscience is also expressed in the novel's use of first-person narration. Of course one could argue that Lucy herself participates in a flaunting of privileged knowledge when she withholds crucial information from the reader, most noticeably at the novel's end. But I will be arguing that Lucy's withholding of information operates very differently and is not an attempt to aggrandize her own power as a narrator.

assembly. Nobody could have brow-beaten her, none irritated her nerves, exhausted her patience, or over-reached her astuteness. In her own single person, she could have comprised the duties of a first minister and a superintendent of police. Wise, firm, faithless; secret, crafty, passionless; watchful and inscrutable; acute and insensate—withal perfectly decorous—what more could be desired? (137)

Lucy displays a wry ambivalence about Mme. Beck's considerable powers: she has harsh things to say about her deception, her impersonal treatment of her children, and her fundamentally extrinsic pedagogy, but she finds herself compelled to admire Mme. Beck's strength, canniness, and "consummate tact," as well as her apparent immunity to the forms of psychological distress that plague Lucy and disrupt her ongoing attempts to maintain tranquillity and stoic calm (181). And indeed, Mme. Beck handles a number of situations with impressive political art: she realizes, for example, that insofar as the English overvalue their personal liberty, the best way to manage Lucy is to bend policy and allow her free rein. In the face of mounting rumors about her association with Dr. Bretton, she remains unruffled, thereby securing both her own reputation and the reputation of her school. Lucy cannot suppress her admiration in this instance: "little Jesuit though she might be, yet I clapped the hands of my heart, and with its voice called 'brava!' as I watched her able bearing, her skilled management, her temper and her firmness on this occasion" (165).

Ultimately, however, Lucy insists on certain moral and practical distinctions. Mme. Beck's ethics and her pedagogy are seen as inadequate; and although her force of character is admirable especially where she stands up to a moralistic sexism, her mode of power belongs to a sphere of life—state politics—that Lucy perceives as fundamentally amoral. Insofar as Mme. Beck's power pretends to cover the sphere of character formation (in its focus on child, student, and employee), Lucy both condemns and demystifies it. Lucy's response to Mme. Beck, of course, derives from her own complex investments. Although she herself derives great pleasure from stealthy observation of others, she seeks to divorce such behavior from any imperial exercise of institutional power and to attribute it to a sphere of limited vocation—a vocation that is at once personal, pedagogical, and aesthetic. Indeed, these dimensions of vocation correspond to three sources of her interest in detachment: a psychological interest in characterological ideals of stoicism and muted affect, a social and moral interest in professional demeanor and its infiltration into familial and pedagogical spheres, and an aesthetic interest in practices of observation and representation.

With respect to the categories of moral stoicism and professional demeanor, it can certainly appear difficult to hold to a strong distinction between Mme. Beck and the English characters. Even as Lucy discredits Mme. Beck's inability to show warmth toward her children, arm's-length affection is held up as an admirable characteristic among the English, and as a personal aim for Lucy Snowe. As I stated earlier, Lucy actively cultivates diminished affect and reduced expectations: she persistently attempts to minimize the possibility for any renewal of the sting of loss and deprivation. Somewhat paradoxically, she idealizes attenuated interactions and bonds, suggesting that a more fully realized reciprocal intimacy may shatter her precarious tranquillity. Accordingly, the epistolary relation with Graham takes on an obsessive quality and eclipses his actual presence the night she loses his letter in the attic; likewise, Lucy attests repeatedly to her temperamental preference for the muted kind of attachment she feels for her godmother, Mrs. Bretton, a woman who herself "preferred all sentimental demonstration in bas-relief" (249). Underlying this is a deep apprehensiveness about direct recognition and unguarded affection, which Lucy does not want to let herself desire, and which are imagined as always entailing a threat of violence, as evidenced by the portrayal of the developing relationship with M. Paul.

In several ways, Mrs. Bretton is deliberately contrasted to Mme. Beck: she displays a calm good sense, steady but controlled affection, and, most tellingly, no addiction to constant supervision of those within her charge. On the contrary, she has a tendency to doze off in company, which in the context of the representation of Mme. Beck, Jesuitism, and the continental system can be read as nothing other than a badge of honor. Yet even as Mrs. Bretton manifests a somewhat comic form of maternal possessiveness in relation to her son, it covers a fairly powerful and even watchful exclusivity, as in the theatre scene where it becomes clear that she has noticed Ginevra Fanshawe's slighting attentions to her. But Lucy is never the object of this kind of heightened maternal feeling, which in any event is only given oblique expression in the case of Graham. In depicting the surrogate mother as somewhat distant but still kind, Lucy Snowe, one could argue, is simply constructing a defensive maternal ideal against an overwhelming experience of loss, but it is also the case that Mrs. Bretton's relation to Lucy reflects the cultivated distance that marked the emergent conception of controlled and professionalized motherhood in the Victorian era. All mothers, in this conception, were in some respects redefined as godmothers, as those who were responsible for the moral and spiritual welfare of the next generation, and as those who needed to guard against the dangers of an unchecked intimacy.

What is crucial to any understanding of this novel is that Lucy displays ambivalence toward this alternative as much as she does toward the frustrated ideal it is meant to guard against. On the one hand, Lucy admires Mrs. Bretton's calm control and even temper and clearly shares in Graham's belief that she is an exemplary representative of British middle-class femininity. On the other hand, Lucy cannot always suppress her bitter sense that Mrs. Bretton's impersonality translates into indifference, especially where her god-daughter is concerned. This is hinted at very early in the novel, when Lucy makes the following puzzling remark, in reference to her own presence at Bretton: "One child in a household of grown people is usually made very much of, and in a quiet way I was a good deal taken notice of by Mrs. Bretton" (61). What is so strange about this remark is that Lucy is *not* the only child in the household—Mrs. Bretton's beloved son Graham is also there—and this seems to invite the suspicion that Lucy is, or perceives herself to be, always already supplanted by a more favored child, first Graham, then Polly. Later in the novel, despite the fact that the Brettons provide a haven for Lucy and manifest an allegiance to her, Lucy registers the fact that the Brettons' serene behavior issues in neglect. The most telling indication of Lucy's suppressed anger at Mrs. Bretton comes at the moment when Mrs. Bretton renews contact after a lapse of seven weeks, precisely the time when Polly Home reappears on the scene. This is a moment of great isolation for Lucy: when she does finally receive an invitation from Mrs. Bretton, she transcribes it into the narrative. In the context of Lucy's complaints about her present lot, and Mrs. Bretton's knowledge of Lucy's past troubles, the letter's breezy kindness carries an almost sadistic edge. Indeed, given Lucy's preamble, in which she catalogs her sufferings and refers to herself as a hermit and a caged animal, the letter reflects an immediately jarring carelessness and unknowingness:

> Dear Lucy,—It occurs to me to inquire what you have been doing with yourself for the last month or two? Not that I suspect you would have the least difficulty in giving an account of your proceedings. I daresay you have been just as busy and happy as ourselves at La Terrasse. (354)

The letter goes on to boast about Graham at great length and then finally comes around to an actual invitation. Despite Lucy's claim that "a letter like that sets one to rights" and her expression of relief that her friends are all well, she in the same breath registers the chilling fact that "[t]heir feelings for me were—as they had been" (356).

I suggest that we read the relationship between Mrs. Bretton and Lucy not simply in the context of Lucy's personal history of loss and anxious emotional investment but also as a reflection of a certain tension between feeling and neutrality within Victorian gender ideology. The feminine domestic ideal, particularly the versions that stressed women's roles as moral guardians or superintendents, promoted a certain cultivation of detachment and impersonality within what was at the same time defined as a sphere of intimacy and solicitude: a place where one could fully be oneself, a place where one would be known and cared for. Insofar as excessive passion was associated with sexuality, feminine modesty had always required a certain muting of affect.[26] But a new ideal of cultivated detachment was also operative in understandings of a specifically maternal impersonality or distance. Because it did not require the extravagant forms of innocent consciousness and merely intuitive judgment that the ideology of maiden femininity did, maternity was often characterized by forms of critical and disinterested judgment that existed in some tension with the qualities of devotion, empathy, and even solicitude.[27] The cryptic loss of the mother that inaugurates Lucy's story in this novel might also be read, that is, as the impossibility of a certain idea of motherhood.

In *Family Fortunes: Men and Women of the Middle Class, 1780–1850,* Leonore Davidoff and Catherine Hall provide extensive discussion of early Victorian ideologues who promulgated the notion of professional motherhood, including nationally prominent writers such as Sarah Stickney Ellis and Harriet Martineau.[28] The emphasis on the mother's duty to train her children carefully often involved cautions against emotional indulgenceand calls for appropriate distance. A similar ambivalence toward the virtues of cultivating a certain distance in the practices of motherhood can be seen in Mrs. Henry Wood's *East Lynne*, where the emotional impulsiveness of Isabel Carlyle is contrasted to the more detached approach of Barbara Hale, who acts as the spokesperson for some of the emerging middle-class ideas:

> I hold an opinion, Mrs. Vine, that too many mothers pursue a mistaken system in the management of their family. There are some, we know, who, lost in the pleasures of the world, in frivolity, wholly neglect them: of those I do not speak; nothing can be more thoughtless, more reprehensible; but

---

[26] See Yeazell, *Fictions of Modesty.*

[27] For discussion of the feminine ideal of disinterested analysis in Victorian gender ideology, and the way in which it was defined against interested behavior in the public sphere, see Harman, *The Feminine Political Novel in Victorian England.*

[28] See Leonore Davidoff and Catherine Hall, *Family Fortunes: Men and Women of the English Middle Class, 1780–1850* (Chicago: University of Chicago Press, 1987), 172–92.

there are others who err on the opposite side. They are never happy but when with their children. . . . A child should never hear aught from its mother's lips but persuasive gentleness; and this becomes impossible, if she is very much with her children.[29]

The ideal of feminine detachment appears in the portrayal of not only Mrs. Bretton, Lucy's godmother, but also Paulina Home, the diminutive child-woman who will be matrimonially paired with Dr. Graham Bretton. Paulina represents a more delicate version of maturing femininity, with emotional self-control and modesty replacing an earlier childhood candor and elasticity. As Lucy watches an interaction between Graham and Paulina during the early stages of their reacquaintance, she describes Paulina's new form of character:

> [Graham] was answered by Miss de Bassompierre in quite womanly sort; with intelligence, with a manner not indeed wholly disindividualized: a tone, a glance, a gesture, here and there, rather animated and quick than measured and stately, still recalled little Polly; but yet there was so fine and even a polish, so calm and courteous a grace, gilding and sustaining these peculiarities, that a less sensitive man than Graham would not have ventured to seize upon them as vantage points, leading to a franker intimacy. (371)

This passage suggests that womanliness in general involves an impersonality, what Lucy calls a "disindividualizing" manner. It is not simply that the role eclipses the individual, but that the role defines itself in terms of a kind of unapproachable neutrality. What redeems Paulina, and constitutes her distinctive charm, is that her individuality can still be glimpsed intermittently. Thus it becomes apparent, again, that Lucy's cultivation of a detachment in the service of art is not something that can be sharply opposed to the ideals of English femininity offered up in the characters of Paulina and Mrs. Bretton; she is not so much painfully yet productively alienated from cozy familial life—in the manner of a romanticized artist figure—as surrounded by forms of alienation that are increasingly coming to define the modern family, the modern professions, and institutional life. Any detachment she may wish to cultivate must thus be a delicate mixture of appropriation and opposition.

[29] Mrs. Henry Wood, *East Lynne* (New Brunswick: Rutgers University Press, 1984), 341. For a powerfully nuanced analysis of the ambivalent presentation of professionalism and motherhood in *East Lynne*, see John Kucich, *The Power of Lies: Transgression in Victorian Fiction* (Ithaca: Cornell University Press, 1994), 158–95.

Villette's complex historical cluster of forms of feminine detachment, disinterestedness, and disciplinary power cannot be assimilated to the paradigms I discussed in the first half of the chapter, particularly those that assimilate women to unreflective and efficacious forms of power. Indeed, if we look closely at Mme. Beck and Mrs. Bretton, their familial and institutional practices are not seen as simply coterminous with a form of power that they instantiate. Mme. Beck's system is only partly successful, and her power does not uniformly achieve even its more limited aim of controlling external behavior (she fails to stop Ginevra Fanshawe from eloping, just as she fails to mount an effective barrier between M. Paul and Lucy). Likewise, Mrs. Bretton's mode of muted kindness, whose ambitions and range of effects seem quite limited, does not in any simple way create tranquil or morally "finished" subjects, especially in the case of Lucy, who both admires and resents Mrs. Bretton. Apart from anything else, Mrs. Bretton seems to function as an exemplar rather than as an effective agent: it is unthinkably contemptible for anyone to think of ridiculing the "sensible, admirable old lady," as Graham refers to her, precisely because she is a model of middle-class femininity, sufficient unto herself, composed, calm, unpretentious (296).

If Mme. Beck and Mrs. Bretton represent forms of psychological detachment to which Lucy is ambivalently drawn, she must also labor to articulate a conception of aesthetic distance that will meet her ambitions as well as reflect her moral principles. Lucy is all too aware that her practices of shielded observation come strikingly close to the immoral practices of surveillance pursued by Mme. Beck. Indeed, in large part the novel records Lucy's ongoing attempt to appropriate and transform what otherwise operate as disabling or negative modes of detachment: crippling psychological and emotional exile, instrumental and self-interested forms of surveillance, and complacent stoicism. This is never an easy or completed process, and the novel is in fact ruthless in its portrayals of the serious emotional and psychological liabilities of Lucy's conscious cultivation of detachment. Detachment threatens to become a pathology at times, as in the instance of Lucy's monomaniacal attachment to the letters Dr. Graham sends her. It leads to a full-fledged nervous breakdown during the long vacation she spends only in the company of the crétin in the pensionnat. It can also seem singularly motivated by avoidance of any further loss or pain, most especially the pain occasioned by Lucy's extravagant sensitivity to any experience of nonrecognition. But detachment is also shown as the enabling condition of Lucy's capacity for social critique through artistry, a source of power and pleasure that she takes some pains to distinguish from the highly instrumental and fundamentally self-interested power of Mme. Beck.

Lucy highlights the keen pleasures she derives from her unseen or at least unacknowledged observation of others, much of which coincides with moments of acute narrative tension. Early in the novel, Lucy casts her marginal position in the Bretton household as an aesthetic advantage: Polly's imminent departure after a mere two months is announced with Lucy's somewhat ironic admission that she "was not long allowed the amusement of this study of character" (87). Repeatedly, her exilic condition produces both pleasure and insight, even when it derives from outright exclusion. She is able to enjoy what is represented as the "riveting" experience of recognizing Graham Bretton in Dr. John precisely because he disregards her: "He laid himself open to my observation, according my presence in the room just that degree of notice and consequence a person of my exterior habitually expects: that is to say, about what is given to unobtrusive articles of furniture, chairs of ordinary joiner's work, and carpets of no striking pattern" (162). Lucy outmaneuvers Mme. Beck, repeatedly watching her acts of espionage from under her own nondescript cover. She sums up this strange economy of pleasure and exclusion on the night of the fête: "It gave me strange pleasure to follow these friends viewlessly, and I *did* follow them" (550). These combined activities of observation and immunity amount to what Lucy refers to as "a knowledge of [her] own" in a conversation with M. Paul (444). And indeed, Lucy takes some pains to disavow conventional forms of knowledge and intellectual mastery, the better to lay claim to her distinctive form of detached observation, a form that derives specifically from her status as situated outsider. Before she relinquishes "the enchantment of distance" and begins teaching in the pensionnat (138), for example, she lacks the capacity to understand the sociological category of the "jeune fille":

> I shall never forget that first lesson, nor all the under-current of life and character it opened up to me. Then first did I begin rightly to see the wide difference that lies between the novelist's and poet's ideal "jeune fille," and the said "jeune fille" as she really is. (142)

This is a potent moment, insofar as several scenes in the novel will interrogate the distanced observation of feminine types and anomalies. Indeed, Lucy's own clear aspiration to a form of authentic professional knowledge in this passage contrasts with her representation of Dr. John's disinterestedness. In many ways, and not simply because he is for a considerable portion of the narrative the chosen secret object of Lucy's affection, Dr. John serves as a contrast to Mme. Beck and as a model of professional discretion and genuine altruism. He is praised for his powers of insight and medical solicitude, and he is represented as a truly benevolent philanthropist and pillar of his adopted continental community. Yet Lucy also takes pains to point out a certain myopia and lack of penetration in her ostensible hero. It is not simply that he fails to recognize her or fails without severe trial to see through Ginevra Fanshawe. More damningly, he is capable of sympathy only in the face of a direct and explicit appeal; powerful manifestations of feeling and imagination are lost on him, except insofar as they function as symptoms of nervous excitation. Thus while Dr. John asserts that both he and Lucy have an "observant faculty," she severely indicts him for a failure to respond to the intensity of the actress Vashti, and for his own bias toward conventional femininity. His cool detachment does not lead in the direction of insight or enlightenment, even if it can be productively opposed to Mme. Beck's interested surveillance.

The famous ending of the novel, where Lucy strongly hints but will not state directly that M. Paul dies by shipwreck, and where she teasingly offers a happy ending to those readers endowed with "sunny imaginations," itself plays upon the theme of detachment (596). Like other well-catalogued evasions and withholdings of this narrator, the ending's equivocation can be seen not so much as a power-play on Lucy's part, but rather as a way to forestall attempts to read her into conventional narratives. What is counterposed to such norms, in each case, is an insistence on her identity as someone who derives meaning through *work*. The years without M. Paul were, by her own assertion, the happiest years of her life, and precisely because she worked. The withholding of her recognition of Dr. John and the gift of flowers from M. Paul both serve to forestall giving primacy to any narrative of romance, if only temporarily. Yet as the reaction of Mr. Home to her disclosure of her profession as a teacher demonstrates—for a painful interval he will not look up and acknowledge what she has said—any simple affirmation of her job can issue in profound social invisibility and diminishment. In that light, evasion seems not only rational but effectively critical of the entrapment of each option.

The question of the psychological strains of persistent detachment remains a powerful one in this novel, and, as we shall see in the following chapters, in the culture at large. What is so compelling about Brontë's contribution to the literature of detachment, apart from the considerable light it sheds on cultural forms of feminine detachment, is her rigorous psychological study of detachment's attractions and costs, whether it be conceived as a practice of the self, as an intellectual mode, as a professional demeanor, or as a form of institutional power. Part of the distinctiveness of Brontë's text stems from the fact that it does not subordinate the psychological to the moral, as many other thinkers do. By this I mean that while Brontë does not shy away from making judgments about the moral effects or dimensions of various forms of detachment, she also does not imagine a place where moral and psychological stability easily meet. Dickens, to whom we shall now turn, explores the lure and danger of distance variously construed, yet he is drawn finally to cordon off distinctly pathologized versions of detachment, and to try to protect his morally privileged characters from the psychologically exacting and vertiginous insights that his own narrative nonetheless relies upon. Brontë, who to some extent may be said to veer toward such options, pulls back in an act of astonishing delicacy, allowing to her endorsed model of detachment a fundamentally artful, and honest, precariousness.

CHAPTER TWO

Cosmopolitanism in
Different Voices

CHARLES DICKENS'S *LITTLE DORRIT*
AND THE HERMENEUTICS OF SUSPICION

Charlotte Brontë's critique of cultural conventions and institutions in *Villette* is complicated by the novel's cosmopolitan framework, which on the one hand seems to erect British values as a standard by which continental practices should be judged, and on the other hand generates a disorienting relativism insofar as both national characters, the Labassecourian (Belgian) and the British, are subjected to withering analysis. While it may be tempting to attribute the ambiguities of Brontë's text to her interest in psychological instability, her divided investment in British values is shared by her contemporaries, many of whom were drawn to forms of comparative critique and cosmopolitan practice. The following three chapters will focus on three nineteenth-century writers—Charles Dickens, Matthew Arnold, and George Eliot—whose work reflects deep divisions between the not always compatible values of nationalism and cosmopolitanism. Throughout my analysis, I take pains to show not only the forms of hierarchy and exclusion that structure the thinking of these writers but also those moments where they pointedly extend their internationalist frameworks beyond Europe and the West, or otherwise challenge the logic of Empire. By reconstructing a tradition of cosmopolitan critique in Victorian culture, I hope to amplify our understanding of the multiple kinds of cultivated distance that informed nineteenth-century literary and intellectual methods, particularly the project of the realist novel but also, in the case of Arnold, the development of literary criticism itself.

Victorian views on cosmopolitanism must be situated within the context of nineteenth-century understandings of the term. In general, cosmopolitanism denotes reflective distance from one's original or primary cultural affiliations, a broad understanding of other cultures and customs, and a belief in universal humanity. The relative weight assigned to these three constitutive elements can vary, as can the forms of identification against which "reflective distance" is defined. In antiquity, with the initial elaboration of cosmopolitanism by the Cynics and the Stoics, cosmopolitan detachment was defined against the restricted perspective and interests of the polis. In the Enlightenment, it was defined against the constricting allegiances of religion, class, and, in the Kantian version, the absolutist state. In many of its Enlightenment manifestations, it comprises both intellectual and ethical dimensions, with a prominent emphasis on the practice of self-cultivation.[1] It is not until the nineteenth century, for obvious reasons, that cosmopolitanism begins to be defined in relation to nationalism, though it often carries along with it the ethos associated with the Enlightenment version.[2]

Those nineteenth-century writers who are drawn to cosmopolitan ideals rarely espouse them without conflict, given anxieties about rootlessness and competing investments in national identity and other forms of limited belonging. John Stuart Mill seeks to balance the endorsement of a civic nationalism closely allied to cosmopolitanism with a plea for "national cohesion" based on stable national character.[3] George Eliot laments the "cosmopolitan indifference" promoted by the rootless condition of the Jew, an indifference that threatens to afflict modern "migratory Englishmen" as well; at the same time she valorizes cosmopolitan artistic culture and a reflective relation to tradition, both of which she saw as enabled by cultivated detachment as well as instructive forms of exile.[4] For her, interestingly, the European Jew is ultimately in a position to overcome the threat of rootlessness and achieve an exemplary and considered response to the unavoidably destabilizing conditions of modern cosmopolitan life. Matthew Arnold makes appeal to the

[1] Thomas J. Schlereth, *The Cosmopolitan Ideal in Enlightenment Thought: Its Form and Function in the Ideas of Franklin, Hume, and Voltaire, 1694–1790* (South Bend: University of Notre Dame Press, 1977).

[2] As Pheng Cheah writes, "Kant's notion of cosmopolitan right is not anti- or postnationalist. A pre-nationalist attempt to reform absolute statism, it is not in the least an ideal of detachment opposed to national attachment. It is instead a form of right based on existing attachments that bind us into a collectivity larger than the state: it can be claimed against states because 'individuals and states, co-existing in an external relationship of mutual influences, may be regarded as citizens of a universal state of mankind.'" Pheng Cheah, "Introduction, Part II: The Cosmopolitical—Today," in *Cosmopolitics: Thinking and Feeling Beyond the Nation*, ed. Pheng Cheah and Bruce Robbins (Minneapolis: University of Minnesota Press, 1998), 24.

[3] John Stuart Mill, "Coleridge," in John Stuart Mill and Jeremy Bentham, *Utilitarianism and Other Essays*, ed. Alan Ryan (Harmondsworth: Penguin, 1987), 195–96.

[4] George Eliot, "The Modern Hep! Hep! Hep!" in *The Essays of Theophrastus Such* (London: Everyman, 1995), 146, 147.

need for the state to provide the binding glue of culture, yet he defines culture itself as the inward cultivation of "general intelligence" as well as a form of detachment from all parochial or sectarian interests.[5] Last but not least, Marx too, writing contemporaneously with these figures—and in their own capital city—was of course also deeply ambivalent about capitalist cosmopolitanism, which for him was an ideological displacement of the truly universal consciousness of the proletariat that was emerging precisely because of the increasingly international character of capitalist production.

Contemporary critiques of cosmopolitanism often draw on a particular Marxist tradition solidified by Gramsci to censure what they construe as disastrous detachment from the vital and necessary task of developing "national culture." In a recent book, Tim Brennan pursues this line of argument, along with the claim that cosmopolitanism, particularly in present-day America, is fully compatible with a neocolonial nationalism. Indeed, he argues that America ideologically forwards its own culture as *the* global culture, using a mystified cosmopolitanism to advance its own interests through global capitalism.[6] Related arguments about the complicity between nationalist and cosmopolitan ideologies within Europe have been forwarded by Jacques Derrida in *The Other Heading*.[7] Certainly some versions of nineteenth-century British cosmopolitanism—particularly those associated with the ennobling effects of the Grand Tour—are fully comfortable with the ways in which cosmopolitanism can reinforce ties to the home country. As James Buzard demonstrates, discourse on the Grand Tour frequently manifested the view, as for example in Frances Trollope's travel writing, that "exposure to the artistic treasures of Europe can liberate the English from their cultural insularity, but a view of the social and political systems of foreign countries will only convince Englanders that they are better off at home."[8]

While certain versions of cosmopolitanism can be shown to support nationalism, the cynical certainty that they necessarily do fails to pursue, in many particular cases, what is most interesting in the configured tensions

---

[5] Matthew Arnold, *Culture and Anarchy*, in *The Complete Prose Works of Matthew Arnold*, vol. 5: *Culture and Anarchy with Friendship's Garland and Some Literary Essays*, ed. R. H. Super (Ann Arbor: University of Michigan Press, 1965).

[6] Tim Brennan, *At Home in the World: Cosmopolitanism Now* (Cambridge: Harvard University Press, 1997).

[7] Jacques Derrida, *The Other Heading: Reflections on Today's Europe*, trans. Pascale-Anne Brault and Michael B. Naas (Bloomington: Indiana University Press, 1992).

[8] James Buzard, *The Beaten Track: European Tourism, Literature, and the Ways to "Culture," 1800–1918* (Oxford: Clarendon Press, 1993), 100.

between the terms.[9] As the default setting of an argument—the form it takes in Brennan's book—such cynicism obscures more than it reveals, allowing for a complacent rather than productive hermeneutics of suspicion. It remains unable to distinguish cosmopolitanism as national aggrandizement from those instances where writers seek to correct the insularity of nationalism by insisting that it incorporate an internationalist aspiration. Eliot takes this route in her treatment of Jewish nationalism in *Daniel Deronda*. The suspicious approach also cannot do justice to Dickens, who in *Little Dorrit* not only critically acknowledges the unholy alliance between British nationalism and global capitalism, but conveys a highly complicated understanding of the gains and losses of detachment cultivated in the service of systemic critique.

The opening scene of *Little Dorrit* might lead one to assume, it is true, that the novel is simply anticosmopolitan. Set in a prison in Marseilles, it introduces two characters: Rigaud, an imperious, self-vaunting prisoner whose pretenses are baldly exposed by the narrator, and his cell-mate, John Baptist Cavelletto, whose underlying goodness is betokened by his name and by his instinctive attraction to the angelic innocence of the jailer's daughter, who herself prefigures the eponymous heroine. Rigaud, later known as Blandois, is generally taken to be a rather starkly drawn, melodramatic villain, and his limited number of appearances in the novel—as well as his capricious function in the plot—establish him as a character of limited interest and complexity. But there is an element of his initial self-presentation that is fundamental to the thematics of detachment and belonging in this novel. Among a series of histrionic claims that seek to assert his status as both a "sensitive" gentleman and a victim of society's false understanding, Rigaud states, "I am a cosmopolitan gentleman. I own no particular country. My father was Swiss—Canton de Vaud. My mother was French by blood, English by birth. I myself was born in Belgium. I am a citizen of the world."[10]

Rigaud's cosmopolitanism—he has refined tastes, smokes cigarettes (an

---

[9] There are current arguments that assert, in contrast to the position advanced by Brennan, that nationalism and cosmopolitanism can exist in a mutually reinforcing relation that preserves the best principles of democracy at both the national and the international levels. This typically involves asserting an affinity between civic nationalism and cosmopolitanism: both share liberal-humanist values and privilege democratic practices, voluntary associations, and a self-reflective relation to cultural heritage and cultural difference. See, for example, David A. Hollinger, *Postethnic America: Beyond Multiculturalism* (New York: Basic Books, 1995).

[10] Charles Dickens, *Little Dorrit* (Harmondsworth: Penguin, 1967, 1985), 48. Subsequent page number references will be cited parenthetically in the text.

unusual delicacy at the setting of the novel), and projects the habitus of a cultivated traveler—is exposed to be a mere mask covering over brute desires, evil motives, and homicidal violence. In contrast to Rigaud's cultivated refinement, Cavelletto is impetuous, lively, passionate, and as such, immediately expressive of a distinct national culture: "In his submission, in his lightness, in his good humour, in his short-lived passion, in his easy contentment with hard bread and hard stones, in his ready sleep, in his fits and starts, altogether a true son of the land that gave him birth" (52).

The opening contrast between Rigaud and Cavelletto suggests, that is, that Dickens understands claims to detachment from national identity, or from communities of manageable scale, as illusory and suspicious, as forces that undermine an individual's sense of place and purpose, and vitiate national cohesion and vigor. Certainly the affectation of ennui, carelessness, or languid indifference forms an object of critique throughout the body of Dickens's work and is especially targeted in this novel's trenchant critique of the British bureaucracy, or "Circumlocution Office," and the hollow pretenses of "Society." Two key characters who share symbolic affiliations with Rigaud, the cynical artist Gowan and the paranoid, embittered Miss Wade, might be seen to further embody the evils of rootlessness and to set in higher relief the negative forces that constantly seek to thwart the energies and commitments of the "good" characters, particularly the hero Clennam, the engineer Doyce, and the heroine, Little Dorrit.

But the novel ultimately will not sustain such an interpretive approach. The most cosmopolitan of Dickens's novels in terms of setting, *Little Dorrit* has more continental scenes than any of his other novels, with the exception of a *A Tale of Two Cities*, which for very specific reasons is focused, in its French sections, on Paris.[11] *Little Dorrit*, by contrast, is populated by diverse travelers and exiles, and offsets the center of cosmopolitanism, Paris, by opening in Marseilles, which functions here not as the Eurocentric relay port to Italy, destination on the Grand Tour, but rather—with the jolt of an unexpected turn—as a more radically international link to Eastern trade. The city is populated by "strangers" and a teeming mass of nationalities who have "come to trade at Marseilles": "Hindoos, Russians, Chinese, Spaniards, Portuguese, Englishmen, Frenchmen, Genoese, Neopolitans, Venetians, Greeks, Turks, descendants from all the builders of Babel" (39). Transnational trade has eclipsed any national character this only nominally French city might have, and even Frenchmen "come to trade at Marseilles" as though it were another country or, rather, no country. The second chapter

[11] William M. Burgan, "Little Dorrit in Italy," *Nineteenth-Century Fiction* 29 (1975): 393.

introduces a group of quarantined travelers who have come from the East, including the hero Arthur Clennam, the Meagles family, and Miss Wade. The portrayal of Mr. Meagles immediately sets up a critique of provinciality through satirizing his references to French "allonging and marshonging" (53), and it becomes apparent that the hero's preceding twenty-year exile in China has served not only to estrange and disempower him but also to enable a critical perspective on English customs and practices once he returns to London.

Moreover, evidence elsewhere in Dickens suggests that he does not opt for any complacent patriotism. He certainly believes, as does Frances Trollope, that travel will promote a greater capacity for cosmopolitan aesthetic judgment. Writing from Italy to Forster in 1853, Dickens comments,

> I am more than ever confirmed in my conviction that one of the great uses of travelling is to encourage a man to think for himself, to be bold enough always to declare without offense that he does think for himself, and to overcome the villainous meanness of professing what other people have professed when he knows (if he has the capacity to originate an opinion) that his profession is untrue. The intolerable nonsense against which genteel taste and subserviency are afraid to rise, in connection with art, is astounding.[12]

A similar argument is put forth in an 1856 *Household Words* essay entitled "Insularities."[13] But we know from the biting critiques in *Little Dorrit* that Dickens did not share Trollope's view that travel was a salutary means of fostering patriotism, and this attitude is confirmed elsewhere, as when he writes to Forster complaining of the British painters on display at the Paris Exhibition, noting that comparative contexts do not show the English to advantage: "Don't think it a part of my despondency about public affairs, and my fear that our national glory is on the decline, when I say that mere form and conventionalities usurp, in English art, as in English government and social relations, the place of living force and truth."[14]

The remarks and views that I instance here date from the period just prior to the writing of *Little Dorrit*. They confirm the opinion, evinced by Burgan, that Dickens's continental travels in the 1850s promoted a markedly wider, more cosmopolitan perspective than his earlier continental sojourns

[12] Quoted in Richard Lettis, *The Dickens Aesthetic* (New York: AMS Press, 1989), 68.

[13] Charles Dickens, "Insularities," *Household Words*, January 19, 1856.

[14] Quoted in Janet Larson, "The Arts in These Latter Days: Carlylean Prophecy in *Little Dorrit*," *Dickens Studies Annual* 8 (1980): 141.

during the 1840s. As Burgan puts it, "it is in the later period that foreign culture appears to have attracted him as an urgently needed alternative to English manners, rather than as a mere refreshing change of scene."[15] In *Little Dorrit*, Dickens unmistakably satirizes expressions of vulgar nationalism, not only in the case of Mr. Meagles, whom he otherwise portrays sympathetically, but even more trenchantly when he exposes the working-class community's prejudicial and xenophobic response to Cavelletto (who ends up living and working in London), a response he ultimately lays at the door of the powerful classes, who promote such ideologies among "the people":

> It was uphill work for a foreigner, lame or sound, to make his way with the Bleeding Hearts. In the first place, they were vaguely persuaded that every foreigner had a knife about him; in the second, they held it to be a sound constitutional national axiom that he ought to go home to his own country. They never thought of inquiring how many of their own countrymen would be returned upon their hands from divers parts of the world, if the principle were generally recognised; they considered it particularly and peculiarly British. In the third place, they had a notion that it was a sort of Divine visitation upon a foreigner that he was not an Englishman, and that all kinds of calamities happened to his country because it did things that England did not, and did not do things that England did. In this belief, to be sure, they had long been carefully trained by the Barnacles and Stiltstalkings, who were always proclaiming to them, officially, that no country which failed to submit itself to those two large families could possibly hope to be under the protection of Providence; and who, when they believed it, disparaged them in private as the most prejudiced people under the sun. (350)

But one would not want to overemphasize Dickens's cosmopolitan leanings and consequently fail to register an underlying investment in a reinvigorated England. Dickens's vehement critique of the British state's bureaucratic inefficiency, which assumes prominence in this novel, rests upon a lament for the lost opportunities to foster and benefit from the energies of its subjects. There is, in other words, a failed national opportunity being recorded in the Circumlocution Office's impassive responses to the inventive enterprises of engineers like Doyce. As I shall elaborate in the course of my analysis, there is consequently a divided set of attitudes displayed toward British nationalism.[16]

---

[15] See Burgan, "Little Dorrit in Italy," 393, n.1.

[16] Suvendrini Perera and Deirdre David have exposed a similar schizophrenia on

CRITICAL COSMOPOLITANISM

Dickens's attitude toward cosmopolitanism must partly be reconstructed in light of his concerns with English provinciality and myopic nationalism, as these preliminary pieces of evidence and the example of the two prisoners demonstrate. The attitudes in evidence here will find novelistic elaboration throughout *Little Dorrit*: in the depiction of foreign travel undertaken by English characters; in the comments on English responses when foreigners visit their country; and in the portrayal of more extended cosmopolitan experience on the part of several of its main characters. But in addition to these topically pertinent sites, any consideration of Dickens's attitude toward cosmopolitanism must also be placed within the context of his deep ambivalence toward the very forms of cultivated distancing that enable a systemic critique of the social totality. On the one hand, Dickens ambitiously strove in his novels to comprehend a social whole, and his narratives repeatedly assert omniscient and comparative knowledge as an intellectual and ethical value. On the other hand, insofar as the knowledge embodied in the narratives, and accessible to select characters, involves exposure to scathing truths about economic inequities or systemic corruption, it actually becomes a negative force as well, threatening the individual's sense of purpose and capacity for clear moral vision when dealing with others, who are suddenly viewed as fully complicit in the forms of power that structure the social world more broadly. The apprehension of this negative force prompts the assertion of those curative ideals so prominent in Dickens, ideals of community and purposive vocation that are defined largely in terms of their deliberately limited scope, a scope that can only be called willfully provincial.

The interrelation of these various valuations of cosmopolitanism and social critique establish Dickens, and *Little Dorrit* more particularly, as centrally important to any larger study of the Victorian response to the powers of modern distance. A number of critics have recently explored Dickens's

---

the related question of imperialist attitudes in Dickens. While his notorious support in 1864 for Governor Eyre of Jamaica is well known, as well as his support for the suppression of the India Mutiny, he nonetheless promotes critiques of imperialism and bald chauvinism in many of his novels, particularly through the representation of Mr. Dombey and Major Bagstock in *Dombey and Son*, Mr. Merdle and the Barnacles in *Little Dorrit*, Mr. Podsnap in *Our Mutual Friend*, and Sapsea in *Edwin Drood*. Suvendrini Perera, *Reaches of Empire: The English Novel from Edgeworth to Dickens* (New York: Columbia University Press, 1991); Deirdre David, *Rule Britannia: Women, Empire, and Victorian Writing* (Ithaca: Cornell University Press, 1995).

attitude toward empire, thereby placing his novels, and the tradition of criticism that treats him as a particularly trenchant social critic, within a larger global context.[17] Likewise, there is a significant body of work on Dickens as an especially acute analyst of modern alienation, itself a crucial form of detachment, though one that is visited upon, and not typically cultivated by, the subject.[18] In this reading of Dickens, I examine *Little Dorrit* by situating these two foci in relation to one another, with several aims in mind. First, I hope to reconstruct a particular form of critical cosmopolitanism in Dickens, one that allows us to expose naïve forms of cosmopolitanism that fail to take structural economic inequalities into account. Dickens is unique among the writers I examine in bringing to the fore the many ways in which intercultural exchange was marked by profound inequities of power and congratulatory delusions of self-cultivation. Second, and equally, I want to explore Dickens's portrayal of psychological estrangement in the context of a broader anxiety about the forms of systemic critique animating the formation of the human sciences as well as the project of the realist novel.[19] My argument is that Dickens's dramatic portraits of estranged, disillusioned, or embittered characters reflect not only their particular social histories but also the perceived consequences of cultivated critical stances, stances intimately related to the sociological, novelistic, and political project of understanding and potentially transforming the social totality. Ultimately, Dickens's internationalist concerns are intricately connected to this portrayal of critical detachment, and analyzing Dickens's representation of defamiliarizing travel and the global economy is central to the project of reconstructing his attitude toward a deliberately distanced or objectivist perspective on the social totality.

One particularly radical element in this novel's approach to cosmopolitanism emerges in the story of Arthur Clennam, which, along with the early

[17] See, for example, Perera, *Reaches of Empire*; Jeff Nunokawa, *The Afterlife of Property: Domestic Security and the Victorian Novel* (Princeton: Princeton University Press, 1994); David, *Rule Britannia*.

[18] See Raymond Williams, "Social Criticism in Dickens: Some Problems of Method and Approach," *Critical Quarterly* 6 (1964): 214–27; William Myers, "The Radicalism of *Little Dorrit*," in *Literature and Politics in the Nineteenth Century*, ed. John Lucas (London: Methuen, 1971), 77–104. For more recent discussion of Dickensian self-estrangement within a Foucauldian framework, see D. A. Miller, *The Novel and the Police* (Berkeley: University of California Press, 1988), ch. 6.

[19] In this sense I am extending arguments I earlier made about Dickens's anxieties regarding the forms of consciousness associated with scientific approaches to self and society. See Amanda Anderson, *Tainted Souls and Painted Faces: The Rhetoric of Fallenness in Victorian Culture* (Ithaca: Cornell University Press, 1993), ch. 2.

descriptions of Marseilles, forces upon us a larger cosmos than that typically indicated by European cosmopolitanism, and certainly larger than the disproportionately Gallic and aristocratic version that Rigaud assumes. As the novel opens, a forty-year-old Clennam is returning to London and his mother after having spent twenty years in China, where he had worked with his father in what remains throughout the novel an unnamed business. (British commercial involvement with China in the nineteenth century consisted in large measure of the opium trade, which the British pursued aggressively, even to the point of war.)[20] Returning to England one year after the death of his father, Clennam is haunted by the conviction that the family business has done some specific harm to a specific person or persons, and he is anxious to uncover and repair the loss, if at all possible. Although the novel does in the end expose a discrete harm that Clennam's mother has perpetrated, the suppression of an inheritance that should have gone to Little Dorrit, the vague sense of guilt haunting this commercial traveler from the east, and his forceful resigning of all connection with Clennam and Co. upon his return to England, suggest a wider sensitivity to the violence of British global capitalism and imperial concerns, and to the vast economic imbalances generated thereby. Indeed, despite Arthur's and the novel's ultimate reduction of this broad sense of obligation to a very local and seemingly idiosyncratic wrong, the narrator reports at one point that Arthur's unease on the subject was "so vague and formless that it might be the result of a reality widely remote from his idea of it" (368).[21] Moreover, the representation of the

[20] The question arises as to why Dickens chooses China as the site for the Clennam business and for Arthur's long "exile," as Arthur himself calls it. I would suggest two reasons: first, symbolically China is associated in much British (orientalist) discourse with stationariness, with being trapped by the past, and Dickens clearly means this to resonate with his representation of Clennam's own particular paralysis. This is obviously not a particularly enlightened aspect of the text, but one must set these kinds of racial judgments next to Dickens's stinging critiques of Englishmen. Indeed, an explicit deconstruction of any opposition of Chinese cultural immobility to British enlightenment takes place in Dickens's 1848 essay, "The Chinese Junk," though this deconstruction involves faulting England for the same tendency to cling to convention and "absurd forms" that he charges the Chinese with. See Charles Dickens, "The Chinese Junk," in *Miscellaneous Papers* (London: Chapman and Hall, 1908), 102–5. Secondly, it does keep the sense of guilt from seeming to settle too directly on explicitly colonial crimes, though there was a strong economic aggressiveness in England's relation to China, which involved going to war to secure its hold on the opium trade. This can be interpreted both as a protection of the hero (and hence diminishment of critical cosmopolitanism) and as indicating that we need to look beyond the simple category of colony in thinking about British global reach.

[21] In a related Marxist interpretation of the novel, Jeff Nunokawa reads this pas-

global reach of British economic concerns in the portrayal of the capitalist Mr. Merdle encourages the understanding of England's particular patholo- gies—its lack of true vitality and its faulty government—within a global soci- oeconomic context.

Dickens's own approach to cosmopolitanism in the beginning of this novel, then, suggests a standard Marxist critique of cosmopolitanism, one that exposes cosmopolitan ideals as a ruse of power and understands itself as *internationalist* rather than cosmopolitan. The unmasking of the violent underside to the aristocratic cosmopolitanism of the narrowly European Ri- gaud, along with the insistence on a transnational economic context, is even- tually continuous, in fact, with Dickens's critique of tourism in the sections of the novel treating the Dorrit travels.[22] Dickens mounts a biting satire of the nouveau tourism promoted by the newly hired Dorrit governess and companion, Mrs. General, who mechanically duplicates tour-guide re- sponses, and who reminds Little Dorrit that it "is scarcely delicate to look at vagrants with the attention which I have seen bestowed upon them by a very dear young friend of mine" (530). Little Dorrit, who has spent her whole life dutifully devoted to easing her father's suffering in debtors' prison, simply hates to travel: not only is she entirely alienated by the artificial forms of tourism that Mrs. General forces upon her, but she literally loses her sense of self during the journey, experiencing it as a dreamlike state of detachment from the purpose, duty, and affection that animated her earlier life and that have always grounded her existence. "To have no work to do was strange, but not half so strange as having glided into a corner where she had no one to think for, nothing to plan and contrive, no cares of others to load herself with" (516). For Little Dorrit, all that remains real is the blunt materiality of the prison life she has left, and the beggars that appear to her as "the only realities of the day" (518). Her newly acquired maid, moreover, is "a weight on Little Dorrit's mind—absolutely made her cry at first, she knew so little what to do with her" (518). This entirely demystifies the ideology of travel as horizon-expanding self-cultivation—which Dickens translates into the arti- ficial process of "forming a surface"—and exposes it as a privilege of the wealthy, who myopically turn their eyes from the social realities of other

---

sage as indicative of a larger apprehension informing the novel, that all acts of owner- ship, all forms of possession, involve an act of appropriation. Clennam's vague sense of guilt thus gives expression to the "rule that ensures that anything taken will be taken away." See Nunokawa, *The Afterlife of Property*, 20–22.

[22] My reading of Dickens's critique of tourism is indebted to Buzard, *The Beaten Track*.

countries, social realities entirely continuous with those they have left behind in England.

Little Dorrit's relation to travel, however, does undergo an important development over the course of her journeys through Italy. Initially, it is true, she serves as the inassimilable counterpoint to the empty, status-driven tourism of Mrs. General and the rest of the family. Deeply unfeeling is her father's criticism that in holding to the past she "systematically reproduce[s] what the rest of us blot out," yet it remains the case that Amy is unable, for reasons very different from those that afflict the rest of the Dorrits, to actually undergo any horizon-expanding experience of the cultures, artistic achievements, and celebrated sights that she encounters: everything is reduced to the common denominator of poverty or rendered fantastic in the face of more acutely felt memories, "all lasting realities that had never changed" (532, 520). But gradually Amy appears to undergo an adjustment, and once the family proceeds from the "crowning unreality" of Venice to archeological Rome, she becomes a different kind of traveler (519).

Amy's alteration is most apparent in the description of her forays among the ruins of the ancient city, but the new form of experience here is crucially prefigured in a letter to Clennam written from Rome. In writing to Clennam, Amy exhibits a desire to enter into the perspective of the experienced traveler as well as an anxiety that she will fail in her attempt:

> If you should ever get so far as this in this long letter, you will perhaps say, Surely Little Dorrit will not leave off without telling me something about her travels, and surely it is time she did. I think it is indeed, but I don't know what to tell you. Since we left Venice we have been in a great many wonderful places, Genoa and Florence among them, and have seen so many wonderful sights, that I am almost giddy when I think what a crowd they make. But you can tell me so much more about them than I can tell you, that why should I tire you with my accounts and descriptions? (608)

Though marked by deferral and evasion, this passage reveals that Amy could indeed produce accounts and descriptions of her experiences, something that her earlier dreamlike state precluded. Moreover, she also reports that, having remembered that Clennam knew foreign languages, she herself is beginning to make headway: "I have begun to speak and understand, almost easily, the hard languages I told you about" (610). In light of these suggestive epistolary moments, very much propped on her desire to emulate Clennam and adopt his values, Amy's experience of the Roman ruins is not quite such an abrupt reframing of her earlier attitude toward travel. Indeed, what stands out in the description of her repeated visits to the ruins is her capacity for a kind of double vision, one that remains true to the experience of cultural otherness as well as to her own psychological past:

> The ruins of the vast old Amphitheatre, of the old Temples, of the old commemorative Arches, of the old trodden highways, of the old tombs, besides being what they were, to her were ruins of the old Marshalsea—ruins of her own old life—ruins of the faces and forms that of old peopled it—ruins of its loves, hopes, cares, and joys. Two ruined spheres of action and suffering were before the solitary girl often sitting on some broken fragment; and in the lonely places, under the blue sky, she saw them both together. (671)[23]

This insistence on maintaining ties to the past actually derives not from any organic investment in natural origins or roots, but rather from the fact that exile is perceived as a primary condition, one which the individual must try to mitigate through privileging early associations and cultivating new ones. In the novel, traveling and imprisonment are predominantly indistinguishable from one another; both constitute an original condition of exile against which precariously constructed homes and vocations must be asserted.[24] Little Dorrit is born in prison. There is no home to which Clennam

[23] See Burgan, "Little Dorrit in Italy," for a related discussion of the differences between Little Dorrit's experiences of Venice and Rome. Burgan writes, "The appeal of Italy becomes fully authentic for Little Dorrit only as Rome comes at last to embody for her the memories that have converted all earlier beauties into unrealities. Dickens has created his own 'new picturesque' not by purging the old one of associations with 'misery and degradation,' but by permitting those associations to identify its meaning" (406). I would disagree with Burgan's notion here that Amy's own memories are fully identifying the meanings of the ruins, since Dickens is careful to insist that she sees the ruins equally for "what they were."

[24] The most elaborate and explicit deconstruction of the distinction between travel and imprisonment occurs in a description, from Little Dorrit's point of view, of the society of travelers they encounter during their trip through Italy: "It appeared on the whole, to Little Dorrit herself, that this same society in which they lived, greatly resembled a superior sort of Marshalsea. Numbers of people seemed to come abroad, pretty much as people had come into the prison; through debt, through idleness, relationship, curiosity, and general unfitness for getting on at home. They were brought into these foreign towns in the custody of couriers and local followers, just as the debtors had been brought into the prison. They prowled about the churches and picture-galleries, much in the old, dreary, prison-yard manner. They were usually going away again tomorrow or next week, and rarely knew their own minds, and seldom did what they said they would do, or went where they said they would go: in all this again, very much like the prison debtors. They paid high for poor accommo-

can return, because he never had a true home, subjected as he was to the claustrophobic Calvinism of a woman who only called herself his mother, and who made no distinction between the family home and the family business. The necessarily doomed attempt to assert an organically guaranteed relation to the past is indicated in a fantastic metaphor used by the narrator to describe Clennam's attempt to recapture his past after the disillusioning meeting with his old lover, Flora: "To review his life was like descending a green tree in fruit and flower, and seeing all the branches wither and drop off, one by one, as he came down towards them" (207).[25] Alienation in this text is fundamental; attachments are achieved and secondary, not the primary ground that must be guarded or retrieved. In this sense *Little Dorrit* differs markedly from a book like *David Copperfield*, where the hero's early attachments to his mother and to Peggotty become a lost and deeply cherished origin.

It is crucial to note, however, that Dickens does seek at least partly to ground the *capacity* for achieved attachments in individual nature or temperament. Indeed, the true moral distinction that Dickens makes is between those who assert forms of redemptive belief against such bleak conditions and those who fail to do so. As I will show, there is a cluster of negatively portrayed characters who fail to do so, and who manifest Dickens's attempt to guard against the dangers of a persistent detachment. Temperament—and particularly a temperamentally driven impulse to affirm the ties of love, community, and nation—will become the means by which Dickens will ward off the implications of his most radical insights. Yet the radical insights ultimately emerge as both source of corruption and necessary vaccine: without at least a preventive dose, one remains utterly vulnerable to negative social and ideological forces.

---

dation, and disparaged a place while they pretended to like it: which was exactly the Marshalsea custom. They were envied when they went away by people left behind, feigning not to want to go: and that again was the Marshalsea habit invariably. A certain set of words and phrases, as much belonging to tourists as the College and the Snuggery belonged to the jail, was always in their mouths. They had precisely the same incapacity for settling down to anything, as the prisoners used to have; they rather deteriorated one another, as the prisoners used to do; and they wore untidy dresses, and fell into a slouching way of life: still, always like the people in the Marshalsea" (565).

[25] For a reading of the novel that elevates this statement into a kind of touchstone for the entire text, and that reads female storytelling in relation to it, see Nancy Aycock Metz, "The Blighted Tree and the Book of Fate: Female Models of Storytelling in *Little Dorrit,*" *Dickens Studies Annual* 18 (1989): 221–41.

THE CRITIQUE OF BITTER REASON

This larger structure of ambivalence toward radical insight persistently haunts the novel's ostensible championing of affirmed modest duties and cultivated provinciality. To examine how this doubled vision is written into the formal structures of the book, I look at three negatively drawn characters—the murderer Rigaud, the artist Gowan, and, most extensively, the illegitimate Miss Wade. These are all self-described exiles of one form or another: Rigaud is "cosmopolitan," Miss Wade has no legal name, no family, and no home, and Mr. Gowan has been disappointed by Society and hence taken to the life of the dilettante artist, spending a great portion of his time in Europe. In presenting these characters, Dickens would appear to strengthen the case for modest affirmation and solidify the case against disaffiliation. Each of these characters has, at best, the narrator's limited sympathy; they are portrayed as afflicted in various ways by paranoia, sadism, fantasies of persecution, and unearned claims to entitlement. As a number of critics have pointed out, however, such characters in a certain sense come closest to the narrator's own perspective on the social world. Deeply disenchanted, they recognize, in other words, what the critical narrative perspective persistently encourages us to see: that society is a vast prison whose members participate in self-deception, aimless wandering, and the purveyance of ideological mystifications. Thus they occupy a strange position in the novel. As Lionel Trilling puts it, "It is a part of the complexity of this novel which deals so bitterly with society that those of its characters who share its social bitterness are by that very fact condemned."[26]

But to focus on the psychological states of these characters, and to attribute a corresponding psychological attitude to the novel itself, may play too fully into the narrative's own tendency to pathologize what is in effect the cultivation of stances that cannot be accounted for in such narrow psychological terms. The perspective assumed and represented by these characters is one more broadly associated, both by Dickens and by the culture at large, with the aesthetic project of realism and the sociological and political project of understanding the whole of the social totality. I do not mean to dismiss the psychosocial insight Dickens provides into characters who, for justifiable reasons, excessively mistrust what may nonetheless be the heartfelt beneficence of others, for example. Nor do I wish to diminish the psychological and moral dimensions of such cultivated stances, which are a fundamental

[26] Lionel Trilling, *The Opposing Self* (New York: Viking Press, 1955), 58.

concern for Dickens and for my reading of him. But ultimately, in portraying these characters, Dickens uses reductive forms of moral condemnation in order to control his anxiety that systemic knowledge breeds and relies upon a corrupting suspicion. While the narrative does contain glimmers of alternative practices that bring exilic knowledges productively to bear upon ongoing experience, as for example in the representation of Amy in Rome, Dickens's characterology of detachment ultimately lacks flexibility and forestalls elaboration of a more finely tuned ideal of self-reflexive enactment. What is most provocative about these negative characters, however, is the manner in which they are used to work out concerns with omniscience and detachment, revealing the threat to cultivated provinciality Dickens perceives to attend any stance of systemic critique. This threat gets figured as a threat to moral integrity itself, yet the threat must be courted if one is to gain the comprehension of the social totality necessary as the very motive for cultivated provinciality.

The costs of this paradox make themselves felt in strange narratorial dances around the three negatively drawn characters. There are in fact striking moments in which these characters are identified with the narrator's own perspective or method. When Gowan takes up company with Blandois after meeting him in Italy, the narrator writes, "That exaggeration in the manner of the man [Blandois] which has been noticed as appertaining to him . . . was acceptable to Gowan as a caricature, which he found it a humorous resource to have at hand for the ridiculing of numbers of people who necessarily did more or less of what Blandois overdid" (542). This is of course exactly how the narrator himself uses Blandois. And in light of Dickens's own pessimistic representation of the Circumlocution Office and of Society, Gowan's lucid readings of the dominance of the cash nexus appear as bracing demystifications. As Gowan states to Arthur Clennam, "Now here's one of the advantages, or disadvantages, of knowing a disappointed man. You hear the truth" (453). Dickens wrote in a letter to Forster in 1856, "Society, the Circumlocution Office, and Mr. Gowan, are of course three parts of one idea and design."[27] On the one hand, this can be understood to mean that corrupt institutions and social conditions foster attitudes like Gowan's, and vitiate the art whose representative he claims to be—in this sense he is of a piece with the larger social frameworks under critique. But at the same time Gowan stands apart from and analyzes these institutions in ways that other characters who help perpetuate their mystifications—Mrs. Merdle, the Barnacles, the Stiltstalkings—do not.

[27] Quoted in John Forster, *The Life of Charles Dickens*, ed. A. J. Hoppé (London: J. M. Dent & Sons, and New York: Dutton, 1966), 2:183.

Miss Wade represents an even more complicated case. She is given great prominence in the second chapter of the novel, but, as with Rigaud, disappears for long stretches of time, and only makes six appearances in the work as a whole. Quite dramatic, however, is the fact that an autobiographical account of her life, entitled "The History of a Self-Tormentor" and given in writing to the hero Arthur Clennam, stands alone as one of the novel's chapters. Many characters enter into extended self-justificatory narrative in this novel, but Miss Wade is given pride of place in this regard.

In her first appearance in chapter 2, moreover, Miss Wade is linked to the narrative perspective of the novel quite explicitly. As the quarantined travelers are released, Mr. Meagles approaches Miss Wade to take his leave. This is how her response is given:

> "In our course through life we shall meet the people who are coming to meet *us*, from many strange places and by many strange roads," was the composed reply; "and what is set to us to do to them, and what is set to them to do to us, will all be done." (63)

The odd insertion of the passive "was the composed reply" assimilates Miss Wade to the narrative activity (*composing*) precisely through a figure of neutrality or detachment (*composure*) that also allows her the long view. But the attitude that accompanies this seemingly cool composure is implicitly criticized in the closing sentence of the chapter, where the narrator echoes her statement, with some alteration:

> And thus ever, by day and night, under the sun and under the stars, climbing the dusty hills and toiling along the weary plains, journeying by land and journeying by sea, coming and going so strangely, to meet and to act and react on one another, move all we restless travellers through the pilgrimage of life. (67)

The narrative revision of Miss Wade's oracular comment discloses and attempts to redress the anxiety that it may share her perspective, a perspective that it wants to construe as too fatalistic and too bitter. Most obviously the revision attempts to delete the emphasis on the way that power structures all intersubjective relations. While Miss Wade hints at the violence we will both perpetrate and be victim to, the narrator stresses the universal weary struggle of life, and the seeming randomness and potentially interactive quality of social encounters: we are coming and going "to meet and act and react upon one another." Yet in certain respects it hardly seems to exert a difference that makes a difference, especially if we read "react" as "re-act." The more hopeful and beneficient connotations of the term *pilgrimage* seem hardly enough, deferred until the end of the sentence, to fully offset the sense that we are all in endless motion, buffeted by blind forces. As I shall explore presently, it is also significant that, in both cases, travel is emptied out of any geographical specificity and the journey of life is universalized.[28]

In her conversation as well as in her written history, Miss Wade displays bitter cynicism and a profound awareness of social hierarchy and its tendency to rely on mystification. Her story emphasizes her social isolation as an illegitimate child dependent on the patronage of others and presents an incisive representation of the marginal position of the governess. She repeatedly lights up the tendency of others to attribute her acute insights into the workings of power, and the bitterness it produces, to her "unhappy temper." Yet at the same time, Dickens wants us to accept this view of her as well, even as her narrative shows in thick detail the social bases for this supposed disposition of nature.

Miss Wade's most dramatic intervention into the lives of the other characters occurs when she prompts the Meagles's maid Harriet, a girl they have "rescued" from the Foundling Hospital and nicknamed Tattycoram, to leave her employers and come live with her. Miss Wade encourages Harriet to interpret her recurrent fits of outrage as the justified realization that the Meagles's relationship to her is untenably exploitative, paternalistic, and fundamentally dehumanizing—particularly with regard to the nickname. As Miss Wade says when Mr. Meagles makes an appeal to Harriet to return to them,

> "Here is your patron, your master. He is willing to take you back, my dear, if you are sensible of the favour and choose to go. You can be, again, a foil to his pretty daughter, a slave to her pleasant wilfulness, and a toy in the house showing the goodness of the family. You can have your droll name again, playfully pointing you out and setting you apart, as it is right that you should be pointed out and set apart. (Your birth, you know; you must not forget your birth.)" (377)

While Mr. Meagles is shocked to find his motives in helping Tattycoram to be so "perverted," one could easily see his lack of social understanding as entirely continuous with his other deficiences: the deference to rank and mobility that in some sense accommodates the Gowans of the world, and brings his daughter Minnie into the disastrous situation of becoming

---

[28] For related discussions of this pair of passages, see Janice M. Carlisle, "*Little Dorrit*: Necessary Fictions," *Studies in the Novel* 7 (1975): 195–214; Peter Garrett, *The Grasp of Form* (forthcoming).

Gowan's wife; the willful provinciality that results in a philistinism in relation to both art and travel. Miss Wade is in effect adding sting to a critique of Mr. Meagles that the novel has already encouraged, even as it holds up his good nature and seemingly endorses a version of his domestic ideology at the end of the novel. That is, Miss Wade incorporates and amplifies a critique already internal to the novel, in effect extending the critique of mystification from Circumlocution and Society to the inner sanctum of the domestic, which is shown to use an ideology of affection and devotion to cover over its own structuring inequalities.[29] Like Gowan, she in a sense instructs us how to read certain characters.

Miss Wade is importantly portrayed, in this regard, as someone in permanent exile, always wandering, never truly dwelling. When Mr. Meagles and Clennam do go to visit Miss Wade in her lodgings in London, she "appeared to have taken up her quarters there as she might have established herself in an Eastern caravanserai. A small square of carpet in the middle of the room, a few articles of furniture that evidently did not belong to the room, and a disorder of trunks and travelling articles, formed the whole of her surroundings" (375–76). Miss Wade's status as a permanent exile, rendered exotic in her detachment and constant mobility, is expressive of a very different form of traveling from that undertaken by Amy Dorrit, or by Clennam, or by the artificial tourists. Indeed, in her case, homelessness and perpetual motion are symbolic of a constant alienation, a persistent suspicion in the service of critique. Travel in her case is purely negative, the refusal to dwell, or to believe, or to affiliate in any affirmative way: for her, disaffiliation *à deux* is the only form of human alliance. She can connect only with those who are seen to occupy a similar position: Tattycoram, with whose social position she identifies completely, or Gowan, who shares her stance of cynical critique and reminds her that they are both "people of the world" (734). In Miss Wade's case, travel and worldliness become universalized into a metaphor for unrelenting social critique and are not expressive of any actual experience of intercultural discovery or exchange.

The representation of symbolic exile is continuous, in other words, with Miss Wade's tendency to adopt an objectifying stance toward other people, and toward the social conditions and practices she subjects to such withering scrutiny. Watching Tattycoram's outburst on the ship in Marseilles, Miss Wade is described as follows: "The observer stood with her hand upon her

[29] For related readings of Miss Wade's critique of the Dickensian domestic ideal, see Myers, "The Radicalism of *Little Dorrit*," 86–87; David Suchoff, *Critical Theory and the Novel: Mass Society and Cultural Criticism in Dickens, Melville, and Kafka* (Madison: University of Wisconsin Press, 1994), 80.

own bosom, looking at the girl, as one afflicted with a diseased part might curiously watch the dissection and exposition of an analogous case" (65). This scene is accompanied by an illustration entitled "Under the Microscope," in which the only possible referent for "microscope" is Miss Wade herself. Effectively, these figurations allot to Miss Wade an estranging dual consciousness: on the one hand she experiences, acutely, passionately, her own social deprivations; on the other she abstracts herself and views both herself and others from the standpoint of the larger social system.

Ultimately, Dickens seeks to pathologize and discredit Miss Wade by reducing the truth of her character to the forms of distorted passion that underlie her more aloof moments of inspection, which are in turn assessed as failed attempts to suppress her bitter hatred and resentment. The narrator's own earlier vexed identification with Miss Wade becomes immaterial as we discover that her oracular stance in chapter 2 was deceptive, and that she had specific personal reasons for being in the company of the Meagles: as the jealous ex-lover of Gowan, she was driven to find her rival. But I am more interested in the discordant effects the figurations of dual consciousness produce, and what they mean for Dickens. Elsewhere I have argued that many of Dickens's fallen women figure a particular anxiety about objectified self-reading, and in many respects Miss Wade can be read within this context.[30] But she is not as self-condemnatory as the typical Dickensian fallen woman, and she in many ways thwarts commonly held conceptions about femininity, particularly in her strongly expressed homoeroticism, and her cool indifference to her own isolation.

In his own notes for the chapter "History of a Self-Tormentor," Dickens writes: "From her own point of view. Dissect it."[31] In the context of *Little Dorrit*'s own figural logic, Dickens here becomes Miss Wade's Miss Wade. But what he insists upon, through his own dissection, is that Miss Wade, as a dissecting character, is driven by pathologies and lacking in moral integrity and insight. This aspect of the text reflects Dickens's broader anxiety that cultivated detachment—aesthetic, scientific, and cosmopolitan—poses a distinct threat to moral integrity, purposiveness, and forms of belonging. The representations of Miss Wade's dual consciousness give expression to this threat and then attempt to contain it, ironically, through moral and psychological dissection. For example, in a passage describing another moment in which Miss Wade studies Tattycoram, the narrator writes, "Miss Wade

---

[30] Anderson, *Tainted Souls and Painted Faces*, ch. 2.

[31] Paul D. Herring, "Dickens's Monthly Number Plans for *Little Dorrit*," *Modern Philology* 64 (1966): 50.

with her composed face attentively regarding her, and suggesting to an observer, with extraordinary force, in her composure itself (as a veil will suggest the form it covers), the unquenchable passion of her own nature" (377).
There is an implicit *mis-en-abîme* here, with the observer observed, and the
suggestion that "composure itself," the stance of objective assessment, is
objectively readable as veiled passion. Strikingly, Dickens's prose seems to
reproduce the failed suppression that he attempts to displace onto his character, thereby revealing that a lot is riding on this narrative moment: the
observer's own "composed" judgment itself gathers "extraordinary force" as
the sentence proceeds, moving from a seemingly controlled literary parenthesis to the more fierce conviction that Miss Wade's passion is "unquenchable." The narrator's attempt to dissociate himself from this character is once
again thwarted, as distanced observation fails to quench the narrator's own
passionate judgments.

Rigaud, Gowan, and Miss Wade all present versions of what appears to be
Dickens's idea of bad or disabling detachment. The question, in light of the
difficulty Dickens has in creating a viable distinction between reliable observation and hysterical suppression, is whether Dickens can imagine forms
of detachment or critique that do not collapse into what for him are disabling, disqualifying, and morally compromised forms. Given that Dickens
relocates structural violences within the breast of the villain, assigning to
him or her the categories of perversion, willfulness, and cruelty, we may
infer that the radical potentialities I outlined in the opening section of this
chapter simply are relinquished in favor of a smaller scale of duty and a
diminished desire to hold the larger social totality in view. This would make
the movement toward resolution in *Little Dorrit* parallel to the perspective
of *Bleak House*, which promotes Esther's modest circle of duty against, to
take simply one pertinent counterpoint, Mrs. Jellyby's telescopic philanthropy, which is connected not so much to vice but rather to the failure to
develop domestic virtue.[32] As I have indicated, however, in *Little Dorrit* the
costs of relinquishing a wider and more detached perspective are suggested
in the very elaboration of the provincial alternatives. Dickens remains divided against his own resolutions in this novel, and this keeps what is fundamentally the perspective of the three suspicious characters very much
alive in the closing sections of the novel, tempering his ostensibly harsh

[32] For a reading of *Bleak House* that recovers a more complicated attitude toward
telescopic vision, however, see Bruce Robbins, "Telescopic Philanthropy: Professionalism and Responsibility in *Bleak House*," in *Nation and Narration*, ed. Homi K.
Bhabha (New York: Routledge, 1990), 213–29.

judgments against them. I am not simply arguing, as is traditionally done, that this novel's ideals seem especially fragile and precarious in light of the pervasive negative forces that will always remain at work. I am arguing that the ideals themselves are shown to be fatally compromised by their failure to remain alert to that which they oppose. That alertness is reserved for the critical narrative perspective and, paradoxically, for the characters that the narrative perspective portrays most unsympathetically: in this sense, one could say that Dickens is necessarily divided against his own very impulse to pathologize these characters, and the practices they represent.

NARROWING VIEWS

For the purposes of pursuing this argument, I focus on two of the novel's ostensibly most sympathetic characters: Daniel Doyce and the hero, Arthur Clennam. Doyce, introduced as "a smith and engineer," is typically read as the moral counterpoint to Gowan (160).[33] If Gowan represents the man without values, the cynical dilettante artist who works only to sell, Doyce is the earnest, thoughtful craftsman and inventor, dedicated to an ideal of labor channeled by visionary creativity. In this sense, as John Lucas points out, he is something like an amalgamation of Carlyle's ideal poet and Ruskin's think-ing worker.[34] He is particularly troubled by Gowan's lack of true dedication to art, and a prime victim of the Circumlocution Office, which at every turn thwarts his attempt to bring his ingenuity to the service "of his country and his fellow creatures" (160). Doyce is associated with a dedication to craft, a well-honed practical judgment, and, importantly, an instinctive nationalistic spirit. While we learn that his work experience—the steady accumulation over many years of knowledge "theoretical and practical"—involved highly successful positions in France, Germany, and Russia, the narrator tells us that "he had naturally felt a preference for his own country, and a wish to gain distinction there, and to do whatever service he could do, there rather than elsewhere" (233).

Yet there are limitations to Doyce, which places what looks like the un-equivocal endorsement of his nationalistic vocationalism in a new light. It is important that we first encounter him in the company of the provincial Mr. Meagles, who lacks a proper respect for other cultures and remains myopic

[33] Larson, "The Arts in These Latter Days"; Ira Bruce Nadel, "'Wonderful Decep-tion': Art and the Artist in *Little Dorrit*," *Criticism* 19 (1977): 17–33.

[34] John Lucas, *The Melancholy Man: A Study of Dickens's Novels* (Sussex: Har-vester Press, 1970, 1980), 279.

on questions of hierarchy and power. While Doyce is clearly meant to symbolize a spirit lacking in his native country, a spirit which might serve as the basis for a refurbished patriotism, he himself remains unable and unwilling to understand the business side of the partnership he enters into with Arthur Clennam. His tendency to keep everything within the bounds of a narrow phronesis, the very opposite of the critical and systemic views of Miss Wade and Gowan, ultimately makes him a faulty interpreter of social life. He is too situated, too incapable of detachment. Thus, although in book 2 his factory, where he "soberly worked on for the work's sake," is deliberately juxtaposed to the empty tourism of the newly rich Dorrits, the limited scope of his actions is emphasized (569). The true limitations of Doyce's capacity for judgment emerge later in the novel, but in order to make the context clear I must first consider the more complicated case of the hero, Arthur Clennam.

As I suggested earlier, Clennam's alienated relation to his homeland engenders a capacity for critique, and we learn something about the Circumlocution Office through his own frustrating experiences with it. But his sense of alienation is depicted largely in negative terms, as an inability to assert his will and to find something valuable and productive to turn his energies to. His time of exile, then, is generally represented as having cut Clennam off from his past, attenuated his sense of purpose, and caused him to age unnaturally. When during quarantine Meagles asks him where he intends to travel next, he replies, "I am such a waif and stray everywhere, that I am liable to be drifted where any current may set" (59). This hardly conforms to the kind of cosmopolitan experience that is represented as promoting self-cultivation or *Bildung,* thereby enlarging one's mind and horizons. Yet it does promote alienation from the prevailing forms of money-getting and the inefficiencies of government, to which many others have grown accustomed.

As a figure somewhere between the extremes of Miss Wade, on the one hand, and Daniel Doyce, on the other, Clennam is capable of delicate intercultural negotiations, as when he comes to the aid of Cavelletto, who after arriving in London is run down by a mail truck, or when he travels abroad to Calais to deal with business matters pertaining to his partnership with Doyce. He is also capable of forms of social critique and moral insight that appear not to take the extreme forms that Dickens assigns to the three pathologized characters. For example, he sympathetically perceives the limitations of Mr. Meagles:

Clennam could not help speculating, as he seated himself in his room by the fire, whether there might be in the breast of this honest, affectionate, and cordial Mr. Meagles, any microscopic portion of the mustard seed that had sprung up into the great tree of the Circumlocution Office. [Mr. Meagles's] curious sense of a general superiority to Daniel Doyce, which seemed to be founded, not so much on anything in Doyce's personal character as on the mere fact of his being an originator and a man out of the beaten track of other men, suggested the idea. (238–39)

This passage begs to be read in the context of the earlier passage describing Miss Wade's observation of Tattycoram. Both characters are endowed with microscopic vision, but Clennam remains seated comfortably by the hearth, speculating on an absent friend and not objectifying a suffering presence. In Miss Wade's case, recall, "The observer stood with her hand upon her own bosom, looking at the girl, as one afflicted with a diseased part might curiously watch the dissection and exposition of an analogous case" (65). It is hard not to see Miss Wade's own scrutiny as the agent of dissection and exposition that is ostensibly externalized, for Tattycoram is consumed in a fit of passion and certainly not engaged in self-analysis. Clennam, by contrast, is allowed the capacity for a form of character analysis aided by the advances of science but still cushioned by basic moral certainty about the fundamental nature of its object, the "honest, affectionate, and cordial Mr. Meagles."

Clennam's wider perspective and capacity for microscopic vision by the hearth, as it were, is ultimately brought within a more narrow scope. I do not mean here to refer to the domestic enclave that his marriage to Little Dorrit asserts against a world forever beset, as the last sentence of the novel has it, by the "usual uproar" of "the noisy and the eager, and the arrogant and the froward and the vain" (895). I mean rather Clennam's decision to devote his energies to reinvigorating his own country: this he does quite explicitly by hitching himself, wandering waif that he is, to Doyce. In large part, his rejuvenation is guaranteed by his temperament: despite a dark and trying childhood under the iron Calvinism of his mother, Arthur "was a man who had, deep-rooted in his nature, a belief in all the gentle and good things his life had been without" (206). His trajectory is opposed to that taken by Miss Wade and by Gowan, even though he certainly has plenty of grounds for bitterness. A somewhat peculiar scene involving Clennam, Mrs. Clennam, and Blandois illuminates the implications of Clennam's devotion to the vital nationalistic labor of Doyce. Blandois has had previous business dealings with Clennam's mother and has returned to see her on as-yet-unspecified business: it will involve blackmailing her on the basis of his knowledge that she has suppressed the truth of Arthur's birth from him. Coincidentally arriving at the house at the same time as Blandois, Arthur takes a visceral dislike to him, reacts strongly to his insinuating manner, and makes his feelings known. His mother says to him,

> "You have no right . . . to speak to the prejudice of any gentleman (least of all a gentleman from another country), because he does not conform to your standard, or square his behaviour by your rules. It is possible that the gentleman may, on similar grounds, object to you."
>
> "I hope so," returned Arthur. (600)

Arthur's reply admits of different readings here. In the confident refusal of cosmopolitan openness to the variability of custom, this practiced traveler could be indicating that what he is responding to, like the landlady in France who comments upon the case of Blandois, is unregenerate evil, a bedrock of moral character that cannot be affected by circumstance. An absolute moral gulf would thus separate him from his sudden adversary and produce their mutual objections to one another. Yet Dickens may also wish to invoke national differences here, especially against the false cosmopolitanism of Blandois. In her claim that he is "of another country," Mrs. Clennam has reduced this visitor to "Blandois of Paris": thus his cosmopolitanism is exposed as sheer assertion and bluster, and he joins the circle of French murderers in Dickens's works: Madame Hortense in *Bleak House*, Madame Defarge in *A Tale of Two Cities*. This reading would fall in line with Arthur's increasing identification with a renewed nationalism. Arthur, who in earlier listening to the Barnacles and the Stiltstalkings dislikes hearing "a great nation narrowed to such little bounds" (362), has now come to assert his "hopeful" nationalism against the destructive forces he has repeatedly encountered: he holds to the belief that there is goodness beyond power and greed, and he seeks to vitalize a more noble national tradition through the partnership with Doyce. Yet it is important to notice that this refurbished nationalism is purely futural: Clennam *hopes* there is a difference between England and France. As in the case of Arnold, where his nationalism is focused in saying what England lacks—culture—Dickens's nationalism is largely a frustrated ideal, not bald chauvinism. Indeed, frustrated himself, Doyce ends up leaving England for an unspecified amount of time on a commission from a country defined as dedicated to the notion "How to do it" (735). Dickens thereby underscores how little ready the time is for him and his principles. As he takes his leave, and the men cheer him, we read,

> Mr. Baptist, as a grateful little fellow in a position of trust, was among the workmen, and had done as much towards the cheering as a mere foreigner could. In truth, no men on earth can cheer like Englishmen, who do so rally

one another's blood and spirit when they cheer in earnest, that the stir is like the rush of their whole history, with all its standards waving at once, from Saxon Alfred's downwards. (738)

The moments of redirected nationalism in *Little Dorrit* are persistently rendered ambiguous by the many forces that make them unlikely to succeed. After all, Doyce is *leaving*: the owl of nationalism flies only at dusk. And there is an even darker element soon to be revealed in Clennam's seemingly valorized commitment to the country: he becomes susceptible to the force of Merdle, the global capitalist who encourages unbounded speculation, and he disastrously invests his money in Merdle's ventures. Just after Pancks strongly recommends the investment to him, he

> began to think it was curious . . . that [the name of Merdle] should be everywhere, and that nobody but he should seem to have any mistrust of it. Though indeed he began to remember, when he got to this, even he did not mistrust it; he had only happened to keep aloof from it.
>
> Such symptoms, when a disease of the kind is rife, are usually the signs of sickening. (643)

There is a connection, that is, between Arthur's turn to an ostensibly renewed nationalism and his enmeshment in the forces of a global capitalism that operates in alliance with the vitiated national culture that the novel diagnoses so pitilessly. Indeed, the incapacity for mistrust—or is it the inability to remember a prior mistrust?—is what produces the disease that is beginning to afflict Arthur, and that pervades the country. What had earlier been pathologized, nothing other than the suspicion of the negatively drawn characters, now turns out to be the prophylactic that would have prevented disease. So it turns out that suspicion and its lack are both productive of pathologies, and Dickens's ethico-political alternative to the Barnacles and the Circumlocution Office is absorbed into the degenerative forces of global capitalism.

Doyce's reaction to the eventual loss of their business fortune must be read in this context. Brought back to England to help fortify Arthur, who has taken the loss very hard and feels massive guilt for having ruined his partner, Doyce remarks,

> "There was an error in your calculations. I know what that is. It affects the whole machine, and failure is the consequence. You will profit by the failure, and will avoid it another time. I have done a similar thing myself, in construction, often. Every failure teaches a man something, if he will learn; and you are too sensible a man not to learn from this failure." (892)

Perhaps Doyce is just being nice, but this is a blatantly false analogy in several respects. Drawn in by the speculative tendencies of the age, duped by the forces of global capitalism and the idea that all can share in its profits, Clennam's was no simple mechanical misjudgment. It was the result of pervasive and systemic forces that simply cannot be "avoided in the future."[35] An ideal of purposive labor held within the bounds of situated judgment is not sufficient to take on the unavoidable conditions of modern social and economic reality.

The fact that the answers to what are initially portrayed as the disabling and sometimes destructive forces of detachment, exile, and disaffiliation themselves carry their own limitations and damaging effects complicates this novel considerably. Ultimately, the haunting presence of the suspicious social critics, and the highlighted myopia and confusion of the sympathetic characters, seriously impedes any reading of this novel for a reconstituted modest circle of duty. A detached, suspicious reading of nationalism and provinciality is demanded by this text at every turn, keeping the novel, in a deep sense, productively cosmopolitan. Ironically, the more suspicious readings of Dickens fail to see that Dickens's own hermeneutics of suspicion, as a persistent form of radical disaffiliation written in against his own more bounded hopefulness, is itself a form of critical cosmopolitanism.

Dickens's relentlessly critical stance, his novel's insistence on both the value and dangers of habitual wariness, is instructive and salutary, if ultimately somewhat arrested in its self-divisions. These self-divisions ultimately produce a too-stark opposition between a detached critical lucidity condemned to a state of exile and an affirmation of modest duty afflicted by the needful myopia of cultivated affiliations. Another impasse sits uneasily next to this one: *Little Dorrit* suggests that once one has achieved a systemic or global perspective, one is dangerously estranged and one's moral temperament is implicated; yet if one fails to achieve it, one runs the risk of "sickening." A way beyond such dilemmas is not entirely absent from the novel, however, and is perhaps most suggestively hinted at during Amy Dorrit's sojourn in Rome, where her personal history, particularly her capacity for sympathy and awareness of socioeconomic realities, becomes the basis, not the limit, for a larger understanding that remains open to cultural and historical alterity. But while Dickens's wider vision takes in structural forces that are lost to view in many other novels of the period, his characterology largely remains truncated, and reductively moralizing: he cannot imagine

---

[35] My reading of this passage is indebted to Larson, "The Arts in These Latter Days," 164.

any sustained and positive dialectical relation between cultivated suspicion and ethical practice.

This critique of Dickens is easy to make from the standpoint of current cosmopolitan thought, in which these separate forms of practice—the political and the ethical—are often simultaneously affirmed and reflectively combined. Many of the new cosmopolitans display alert awareness of geopolitical conditions as well as active ethical engagement with cultural difference in the name of self-cultivation, intersubjective reciprocity, and democratic ideals.[36] But within the nineteenth-century context of Enlightenment-inflected cosmopolitan thought, such combinations of critical diagnosis and reconstructive ideals were unusual. The tenor of much writing on cosmopolitanism in the nineteenth century, when it was not warning of dangers to nationalist cohesion, was naïvely optimistic: cosmopolitanism was typically seen as an ideal of self-cultivation enabled by European travel and cultural exchange, and international commerce was seen as an aid, not a hindrance, to such ethical and intellectual ideals. In this context, Dickens's divided investments carry a potent critical edge.

[36] Bruce Robbins, *Feeling Global: Internationalism in Distress* (New York: New York University Press, 1999); Paul Gilroy, *Against Race: Imagining Political Culture Beyond the Color Line* (Cambridge: Harvard University Press, 2000); Hollinger, *Postethnic America*; also see the essays collected in Cheah and Robbins, eds., *Cosmopolitics*.

CHAPTER THREE

Disinterestedness
as a Vocation

REVISITING MATTHEW ARNOLD

The Arnoldian concept of disinterestedness has strongly influenced the development of Anglo-American literary studies, both as an ideal and as an object of ongoing and stringent critique. Matthew Arnold's defense of the distanced viewpoint as a positive achievement of character and culture contrasts with Dickens's elaborate suspicions, yet both writers exemplify a more general cultural anxiety about the moral ramifications of modern objectifying practices. Despite the continuing hold that debates over Arnold exert on our profession, this aspect of Arnold's thought has been under-studied, especially in recent criticism. To Arnold is generally attributed the dubious honor of instituting the discipline of English as a humanistic study of works of literature deemed great and timeless, through a method that appeals to standards of objectivity and reason. While there have been a number of appraisals of Arnold that cogently reconstruct the insistently social and historical dimensions of his work, it nonetheless remains the case that his ideals of criticism as disinterestedness and culture as the pursuit of perfection are often assumed to connect seamlessly to his later touchstone theory of poetic greatness.[1] Such a view, however, misses one of the most important underlying investments of Arnold's thought: its persistent concern with the moral and characterological elements of modern intellectual and aesthetic practices. Acknowledgment of this aspect of Arnold's thought, moreover, is crucial to any comprehensive understanding of his conception of cultivated detachment, whether that be conceived in scientific, aesthetic, or cosmopolitan terms.

---

[1] Among the studies that emphasize the historical and social dimensions of Arnold's work are Lionel Trilling, *Matthew Arnold* (New York: Harcourt Brace Jovanovich, 1954; originally published 1939); Frederic E. Faverty, *Matthew Arnold the Ethnologist* (Evanston: Northwestern University Press, 1951); Morris Dickstein, *Double Agent: The Critic and Society* (New York: Oxford University Press, 1992); Donald Stone, *Communications with the Future: Matthew Arnold in Dialogue* (Ann Arbor: University of Michigan Press, 1997).

The preliminary point to be made about Arnold's ideal of disinterestedness is that, from a philosophical standpoint, it is terminologically and conceptually unsystematic, comprising what are elsewhere in the tradition distinguished as clearly different forms of detachment. Many readers of Arnold assume that the principle of objective realism, the endeavor to "see the object as in itself it really is," is meant to be the primary definition of the critical ideal in "The Function of Criticism at the Present Time."[2] Yet also prominent in this 1864 essay is an understanding of criticism as the "free play" of the mind upon conventional or customary ideas. Such flexible judgment is guaranteed, for Arnold, by one's cultivated distance from the practical sphere: criticism must be fully noninstrumental if it is to lay the ground for the fertile growth of future creative epochs. Openly speculative, characterized by constant movement and even a kind of restless negative energy, this form of criticism is celebrated as "a pleasure in itself" (*CPW* 3:268), a formulation that anticipates the tenets of the Aesthetic Movement and that is situated at an oblique angle to the more serious norm of objective realism that has often been associated with Arnold.[3]

When Arnold speaks of the pleasurable play of the mind upon conventional ideas, he combines what in the Kantian tradition are distinguished as the two separate faculties of aesthetic disinterestedness and critical reason. For Kant, critical reason is the interrogation of custom and the self-conscious authorization of principles, while aesthetic disinterestedness is associated with the free play of the mind and autotelic detachment. Critical reason is of course itself to be distinguished from conceptions of objectivity: the former subjects custom and habit to reflexive interrogation; the latter seeks to identify empirically verifiable facts and laws, relying on a fundamental conception of the objective status of the external world. Arnold's

---

[2] Matthew Arnold, "The Function of Criticism at the Present Time," in *The Complete Prose Works of Matthew Arnold*, vol. 3: *Lectures and Essays in Criticism*, ed. R. H. Super (Ann Arbor: University of Michigan Press, 1962), 258. Subsequent page number references will be cited parenthetically in the text as *CPW* 3.

[3] When I say that criticism is characterized by "even a kind of restless energy," I have in mind the section of "The Function of Criticism at the Present Time" in which Arnold criticizes those who insist we move beyond mere negative critique—in this context Arnold insists that criticism must be "perpetually dissatisfied" (*CPW* 3:280). Also relevant here is the early description of culture, in *Culture and Anarchy*, as "eternally passing on and seeking." See Matthew Arnold, *Culture and Anarchy*, in *The Complete Prose Works of Matthew Arnold*, vol. 5: *Culture and Anarchy with Friendship's Garland and Some Literary Essays*, ed. R. H. Super (Ann Arbor: University of Michigan Press, 1965), 111. Subsequent page number references will be cited parenthetically in the text as *CPW* 5.

ideals of disinterestedness and criticism unsystematically make appeal to all three cognitive practices: objectivity, critical reason, and aesthetic flexibility. All three appear not only in "The Function of Criticism at the Present Time," but also in the preface to *Culture and Anarchy*, when Arnold writes:

> The whole scope of the essay is to recommend culture as the great help out of our present difficulties: culture being a pursuit of our total perfection by means of getting to know, on all the matters which most concern us, the best which has been thought and said in the world, and, through this knowledge, turning a stream of fresh and free thought upon our stock notions and habits, which we now follow staunchly but mechanically, vainly imagining that there is a virtue in following them staunchly which makes up for the mischief of following them mechanically. (*CPW* 5:233–34)

In its confident reference to "the best which has been thought and said in the world," a phrase that also occurs repeatedly in "The Function of Criticism at the Present Time," the passage makes an appeal to the objective value of knowledge; in its idea that one should disrupt stock notions and habits, it makes an appeal to reason's interrogation of custom; and in its image of "a stream of fresh and free thought," Arnold's writing obliquely evokes aesthetic free play. Of course, it should be noted that the history of aesthetics beginning with eighteenth-century Enlightenment thinkers in Britain itself manifests different approaches to the question of whether disinterestedness is a distinctively aesthetic mode of apprehension or not. In Addison's writings, for example, the disinterested perception of beauty is opposed to critical reflection, which is construed as overly motivated in its impulse to demonstrate something or to work out a problem. But Shaftesbury, by contrast, directly assigned disinterestedness to the faculty of reason as well as to aesthetic perceptions.[4]

The point here is simply to register the range of forms of detachment to be found in Arnold's work as well as their loose relation to one another. And in addition to the shifting and complex relations among objectivity, critical reason, and aesthetic free play, there is still another form of detachment valued in this essay, a specifically cosmopolitan distance. At key moments, Arnold endorses comparative knowledge and laments English provinciality. Late in the essay, he stresses the need for the English critic to "dwell much on foreign thought" and to "possess one great literature, at least, besides his own; and the more unlike his own, the better" (*CPW* 3:283, 284). Arnold also

[4] See Jerome Stolnitz, "On the Origins of 'Aesthetic Disinterestedness,'" *Journal of Aesthetics and Art Criticism* 20 (1961–62): 131–43.

promotes the idea that commingling of cultures is conducive to an epoch of expansion: indeed, signs of impending expansion are voiced specifically through a metaphor of cosmopolitan openness and imperceptible cultural fusion, made possible by the waning threat of the French Revolution:

> In the first place all danger of a hostile forcible pressure of foreign ideas upon our practice has long disappeared; like the traveller in the fable, therefore, we begin to wear our cloak a little more loosely. Then, with a long peace, the ideas of Europe steal gradually and amicably in, and mingle, though in infinitesimally small quantities at a time, with our own notions. (*CPW* 3:269)

To be sure, Arnold's self-conscious avoidance of nationalist provinciality in his blanket standard of "the best that is known and thought *in the world*" usually reaches no farther than the boundaries of Western Europe, or, at best, leaps temporally to embrace a more geographically expansive antiquity that includes the East (*CPW* 3:282; my emphasis).[5] But transcendence of provincial narrowness, and specifically transcendence of a constraining *Englishness*, is stressed in various ways throughout Arnold's writing on criticism and culture. An implicit ideal of cosmopolitan cultivation informs his characterization of his fellow countrymen as Philistines and distinctly lacking in light (ideas).[6] The corresponding notion that comparative knowledge or an international perspective will illuminate the tasks of criticism is pursued in many of Arnold's literary essays, most notably "A French Critic on

[5] Arnold states in "The Function of Criticism" that the criticism he is advocating "regards Europe as being, for intellectual and spiritual purposes, one great confederation, bound to a joint action and working to a common result; and whose members have, for their proper outfit, a knowledge of Greek, Roman, and Eastern antiquity, and of one another" (*CPW* 3:284).

[6] Arnold was in fact taken to task repeatedly for his lack of patriotism and even went so far, in the pages of the *Pall Mall Gazette*, to acknowledge the need, as he put it, "to disclaim that positive admiration of things foreign, and that indifference to English freedom, which have often been imputed to me." Quoted in Faverty, *Matthew Arnold the Ethnologist*, 4. Interestingly, Arnold's late lecture "Numbers," delivered in the United States in 1883, acknowledges that he may have underestimated the patriotism of his home audience: "Here, so many miles from home, I begin to reflect with tender contrition, that perhaps I have not,—I will not say flattered the patriotism of my own countrymen enough, but regarded it enough. Perhaps that is one reason why I have produced so very little effect upon them." Matthew Arnold, "Numbers; or The Majority and the Remnant," in *The Complete Prose Works of Matthew Arnold*, vol. 10: *Philistinism in England and America*, ed. R. H. Super (Ann Arbor: University of Michigan Press, 1974), 143–44. Subsequent page number references will be cited parenthetically in the text as *CPW* 10.

Milton" and "A French Critic on Goethe."[7] And Arnold identifies as cosmopolitan several of the literary or cultural figures whom he singles out for
sustained attention in his writings. It is clearly no accident that Arnold
stresses Heinrich Heine's hybrid identity when he introduces him, dramatically, as a hero in the war against Philistinism: "a young man of genius, born
at Hamburg, and with all the culture of Germany, but by race a Jew; with
warm sympathies for France, whose revolution had given to his race the
rights of citizenship."[8] Part of the attraction and relevance of Marcus Aurelius lies in the fact that, as Emperor "in a brilliant centre of civilisation," he
maintained a commanding perspective over a highly developed and quin-
tessentially modern empire.[9]

I point to this element of Arnold's thought not because I intend to celebrate him as a champion of cosmopolitanism, thereby answering a well-
developed critique of Arnold's ideals as falsely universal and ultimately
dangerous. There have certainly been some notable instances of such recuperation, both historically and more recently: conceptions of Arnold as promoting marginality, hybridity, or multiculturalism in *On the Study of Celtic
Literature*; or appreciative claims that he is cosmopolitan by method (in his
promotion of international vantage points or perspectives) or temperament

---

[7] Both these essays acknowledge without idealizing the aid of extranational distance in the appraisal of literary figures claimed as national treasures by the home
country. In the essay on Milton, Arnold writes, "A completely disinterested judgment about a man like Milton is easier to a foreign critic than to an Englishman.
From conventional obligation to admire 'our great epic poet' a foreigner is free. Nor
has he any bias for or against Milton because he was a Puritan,—in his political and
ecclesiastical doctrines to one of our great English parties a delight, to the other a
bugbear." Arnold quickly adds, however, that good criticism also requires "a thorough knowledge of the man and his circumstances" and goes on to credit Scherer
with extensive knowledge of Milton and his times, and with a general cosmopolitanism of knowledge and character: "He knows thoroughly the language and literature
of England, Italy, Germany, as well as of France. Well-informed, intelligent, disinterested, open-minded, sympathetic, M. Scherer has much in common with the admirable critic whom France has lost—Sainte-Beuve." Matthew Arnold, "A French Critic
on Milton," in *The Complete Prose Works of Matthew Arnold*, vol. 8: *Essays Religious
and Mixed*, ed. R. H. Super (Ann Arbor: University of Michigan Press, 1972), 174,
174–75. Also compare Arnold's articulation of a comparative imperative in "On the
Modern Element in Literature": "no single event, no single literature, is adequately
comprehended except in its relation to other events, to other literature." *The Complete Prose Works of Matthew Arnold*, vol. 1: *On the Classical Tradition*, ed. R. H.
Super (Ann Arbor: University of Michigan Press, 1960), 20–21. Subsequent page
number references will be cited parenthetically as *CPW* 1.

[8] Matthew Arnold, "Heinrich Heine," *CPW* 3:111.

[9] Matthew Arnold, "Marcus Aurelius," *CPW* 3:140.

He has various forms of disint.

86

various forms of disinterestedness are response to modernism

(in his celebration of diversity and variety).[10] My aim is rather different. Focusing primarily on Arnold's writings of the 1850s and 60s, I want to reconstruct a broader map of Arnoldian detachment, while at the same time arguing that his several conceptions of detachment—disinterestedness, objectivity, cosmopolitanism—all manifest a similar and distinctive pattern of response to the challenge of modernity as Arnold conceived it.[11]

How to reconcile cultivated w/ stance of the subj/ective POV

In developing this reading of Arnold, I reframe the question of how we can reconcile, on the one hand, his advocacy of cultivated stances and, on the other, his emphasis on transcendence of the subjective point of view through impersonal or universal entities such as culture, the best self, or the state. The tension between an appeal to subjective stance and an appeal to impersonal entities as the guarantors of value has been criticized in Arnold as a pattern of circular reasoning, whereby each is supposed impossibly to underwrite the other.[12] We can refocus the question if we discover what drives this seeming division. The unifying concern behind Arnold's elaborations of detachment is how to deal with the dual experiences of modernity, whereby the growth of scientific knowledge is both a form of progress and a "fatal event" with regard to traditional sustaining beliefs, and whereby the critical spirit both liberates and disenchants. As is well known, Arnold was profoundly exercised by the problem of value in its broadest sense and persistently concerned that with the loss of religious traditions the moral life— the resources for responding to the crucial question of the relation between knowledge and conduct, or fact and value—was endangered. By closely examining his approach to detachment, we can trace a pattern of response to the challenge of modernity that considerably complicates the view of Arnold as authoritarian in his appeals to absolute standards or foundational values. For while the appeal to noncontingent and nonsubjective value does emerge in the notion that the authority of the state will undergird the best self, or in the idea of the touchstone line, or in the asserted faith that Hellenism and

modernity itself dual

[10] See Trilling, *Matthew Arnold*; Faverty, *Matthew Arnold the Ethnologist*; Dickstein, *Double Agent*; Stone, *Communications with the Future*.

[11] I restrict the focus of this analysis to the 1850s and 1860s because the pattern of thought that I am identifying takes on a different shape in Arnold's writings on religion in the 1870s, tending toward a kind of mysticism.

[12] The most common target of attack is the series of arguments about the ground of culture in *Culture and Anarchy*, in which the state, culture, and individual perfection all depend upon one another for their validation. See Trilling, *Matthew Arnold*, 254; David J. DeLaura, *Hebrew and Hellene in Victorian England: Newman, Arnold, and Pater* (Austin: University of Texas Press, 1969), 77; Steven Marcus, "Culture and Anarchy Today," in *Culture and Anarchy*, ed. Samuel Lipman (New Haven: Yale University Press, 1994), 178.

Hebraism will work together toward a single overriding spiritual end, there is another line of thinking in Arnold's work, one that raises up temperament, stance, and character as the site where fact and value might be reconciled, or where the promises of modernity might best be glimpsed. The emphasis here is on the successful subjective enactment or embodiment of forms of universality, as distinguished from other moments where he seems to valorize impersonal or objective standards. Such an approach helps to retrieve one key instance of the nineteenth-century approach to detachment as an ongoing achievement: as something that cannot simply be presumed or asserted but rather must emerge out of concrete practices, guided by shaping aspirations, and intimately linked to the crafting of character and moral selfhood.

The reading of Arnold I will offer might be summed up as a more systematic explanation of David J. DeLaura's observation that "whenever Arnold tries to introduce something that transcends the self, he introduces the self in another guise."[13] The discussion proceeds as follows. First, I examine the ways in which an ideal of scientific objectivity is intricately bound up with Arnold's thinking about race, cultural affiliation, and intercultural relations in the mid-1860s, a time in which Arnold briefly called upon the authority of science in order to elaborate the racial bases for the study, and advancement, of culture. As we shall see, race remains a central category throughout Arnold's writings on science and criticism, serving alternately to thwart and enable the project of cultivated distance. During his romance with science, Arnold tries to reconcile fact and value through an ideal of objective stance construed as continuous with moral vision. Scientific detachment ultimately poses more of a threat than a solution to the challenges of modernity, however, and Arnold relinquishes this particular dream of legitimization, placing his faith in "letters." Yet as I show in the second section of the chapter, the yoking of method and ethos that appears with particularly stark clarity in the embrace of science reappears distinctly throughout all of Arnold's writing on forms of detachment, including those analyses that center on disinterestedness, critical reason, and cosmopolitanism.

In general, this reading of Arnold provides a more comprehensive understanding of the forms of detachment that inform Arnold's ideals of criticism and culture. In so doing, it resituates debates about Arnold and race and revises standard thinking about Arnold's relation to Pater and Wilde. By way of conclusion, I try to assess the success and value of Arnold's attempt to embody ideals through the somewhat paradoxical practice of subjectivizing

[13] Delaura, *Hebrew and Hellene*, 77.

categories otherwise associated with the impersonal, the objective, or the universal. If Arnold's elaborations of exemplary stance demand a rethinking of the fundamental critiques of Arnold as authoritarian and foundational, as I contend, it is still an open issue whether his concept of enacted universality is itself in need of further critique or refinement. While I favor the project of imagining how universality might be lived or given a concrete characterology, this does not mean, in other words, that any given articulation of embodied universality is itself above critique. As in the previous chapter, and the study as a whole, I therefore engage in a process of immanent critique, first defending Arnold against what I take to be reductive lines of attack, and then subjecting my own defense, and my reconstructed Arnold, to critical scrutiny.

SCIENCE, RACE, AND THE FAILURE OF NATURALISM

Discussion of the categories of race and nationality in Arnold's thought has taken a number of different forms over the years. Trilling, whose 1939 book on Arnold paid admiring attention to the social and historical dimensions of his work, fairly directly confronted the problem of Arnold's "untenable theory of race."[14] He sought to mitigate judgments against Arnold in two ways: by claiming that he was merely reflecting the unexamined intellectual assumptions of his time—preeminently, the tendency to explain national characteristics on the basis of racial nature—and by asserting that Arnold's aim in identifying racial characteristics was to bring people together, not to separate them.[15] Similarly, Frederic E. Faverty's interesting 1951 study, *Matthew Arnold the Ethnologist*, argued that Arnold's aim in his ethnological writings, in contrast to many of his contemporaries, was reconciliation and productive cultural interchange. A prime example adduced is the influential *On the Study of Celtic Literature*, which challenged the prevalent notion

---

[14] Trilling, *Matthew Arnold*, 236. Subsequent page number references will be cited parenthetically in the text.

[15] Writing in the 1930s, Trilling was acutely aware of the dangers of race thinking. On balance, he sought to defend Arnold, but he also acknowledged that any use of "the racial hypothesis" conduced to legitimize a volatile and dangerous set of practices: "if some used [the racial hypothesis] for liberalizing purposes, as Arnold himself did, still, by their very assent to an unfounded assumption, they cannot wholly be dissociated from the quaint, curious and dangerous lucubrations of Houston Stewart Chamberlain, Richard Wagner, Woltmann, Treitschke, Rosenberg and the whole of official German thought in the present day" (235).

that Celtic blood had been expunged from the English peoples; Faverty also cites Arnold's deep belief that it was destructive to allow any single racial element to dominate the life of the individual or nation: the ideals are measure, balance, integration. These defenses begin a tradition whereby Arnold's category of national culture is shown to be importantly complex or revealingly self-undermining. Trilling observes, for example, that it is contradictory to exhort people to give greater prominence to a particular part of their racial nature: "as soon as a people admits an imperative higher than that of its blood—the imperative of reason, for example—the imperative of blood itself is totally negated" (236). Robert Young, who ultimately emphasizes the fact that race underlies Arnold's conception of culture, also points out that Arnold defines "Englishness" not by what it *is* but by what it *lacks* (culture, ideas, light, universal standards). An opposing tradition insists, however, that no matter how far Arnold's theory of race tends to transmute into culture, no matter how willful or mediated the relation between the cultivated individual or group and its racial characteristics, the fact remains that Arnold necessarily relies upon, or always returns to, a bedrock theory of racial difference.[16]

Other aspects of Arnold's treatment of national culture invite the deconstructive approach evident in Trilling and Young, as he unfailingly introduces negative, critical, or trumping elements into what may have initially appeared as a substantive category of race. Insofar as the French element of novelty serves as a catalyst for modern hybrid formations, French national culture becomes not an essence but a force that transforms any preexistent racial identity it encounters. Similarly, the "hauntings of Celtism" in the English race give rise to an awkward self-consciousness, and thwart spontaneity and naturalness: how can this be simple racial determinism? Beyond these identifications of catalytic or disruptive racial elements,

[16] Robert J. C. Young, *Colonial Desire: Hybridity in Theory, Culture and Race* (New York: Routledge, 1995). "Trilling suggests in Arnold's favour that despite his immersion in racial theory, at least Arnold advocated racial mixture. . . . Arnold does not advocate an amalgamation that results in merging and fusion but rather an apartheid model of dialogic separation: in claiming the continued existence of types, which can still be distinguished by the perceptive ethnologist or literary critic, Arnold keeps to the idea of racial mingling with no loss of distinctness for each racial type, and thus shows his position to be much closer to those on the right such as Edwards, Knox, Nott, and Gliddon" (86–87). This is subsumed as well under a more general set of claims: "Culture has always marked cultural difference by producing the other; it has always been comparative, and racism has always been an integral part of it: the two are inextricably clustered together, feeding off and generating each other. Race has always been culturally constructed. Culture has always been racially constructed" (54).

redeeming?) has racial determinism — mixing, of choice notes to racial idea of balance

Arnold often attributes individual genius to some form of disjunction with respect to national culture: "And yet just what constitutes special power and genius in a man seems often to be his blending with the basis of his national temperament, some additional gift or grace not proper to that temperament" (*CPW* 3:360, 358). (He then goes on to cite as examples Shakespeare and Goethe.) We are now very close to the cosmopolitanism of exemplary figures like Heine, as well as to the illuminations of exile, represented most strikingly in the case of Spinoza's excommunication: his persecutors "remained children of Israel, and he became a child of modern Europe."[17]

Such an interpretive strategy aims to uncover, in the course of Arnold's seemingly pervasive race-thinking, either a saving inconsistency or outright reversal. Against the disturbing ideology of Arnold's ethno-logic, it asserts one or more of the following points: (1) the inherent inconsistency of race thinking, (2) Arnold's own and obviously genuine inconsistencies, which somehow mitigate the charge of racialist thinking, or (3) an underrecognized opposing truth in Arnold, something higher than inconsistency but lower than elaborated alternative, the truth of a kind of ennobling relation to cultural identity, brought on by fortuitous hybridity, or the spark of genius, or the cultivated balance that defines harmonious development.

These debates about Arnold's relation to race reflect a genuine division in his thought. It is crucial to acknowledge both sides of his thinking: the reliance on racial nature and the appeal to any number of ways in which consciousness and culture might intensify, channel, or mitigate those racial forces that can never be fully escaped.[18] In his ringing calls for intercultural fusion or individual perfection, racial elements are thus conceived of as malleable to a certain extent, even if fundamental nonetheless. A key passage appears in *On the Study of Celtic Literature*:

> Modes of life, institutions, government, and other such causes, are sufficient, I shall be told, to account for English oratory. Modes of life, institu-

[17] Matthew Arnold, "Spinoza and the Bible," *CPW* 3:158.

[18] In his appeal to essential racial nature, Arnold is similar to many but not all of his contemporaries. Criticizing Trilling's attempt to defend Arnold by saying that he is simply a product of his time, Young points out that many of Arnold's contemporaries contested racial thinking; he lists Prichard, Buckle, Huxley, Latham, Lubbock, Mill, Quatrefages, Tylor, and Waitz. See Young, *Colonial Desire*, 63. Trilling, on the other hand, admits the existence of challenges from figures like Mill and Buckle but provides an extensive list of racialists, including Gobineau, Moses Hess, Heine, Ludwig Börne, Stendhal, Meredith, Mme. de Staël, Carlyle, J. A. Froude, Kingsley, J. R. Green, Taine, Renan, and Sainte-Beuve. Trilling goes so far as to say, "Indeed, the list could be made to include nearly every writer of the time who generalized about human affairs" (235).

tions, government, climate, and so forth,—let me say it once for all,—will further or hinder the development of an aptitude, but they will not by themselves create the aptitude or explain it. On the other hand, a people's habit and complexion of nature go far to determine its modes of life, institutions, and government, and even to prescribe the limits within which the influences of climate shall tell upon it. (*CPW* 3:353)[19]

My primary aim here is to show that the shifting emphases and underlying presupposition of Arnold's writings reflect the privileged place that race and cultural heritage play in Arnold's obsessions with the modern project of achieving psychological, moral, and cultural distance from the "given." Arnold is drawn to and wants to believe in the possibility of transformative and critical relations to what he construes as natural racial forces, but he is also haunted by the fact that such forces are starkly determining. It is in response to this more general apprehension that Arnold's thought produces some of its most distastefully racist moments, as he asserts distinctions among different races and nationalities precisely on the basis of their capacity to respond to the challenges of modernity. (I will discuss in the second half of this chapter the distinctive form his hierarchical thought takes.)

The "modern" was of course a key concept for Arnold throughout his work and foundational in structuring his famous turn from poetry to prose. This is evident in the opening paragraph of the "Preface to the First Edition of *Poems*," in which Arnold explains his decision not to include *Empedocles on Etna* in the collection. For Arnold, the Greek figure Empedocles represents a form of consciousness that should no longer be indulged by poets or critics:

> What those who are familiar only with the great monuments of early Greek genius suppose to be its exclusive characteristics, have disappeared: the calm, the cheerfulness, the disinterested objectivity have disappeared; the dialogue of the mind with itself has commenced; modern problems have presented themselves; we hear already the doubts, we witness the discouragement, of Hamlet and of Faust. (*CPW* 1:1)

While this passage identifies modernity as something negative that befalls the self, Arnold's inaugural lecture as professor of poetry at Oxford, "On the Modern Element in Literature," views modernity as a constellation of

[19] One might contrast this with the following statement by Mill, in *The Principles of Political Economy*: "of all vulgar modes of escaping from the consideration of the effect of social and moral influences on the human mind, the most vulgar is that of attributing diversities of conduct and character to inherent natural differences." Quoted in Trilling, *Matthew Arnold*, 234.

positive conditions: a civil life relatively secure from any intrusions of war or crime, the growth of tolerance, an increase of conveniences, the formation of taste, the capacity for refined pursuits, and above all and supremely, "the intellectual maturity of man himself; the tendency to observe facts with a critical spirit; to search for their law, not to wander among them at random; to judge by the rule of reason, not by the impulse of prejudice or caprice" (*CPW* 1:24).

At issue for Arnold in both the "Preface to *Poems*" and the inaugural lecture as professor of poetry is what precise posture should be adopted toward the distinct conditions and challenges of modernity: "On the Modern Element in Literature" describes modernity as "the spectacle of a vast multitude of facts awaiting and inviting [one's] comprehension"; the proper response involves finding "the true point of view from which to contemplate this spectacle" (*CPW* 1:20). It is a question of stance, articulated as a need for some perspective from which one can both contemplate and comprehend; the suggestion is that one must ascend to a point of lofty detachment; indeed, Arnold states that "he who adequately comprehends this spectacle, has *risen* to the comprehension of his age" (*CPW* 1:20: my emphasis). For Arnold, as for a thinker like Hegel, modernity is not so much a historical epoch as a form of consciousness—one that appears throughout human history as a response to momentous cultural transitions. The literature of Periclean Athens represents just such an ennobling response to modern complexities, while the Roman writer Lucretius is modern but *inadequate* because he displays negative versions of contemplation, namely, depression and ennui. (The comments on Lucretius, of course, parallel Arnold's indictment of the brooding and subjective tendencies of Romantic poetry.)

As indicated by Arnold's dramatic emphasis on "the intellectual maturity of man," Arnold follows Kant in identifying modernity largely with the critical spirit, or, to adopt Habermas's terminology, with the postconventional interrogation of prevailing customs, routines, habits, and norms. In the second section of this chapter, I will examine this aspect of Arnold's understanding of modernity. But for Arnold modern also means "scientific," and it is in conjunction with what he sees as the distinct promises and limitations of contemporary science that the issue of race arises most forcefully and dramatically in his work; any full treatment of Arnold's conception of cultural affiliation and detachment, then, must take into account the dimension of his writings that brings science to bear upon the question of racial culture.[20]

[20] I use the term "racial culture" here in part to indicate that for Arnold, as for

It is important to clarify in a preliminary way how Arnold uses the term *science*.[21] Throughout his career, he moves back and forth between a general conception of science as simply disinterested and systematic study, "seeing the object as it really is" in any intellectual domain, and a more narrow conception of the natural sciences. In the first instance, there is no tension between humanistic studies and the sciences, as Arnold states explicitly in the late essay "Literature and Science": "all learning is scientific which is systematically laid out and followed up to its original sources, and . . . a genuine humanism is scientific."[22] But insofar as a privileging of the natural sciences threatens the study of letters, both in the practical sphere of education and as a larger question of culture, then science must not eclipse literature or humanistic studies. To the latter falls the crucial task of relating new scientific knowledge, with its fatal effects on traditional beliefs and ideas, to the supremely important conduct of life, to the moral and spiritual sphere which makes up, to invoke Arnold's famous formulation, three-fourths of life. This is in fact the ultimate argument of "Literature and Science." But in the mid-1860s, Arnold briefly called upon the authority of natural science in order to elaborate the racial bases for the study of culture.[23] This was actually a two-pronged effort. On the one hand, Arnold seemed genuinely fascinated by the project of ethnology and was clearly a true believer in the forms of racial generalization that inform his writings on national characteristics and historical trajectories. Such a commitment to ethnological science lies behind the magisterial claim, in *Culture and Anarchy*, that "Science has now made visible to everybody the great and pregnant elements of difference which lie in race" (*CPW* 5:173). On the other hand, Arnold saw the project of ethnology as subordinate to the larger, normative project of ideal

---

many nineteenth-century thinkers, "race" was used in a loose way, sometimes with strict reference to physical characteristics, sometimes more expansively, along the lines of what we now call "culture." On this issue, see Young, *Colonial Desire*, 86; George W. Stocking, Jr., *Victorian Anthropology* (New York: The Free Press, 1987), 138–39.

[21] The sketch provided in this paragraph is largely drawn from Fred A. Dudley, "Matthew Arnold and Science," *PMLA* 57 (1942): 276–86.

[22] Matthew Arnold, "Literature and Science," *CPW* 10:57.

[23] "Nowhere else did Arnold make such cordial overtures to science as in the Celtic lectures of 1865 and 1866. Students of ancient Welsh and Irish literature, he believed, should try to be as objective as the philologists and anthropologists, whose contributions toward the understanding of race, led him repeatedly to attribute to science that very power of integration which he found more usually in poetry." Dudley, "Matthew Arnold and Science," 289.

culture for the individual, for the nation, and for humanity as a whole. The attempt to build the project of culture upon the findings of ethnology in fact stands at the heart of both *On the Study of Celtic Literature* and *Culture and Anarchy*.

On the Study of Celtic Literature holds out science as the basis for inter-cultural understanding and reconciliation, particularly with regard to long-standing tensions between the Celt and the Saxon. Indeed, one might say that this work attempts to fuse fact and value through a cosmopolitan science of racial unity. Admittedly, Arnold begins by simply displacing one line of racial demarcation by another, claiming that science has laid the basis for reconciling the Irish and the English by revealing the "native diversity be-tween our European bent and the Semitic bent" (*CPW* 3:301). Later in the text, however, he asserts that science will gradually tend, despite its method of dividing and separating, toward "the idea of the substantial unity of man" (*CPW* 3:330). Although it will be long in coming, ultimate fusion is prefig-ured insofar as science is continually "showing us affinity where we imag-ined there was isolation" (*CPW* 3:330).

What is important to recognize here, insofar as it characterizes Arnold's approach to forms of detachment more generally, is that scientific objectivity is conceived of as both constitutive and productive of moral value—largely in response to an underlying anxiety that it is entirely divorced from value.[24] In a way, Arnold attempts in this phase of his intellectual life to give to science the task he later assigns to literature: the task of promoting harmoni-ous unity. As conceived by Arnold, the science of race both renders compre-hensible the conditions of racial and cultural makeup and illuminates the unity that lies behind seeming divisions. Science aids comprehension by discerning the hybrid formations that make up contemporary nationalities as well as "the genius of each people" (*CPW* 3:325). For example, science dem-onstrates English hybridity by showing that the Celtic element has not, con-trary to widely held belief, been expunged from the English race. It secures this claim in a broadly scientific way, "by external and by internal evidence," and across a range of domains: "the language and the physical type of our race afford certain data for trying it, and other data are afforded by our liter-ature, genius, and spiritual production generally" (*CPW* 3:337).

[24] In this Arnold manifests the more general tendency among nineteenth-century scientists to "moralize" objectivity. See Lorraine Daston, "The Moral Economy of Science," *Osiris* 10 (1995): 3–24; Lorraine Daston and Peter Galison, "The Image of Objectivity," *Representations* 40 (1992): 81–128; and Lorraine Daston, "Objectivity and the Escape from Perspective," *Social Studies of Science* 22 (1992): 597–618. Also see my introduction for further discussion of the work of Daston and Galison.

A significant portion of *On the Study of Celtic Literature* is thus devoted to uncovering and praising the influence of Celtic sentimentalism on English culture, with the aim of scientifically solving, by essentially rendering moot, a problem of political division.[25] Yet the scientific analysis promoted by Arnold in this text cannot uniformly guarantee the happy results it predominantly and cheerfully offers to us. Indeed, one crucial analysis of the disparate elements that make up the English race yields a dispiriting result:

> The Englishman, in so far as he is German,—and he is mainly German,— proceeds in the steady-going German fashion; if he were all German he would proceed thus for ever without self-consciousness or embarrassment; but, in so far as he is Celtic, he has snatches of quick instinct which often make him feel he is fumbling, show him visions of an easier, more dexterous behaviour, disconcert him and fill him with misgiving. No people, therefore, are so shy, so self-conscious, so embarrassed as the English, because two natures are mixed in them, and natures which pull them such different ways. (*CPW* 3:360)

This passage reveals the anxiety that perpetually haunts Arnold's embrace of modernity, his embrace of science specifically and critical detachment more generally. Revealed here is not so much the promise as the threat of science: science contributes to the project of seeing the object as it really is but seems to do so by seeing the object as it *ineluctably* is. That is, science does not so much provide the basis for a reassuring comprehension of the multitude of facts but rather simply uncovers determinations painful to contemplate. In the report of his second official tour of the Continent, written during the same year that he composed the lectures on Celtic literature, Arnold makes the following distinction between letters and science: "The study of letters is the study of the operation of human force, of human freedom and activity; the study of nature is the study of the operation of human limitation and passivity. The contemplation of human force and activity tends naturally to heighten our own force and activity; the contemplation of

---

[25] *On the Study of Celtic Literature* was written in the midst of Fenian violence and anti-Irish reaction. Arnold consistently opposed Home Rule (which he feared would spark a civil war) but did campaign for landlord reform and a federalist system of local provincial government; he also supported concurrent endowment of the Protestant and Catholic churches in Ireland, departing from his usual disestablishmentarian views. See David Lloyd, "Arnold, Ferguson, Schiller: Aesthetic Culture and the Politics of Aesthetics," *Cultural Critique* 2 (1986): 137–69; Thomas S. Snyder, "Matthew Arnold and the Irish Question," *The Arnoldian* 4 (1977): 12–20.

human limits and passivity tends rather to check it."[26] This is a far cry from the promises of unity and reconciliation that inaugurate the discussion in *On the Study of Celtic Literature*; the passage describing the fumbling Englishman seems precisely to identify human limits and passivity, insofar as the Englishman is literally, physically, manifestly at the mercy of forces that thwart his freedom and activity. Even more: what results from forces of nature in this case is a negative version of the critical spirit, elsewhere heralded as a manifestation of the modern. For the Englishman is modern to the extent that he is self-conscious, but his self-consciousness is limited here to the painful apprehension of his own faltering freedom, which is also, for Arnold, the dire sentence of being unable to maintain a heroic stance precisely because the ideal of equipoise (in the face of forces beyond one's control) is here definitively thwarted by forces beyond one's control. The Englishman as object of scientific study becomes in a sense representative also of the limits of the modern scientific subject, whose strenuous objectivity discloses only the intractability of nature.

Arnold himself does not remain passive in the face of these tragic versions of the modern—a science divorced from value and progress, a self-awareness that does not liberate. As Trilling makes a point of emphasizing, Arnold asserts, in a kind of surprise ending to *On the Study of Celtic Literature*, that natural forces can themselves be subjected to the powers of reason: "So long as we are blindly and ignorantly rolled about by the forces of our nature, their contradiction baffles us and lames us; so soon as we have clearly discerned what they are, and begun to apply to them a law of measure, control, and guidance, they may be made to work for our good and to carry us forward" (*CPW* 3:383). It is interesting that a potent, indeed virtually instrumental, form of self-critical reason (applying a law of measure, control, and guidance) is brought in to guarantee the scientific project. Arnold thereby recasts the stalled and painful self-scrutiny of the Englishman as heroic self-overcoming. We are now baffled and lamed only *before* the project of science and reason has gotten underway, and not, as before, in the quasi-enlightened wake of its ineffectual realizations. Beyond asserting the possibility for the critical channeling of natural forces, Arnold also insists that value resides within the very processes of scientific activity and understanding. Rather than being value-neutral and disturbingly unanswerable in its identification of extrinsic forces, science in this aspect becomes the emblem and generator of moral value. As I have discussed, for Arnold science ideally breaks down the Englishman's alienation from the Irish and thereby

[26] Quoted in Dudley, "Matthew Arnold and Science," 290.

fosters a sense of kinship and reconciliation between two groups who exist in antagonism with one another. But, as Arnold himself is keenly aware, this action on the part of science is more fortuitous than guaranteed: reconciliation here issues out of the unknown fact of racial affinity, but elsewhere science could just as easily identify race-based antipathies, as is clear when Arnold tells us that science "[teaches] us which way our natural affinities and repulsions lie" (*CPW* 3:301). To avoid the unsettling consequences of such contingency—the fact that increased sympathy is in this case merely "an indirect practical result" (*CPW* 3:301)—he generates a double argument:

> However, on these indirect benefits of science we must not lay too much stress. Only this must be allowed; it is clear that there are now in operation two influences, both favourable to a more attentive and impartial study of Celtism than it has yet ever received from us. One is the strengthening in us of the feeling of Indo-Europeanism; the other, the strengthening in us of the scientific sense generally. The first breaks down barriers between us and the Celt, relaxes the estrangement between us; the second begets the desire to know his case thoroughly, and to be just to it. This is a very different matter from the political and social Celtisation of which certain enthusiasts dream; but it is not to be despised by any one to whom the Celtic genius is dear; and it is possible, while the other is not. (*CPW* 3:302–3)

After noting the overcoming of estrangement through the fortuitous discovery of shared origins, that is, Arnold then forwards the noncontingent claim that "the scientific sense generally" is a force for good, because it produces a desire for comprehensive knowledge and fosters forms of objectivity that Arnold equates with justice. Here, the scientific stance is also a moral one: objectivity *is* impartiality, knowledge *is* justice.

In the end, however, Arnold does not maintain his optimism about the moral potentialities of science. Perhaps this is because Arnold cannot shake the sense that science too definitively discloses the ineluctable facticity of racial determinations. Perhaps it is because of the politics of the education systems he inspected, and his need to combat the dominance of science over humanistic studies. We can only speculate as to the relative force of contributing causes, but Arnold's talk of the ultimately unifying aim of science dissipates, and the claim that scientific objectivity produces just appreciations is replaced with a very explicit call to assign questions of morality to the domain of letters. Arnold's early separation between reason and faith, which animated his essays on the dangers of bringing the results of speculative thinking too suddenly to the masses, reappears in a different guise, remapped onto the distinction between Hellenism and Hebraism. But the concern about the contingency of value reappears in Arnold's discussions of the ideals of critical reason and cosmopolitan detachment, which, as I shall argue, more deeply engage the distinctly modern question of whether universal or impersonal value can find subjective embodiment.

COSMOPOLITANISM, RACE, AND ALLEGORIES OF THE MODERN

Arnold's reflections on modernity take the form, in his ethnological or cosmopolitan modes, of emblematic stories about racial and cultural genealogy. The stories that he tells about specific peoples or noteworthy individuals often foreground how racial heritage inflects the challenges of modernity, both the opportunities and struggles associated with living in a disenchanted world. The Englishman carries the burden of a flickering consciousness of thwarted ease: he is self-aware, but only as a stumbler is self-aware. Negative versions of modernity also appear when a particular people is seen as lacking sufficient capacity for science, for critical thinking, for self-control. Thus the situation of the Celt is lamented because, while his capacity for sentiment is laudable and a key component of artistic culture, he has failed to control it: "do not let us wish that the Celt had had less sensibility, but that he had been more master of it" (*CPW* 3:346–47). The English, dominated by Philistinism, are "in a certain sense, of all people the most inaccessible to ideas" (*CPW* 3:113); their failure to establish anything akin to the French Academy bespeaks an inability to perceive that there is "a high, correct standard in intellectual matters" (*CPW* 3:243).

By contrast, some stories tell of a heroic or exemplary relation to modernity enabled by a distinctly disjunctive relation to national culture, one that is ennobling rather than constraining. Heine is a genius because of his cosmopolitanism and his possession of both "the spirit of Greece and the spirit of Judaea"; he is also singled out, dramatically, for his paradoxical ability to detach himself from his own powerful racial determination: "His race he treated with the same freedom with which he treated everything else, but he derived a great force from it, and no one knew this better than himself" (*CPW* 3:127). Heine understands, in the spirit of the modern scientific attitude, what effect his cultural heritage has on him, yet he also has the capacity to subject that heritage to the free play of the critical mind. Thus he delivers on the promise of modernity in his capacity to reflect upon—and transmute through art—that which otherwise operates as unconscious nature or unexamined custom. In more general terms, the French are commended for their devotion to ideas and to the power of reason, and for their high intellectual standards and conscience. Insofar as these are forces that characterize the progressive nature of modernity, the French exemplify and forward the pursuit of culture. Likewise, the Germans are commended for their scientific powers and accomplishments.

Now from one point of view it could appear that Arnold is simply replaying prevalent nineteenth-century assumptions that certain races of Western Europe are more civilized than various other races construed as barbaric. Thus not only the Celt but the Jew and specific Eastern races are seen as lacking in elements that promote intellectual, spiritual, and artistic achievement. Along the same lines, one could indict Arnold's ostensible championing of hybridity or cultural fusion as a distinctly narrow cosmopolitanism, cozily European and Western. Indeed, there was a general assumption within nineteenth-century racial theory that intra-European hybrids were culturally productive while the interbreeding of Europeans with those of geographically distant races was likely to be infertile. A carefully bounded cosmopolitan hybridity, in other words, was fully compatible with a starkly hierarchical racialism.[27] But Arnold is here largely distinguishing races and individuals from one another on the basis of their *relation* to modernity as much as or more than their exemplification of modern achievements. The former requires a certain ingenuity or heroism in the face of modernity's Janus face—it is in no sense simply modernity or civilization triumphant. To that extent it exists at a remove from any simple spectrum of more or less "progressive" races, since ambivalence toward progress, and toward modern forms of detachment themselves, lies at the heart of Arnold's thinking. This in turn produces a parallel ambivalence on Arnold's part toward the characteristics of each national or individual character that he constructs. Heine may be wonderfully hybrid and flexible, but he has an insufficient moral sense; the French devotion to ideas and reason is laudable, but their sensuality and amorality is not; the German may be scientific, but he is also dragged down by the very steady-going nature that ensures his intellectual achievement. Correlatively, as Arnold argues in *Culture and Anarchy*, even though the English suffer from a deficiency of ideas and general intellectual narrowness, they stand out for their honesty and morality; if they can become intelligent, then they will not be undermined by the faults of the French.[28]

[27] See Young, *Colonial Desire*, 16.

[28] On the issue of Arnold's pervasive ambivalence about specific racial characteristics, see Faverty, *Matthew Arnold the Ethnologist*, 8.

The valorized forms of reflective distance that appear in Arnold's emblematic ethnographies pull in two directions. On the one hand, cosmopolitan detachment is presented as a highly particularized practice of taking one's distance from a specified set of conditions, through critical reflection, through discipline and self-control, and through a cultivated posture of contemplation, calm, or aloofness; yet, on the other hand, it is the transcendence of situatedness *tout court*. There is a tension, in other words, between Arnold's valorization of exemplary stances toward the modern and his valorization of a trajectory that escapes contingency into universalism. One could characterize this tension as one between a kind of layered cosmopolitanism and an abstract universalism.[29] In a useful essay, Alan D. McKillop distinguishes between inclusive and exclusive cosmopolitanism: exclusive cosmopolitanism constitutes an abstract universalism, a neutral thinning out of affiliation; inclusive cosmopolitanism embraces multiple affiliation, dialogue, and intercultural experience.[30] I call Arnold's cosmopolitanism "layered" because of the many ways in which it courts multiple affiliation and intercultural perspectives, as for example in the recognition and celebration of hybrid individuals, in the definition of genius as a fortuitous moment of cultural mixing, and in the appreciation of the comparative method in criticism. I refrain from calling it "inclusive," however, because his conception lacks a reciprocal intersubjective dimension, though one could say that there is a highly sublimated form of inclusive cosmopolitanism in Arnold, evident in the dialectical conception of cultural fusion or in the notion of recognizing other races in one's own internal cultural hybridity.

Arnold's abstract universalism, in contrast to his layered cosmopolitanism, removes itself from the embedded context of cultural practice or exchange so as to posit absolute standards. Abstract universalism comes up most notably as counterpoint to forms of provinciality variously construed. In "The Literary Influence of Academies," for example, Arnold holds up the high intellectual standard of the French, contrasting it to the "note of provinciality" that marks the literature of those nations without an academy. Only when a nation has gotten rid of provinciality, moreover, is one brought "on

---

[29] This tension between abstract universalism and a more expansive conception of cultural fusion or perspectivalism in many ways replicates the oft-noted tension between Arnold's appeal to objective and timeless standards and his relativist historicism.

[30] Alan D. McKillop, "Local Attachment and Cosmopolitanism: The Eighteenth-Century Pattern," in *From Sensibility to Romanticism*, ed. Frederick W. Hilles and Harold Bloom (New York: Oxford University Press, 1965), 191–218.

(but our absolute standard is also singular)

provinciality
v. totality

to the platform where alone the best and highest intellectual work can be said fairly to begin. Work done after men have reached this platform is *classical*" (*CPW* 3:245). Similarly, in the preface to *Culture and Anarchy*, Arnold opposes the term *provinciality* to the term *totality*. Those who are provincial allow only one side of their humanity to develop—Arnold has in mind here the unmeasured religious zeal of the Nonconformists, their overwhelming Hebraism—whereas those who belong to the ordered and balanced Establishments come nearer to approaching totality, are on the way to perfection.[31] In this instance, Arnold associates sectarianism and pluralism with a loss of guiding standards, standards that must underwrite any pursuit of culture or totality. To allow freedom of religion would only "provincialise us all round" (*CPW* 5:240). Likewise, further in the essay Arnold laments the limitations of class bias, or the ordinary self motivated only by his or her contingent and situated interests. The goal is to foster one's "best self": "By our everyday selves . . . we are separate, personal, at war. . . . But by our *best* self we are united, impersonal, at harmony" (*CPW* 5:134). Culture, the best self, reason and the will of God—all of these ideals are defined against situated bias, which is seen systematically to distort the pursuit of perfection.[32]

How do we place Arnold's abstract universalism in relation to the advocacy of the comparative method, the celebration of illuminating hybridity, and the seductive way that less austere forms of detachment seem recurrently to hold his admiring attention? One could argue that Arnold's particular versions of cosmopolitanism are actually in the service of his abstract universalism. By this reading, those cosmopolitans that he intermittently invokes throughout his prose writings are heroes, or intermittently heroes, not because they embrace diversity, comparatism, or the illuminations of multiple affiliation, but because their particular histories and cultural make-ups promote the establishment of universal standards—in other words,

---

[31] In making this argument, Arnold significantly exempts the Jew and the Catholic: because these two religions are, to use Arnold's word, "cosmopolitan," they overcome the deficiencies of other non-Establishment religions (*CPW* 5:238). Cosmopolitanism here, however, is simply expressive of a higher totality, via the religions that transcend provinciality, whereas the Protestant sects in England are both provincial and factionalizing. Both the Establishment and cosmopolitan religions differ from the domestic sects insofar as they exist above and beyond the mere concerns of the local.

[32] It is of course interesting that Arnold never attributes insight to the distancing effects of class difference, but only to international or intercultural viewpoints. Young argues that in *Culture and Anarchy* Arnold displaces class conflict by invoking larger racial forces as the determinants of England's cultural history. Young, *Colonial Desire*, 60.

complex cosmopolitanism that leads to higher totality

solution to contradiction?

character

because their particular histories and cultural make-ups paradoxically promote the transcendence of particularity. This would be true not only of exemplary individuals but also of opportune conjunctions in the life of a people or race. So understood, Arnold's approach is everywhere unified by its dialectical approach, where intercultural mixing and contingent historical conditions are ultimately in the service of a higher totality.

Admitting the complexity of Arnold's cosmopolitanism while ultimately underscoring its abstractive ascent toward universalism allows us to account more fully for Arnoldian detachment. It is important to acknowledge, however, that Arnold's thought displays a recurring impulse, even in his appeals to universalism, toward an ideal that is enacted characterologically. What I have been referring to throughout the chapter as enactment and embodiment always matter profoundly to Arnold, and it is crucial to explore more closely what it means for Arnold to conceptualize temperament, stance, and character as the means through which embodied universality can best be represented. This is an argument that requires a rethinking of the tendency to read the revisions of Arnold by Pater and Wilde as expressive of a decisive shift from objective to subjective standards. And it is also an argument that might help us to understand better Arnold's own revisions of himself, particularly his constant protesting that he had been misunderstood and did not advocate a conception of culture as effete aestheticism. For the crucial element in Arnold's emphasis on individual attitude or character lies in the particular way that it reconciles ideals of objectivity and reason with subjective stance and moral value—and it does so in a way very similar to the pattern discerned in his writings on the promises and limits of science.

Arnold's attraction to specific historical and literary figures had to do with two things: his rejection of what he saw as the ignoble subjectivism of the Romantics, which his own turn from poetry to prose was calculated to enforce, and his correlative heroicizing of those who expressed the ideals of detachment that he sought to advance through his own critical writings. But what emerged was an anxiety that the forms of detachment that he valorized were themselves easily detachable from moral substance: this anxiety encompassed not only the realm of science but also the spheres of critical reason and aesthetics (spheres that, as I noted at the outset of the chapter, are frequently undifferentiated in Arnold). This anxiety also prompts his insistence that highly speculative intellectual work, especially modern criticism of the Bible, could have a dangerous effect on the masses and should therefore remain esoteric until its findings had been reconciled to the popular domains of conduct and belief. It also lay behind his need to isolate flaws in those figures who displayed an otherwise admirable detachment: thus the

master of irony Heine or the aesthetic, noncomittal Maurice de Guerin are
suddenly convicted of amorality after long appreciations of their intellectual
and aesthetic modes. The fear that it might be impossible to recover moral
substance in the flight from the opposing dangers of subjectivism and traditionalism—both defined against the free play of the creative powers or of
disinterested criticism—also lies behind the compensatory insistence that
criticism will "naturally and irresistibly" make its benefits felt in the practical
sphere, or that culture must be made to prevail, or that Hebraism will provide the moral ballast to Hellenism.

Another key way in which Arnold counteracts this fear—and the one I
want to isolate here—is to represent as moral character the very form of
detachment he is advocating, to try to make detachment ultimately indistinguishable from moral stance or ethos. This move corresponds to a more
general tendency in the culture to articulate the methods of modern intellectual practice as productive not only of new knowledges but of refinements of character among those who practice them with the proper rigor and
self-control. In the introduction, I discussed how recent work by Lorraine
Daston and Peter Galison has established this tendency within the natural
sciences. Versions of this cultural formation also inhere in other nineteenth-
century intellectual and disciplinary spheres. They take on a particularly
interesting form when pursued, as they are in Arnold, in the face of elaborate
apprehensions about the potential groundlessness of modern life. The force
of Arnold's investment is rendered more vivid when we consider that he is
insisting on detachment as an achievement of character at the same time that
he is condemning certain individuals for lacking moral character precisely
because of their detachment. He repeatedly insists that forms of detachment
are in the service of perfection, thereby effectively making a virtue of what
otherwise appears to him as an alternative to a moral position. At such moments, he will articulate his model of criticism as a blend of impersonal and
personal values, through pivot terms that lend flesh to otherwise abstract
principles.

A primary example is the famous passage on Goethe from the essay on
Heine:

> Goethe's profound, imperturbable naturalism is absolutely fatal to all rou-
> tine thinking; he puts the standard, once for all, inside every man instead of
> outside him; when he is told, such a thing must be so, there is immense
> authority and custom in favor of its being so, it has been held to be so for a
> thousand years, he answers with Olympian politeness, "But *is* it so? Is it so
> to *me*?" Nothing could be more really subversive of the foundations on

113

which the old European order rested; and it may be remarked that no persons are so radically detached from this order, no persons so thoroughly modern, as those who have felt Goethe's influence most deeply. (*CPW* 3:110)

This passage identifies modernity with the capacity for self-authorization of belief that forms the core of the Enlightenment conception of autonomy. It identifies self-authorization as a radical detachment from the preexisting, traditional, or conventional social order. While one might feel a resurgent subjectivism in the passage, a danger that the whims of individual *me*'s might threaten the capacity for any truly justified examination of custom, the passage appears within a context that opposes unthinking custom to rational reflection, and so elevates a principle of reason above the mere whims of the individual. But what is equally prominent in the passage, and also offsets the suggestion of idiosyncrasy, is the notion that Goethe's naturalism is "imperturbable" and that his interrogations are conducted with "Olympian politeness." In both instances, Arnold characterizes Goethe's intellectual stance as an expression equally of manner, a manner that rises above bias, that is in no way reactive or driven by the vicissitudes of impulse or passion. Manner is here utterly continuous with method and principle and gives seamless expression to it.

This example represents a general pattern in Arnold's conception of detachment: it is an ideal that is at once characterological and impersonal. All of its key terms seem to mark the transcendence of subjectivity, yet Arnold repeatedly indicates that it is as much a moral and psychological achievement as a purely intellectual one. We saw this as early as the preface to *Poems*, where he yokes distinctive psychological states—"the calm, the cheerfulness"—to the "disinterested objectivity" that marks Greek genius; similarly, modern "doubt" is also "discouragement." Likewise, in "The Literary Influence of Academies," Arnold stresses that the provincial spirit lacks "graciousness"; that it is betrayed by its "tone," which is marked by violence and "seems to aim rather at an effect upon the blood and senses than upon the spirit and intellect" (*CPW* 3:249). It is commonly noted, of course, that the Arnoldian ideal is an ideal of *Bildung*, and that the achievement of culture involves the cultivation of character. What has been insufficiently explored is the extent to which the ideal of character that Arnold advances involves the attempt to enact, through a distinctly subjective embodiment, the modern promise of universal reason.[33]

[33] In *Matthew Arnold*, Trilling explains that "[c]ulture is reason involving the whole personality" (265), though without exploring the precise forms of reconcilia-

give reason ethical dimension by casting it in terms of character

state to replace aristocracy

At those moments where Arnold directly addressed the need to replace the gap left by the loss of aristocratic nobility, he pointed not to individual temperament but to the state as that which might provide the ballast needed in an increasingly anarchic (i.e., liberal-pluralist) world.[34] He also of course famously yoked reason to the will of God in *Culture and Anarchy*, thus at once highlighting and refusing the question of whether reason can so easily be conflated with a singular conception of the good. It is my argument here that Arnold persistently sought, in less absolutist terms, to give critical reason an ethical dimension, though not exactly a specific content, by casting it as an ideal of temperament or character, whose key attributes bespeak a kind of value-laden value-neutrality: impartiality, tact, moderation, measure, balance, flexibility, detachment, objectivity, composure.[35] These attributes, and the curious conception of an embodied universality to which they give voice, can be summed up by the term pervasive throughout Arnold's writings on culture: perfection. It, like Arnold's Hellenism more generally, points to the transcendence of any rule-governed conception of identity or practice, but nonetheless accords an objective value to what is repeatedly portrayed as not a science but rather an art of reason.[36]

perfection; embodied universality

art (not science) of reason

---

tion that I have analyzed here: fact and value, manner and method, reason and tact. Arnold also addresses the issue of character in "Democracy": "It is common to hear remarks on the frequent divorce between culture and character, and to infer from this that culture is a mere varnish, and that character only deserves any serious attention. No error can be more fatal. Culture without character is, no doubt, something frivolous, vain, and weak; but character without culture is, on the other hand, something raw, blind, and dangerous." Matthew Arnold, "Democracy," in *Culture and Anarchy and Other Writings*, ed. Stefan Collini (Cambridge: Cambridge University Press, 1993), 21. *culture can't be divorced fr character*

[34] I have in mind here *Culture and Anarchy*, but also the essay "Democracy."

[35] In some instances, the ideal of temperament animates and informs his description of critical method such that odd personifications—of culture and criticism— appear. I consider these symptomatic distortions—or reversals—of the tendency I am describing. Hence we get formulations such as "culture hates hatred; culture has but one great passion, the passion for sweetness and light" (*CPW* 5:112).

[36] This claim needs to be distinguished from those interpretations of Arnold that give centrality to his conception of imaginative reason in "Pagan and Mediaevel Religious Sentiment." Arnold certainly sought to reconcile a series of opposing terms through the concept of "imaginative reason," most centrally reason and faith. And the synthesis offered up by *Culture and Anarchy* is, as DeLaura points out, another version of such a reconciliation, in this case between the moral and the intellectual. I am arguing more generally that the ideal of Hellenism seeks to give an ethical dimension to those stances that Arnold repeatedly feared were divorced from the realm of value.

DETACHMENT AS A PRACTICE OF THE SELF

[handwritten: still tied to race]

Arnold's ideal of embodied universality is marked throughout by Hellenism and thus yoked to a very specific cultural heritage even as it can seem to transcend all racial and cultural specificity. The term "Olympian" perfectly captures this inherent tension; it carries a Hellenistic reference, but it denotes the capacity to rise above any mortal interest. In its tendency toward a logic of exemplarity, Arnold's universalism here might be compared to the French and European claims of cosmopolitan or universalist exceptionalism criticized by Jacques Derrida in *The Other Heading*.[37] Still, the centrality of the ideal of temperament and stance does establish a line of thinking in Arnold that can be seen as an alternative to his less nuanced appeals to impersonal entities as guarantors of value. Moreover, it partly reconstrues his relation to the later Victorian aesthetes, particularly Pater. Pater is commonly understood to have subjectivized the Arnoldian dictum, especially insofar as the preface to *The Renaissance* famously rewrites Arnold: "in aesthetic criticism the first step towards seeing one's object as it really is, is to know one's own impression as it really is, to discriminate it, to realise it distinctly."[38] Pater and Wilde are seen as holding up stance or temperament as the key to aesthetic experience and criticism, where Arnold believed it was possible to pursue objective standards.[39] Others have certainly pointed to pre-Paterian moments in Arnold, but the point I want to make is that whereas Pater elevates stance itself as a value, Arnold promotes a particular kind of stance, one that can reconcile the objective and the subjective, the universal and the particular. He does so in part so that he may provide an alternative to the aesthetic overvaluing of reflective stance divorced from value (via irony or the protean pursuit of experience), and this desire accounts for his ambivalent critiques of Heine and Maurice de Guerin.

[handwritten left margin: Pater]

[handwritten left margin: value stance that to reconcile universal particular. As alternative to overvaluing of reflective stance value]

A central question raised by my reading of Arnold is whether his attempt to integrate an ethical dimension into certain practices of detachment is either successful or even credible as an alternative ideal. This is a question that goes beyond the problems raised by Arnold's move toward racial exem-

---

[37] Jacques Derrida, *The Other Heading: Reflections on Today's Europe*, trans. Pascale-Anne Brault and Michael B. Naas (Bloomington: Indiana University Press, 1992), 48.

[38] Walter Pater, *The Renaissance: Studies in Art and Poetry*, ed. Donald L. Hill (Berkeley: University of California Press, 1980), xix.

[39] See, for example, David Bromwich, "The Genealogy of Disinterestedness," *Raritan* 1 (1982): 62–92.

[handwritten: can ethical dimension be incorporated into practices of detachment]

plarity. Put simply, can fact and value (in the case of science) or reason and ethos (in the case of the critical spirit) be reconciled in this way, or is this simply a fantasy of reconciliation? In the case of scientific objectivity, I suggest, Arnold's notion of a "scientific sense" that comprises both epistemological and ethical motives (insofar as it "begets the desire to know [the Celt's] case thoroughly, and to be just to it") is simply untenable. Epistemology does not absorb or generate ethics, though knowledge is certainly requisite to the tasks and pleasures of intercultural recognition, and to the larger project of "justice." In the case of criticism or culture—the detachment associated with critical reason rather than science—the question is perhaps more complicated. On the one hand, Arnold's emphasis on stance—and his particular articulation of method as ethos—importantly conceives of cultural ideals as always *enacted*, and not simply pregiven or independent essences. This strain in Arnold, and its link to classical culture, can be assimilated to the "aesthetics of existence" that interested Foucault in his late work, and that served as the basis for a renewed attention to ethics in both his own project and much of the work that has been influenced by the second and third volumes of the *History of Sexuality*. Certainly it is possible to see Arnold's Hellenism, or the ongoing project of perfection, as a technique of the self, one that moreover significantly contrasts with the strongly "code oriented" discipline of Hebraism, though Arnold's classically inflected notion of self-discipline always imported the aversion to physicality that marks Christianity.[40]

On the other hand, many of the specifically ethical problems that attend Foucault's turn to the aesthetics of existence, so resonant for study of Victorian aestheticism and Victorian Hellenism, also can be seen to inhere in Arnold's works. As Thomas McCarthy has argued, one of the central problems with Foucault's late works is the absence of any truly social or intersubjective dimension, the fact that the only zone of liberty resides in the self's action upon the self.[41] Arnold's is an ideal articulated almost exclusively in individualist terms: the only relation is that between the singular subject and those forces and conditions (both intrinsic and extrinsic) that must be controlled, balanced, or heroically faced; missing is any intersubjective or

---

[40] This points to another key limitation to Arnold's conception of embodied universality: its paradoxically aversive relation to the bodily and other forces of nature. Indeed, as we saw in the case of *On the Study of Celtic Literature*, Arnold's conception of stance can take the form, at times, of a stark and repressive relation between the controlling individual and forces of nature—the body, desire, racial nature.

[41] Thomas McCarthy, *Ideals and Illusions: On Reconstruction and Deconstruction in Contemporary Critical Theory* (Cambridge: MIT Press, 1991), 72–73.

public dialogue. Arnold's aversion to transformative dialogue must be described as crucially different from Foucault's failure to articulate freedom in intersubjective terms: Foucault's avoidance of a dialogical conception of freedom stems from his concerns about the normalizing effects of any social norms; Arnold is worried not about the institution of norms but rather about the disruptive effects of dissent and debate. The point of convergence between the two, however, lies in the inability to imagine reciprocal social relations as a site where one's own principles might be enacted. His protestations about the social dimensions of culture notwithstanding, Arnold seems incapable of construing social interaction in concrete terms. The dialectical model of cultural fusion, wherein Hebraism and Hellenism slowly come into balance, remains a wholly transpersonal form of cultural interaction. Likewise, in *On the Study of Celtic Literature*, recognition and reconciliation are routed through an intellectual project, and genuine politics is dismissed as a "dream."[42]

Arnold's attempt to cast detachment as an *inherently* ethical practice ultimately manifests the limits of his social and political vision. In the new cosmopolitanisms that I discussed in the introduction, enacted universalism stresses the cultivation of phronesis, sensibility, and tact as a response to the inescapably delicate intercultural conditions that obtain in a widening world. Indeed, it is precisely in the rigorous imagining of how universalism might be lived that a more supple, intersubjective, and self-critical characterology comes into play. As I have shown, Arnold does introduce valuable cosmopolitan elements into his articulations of criticism, especially when he considers the value of comparative method and the need to cultivate a distanced relation toward one's own heritage. The problem, however, resides in the highly individualized nature of Arnold's ideals—their heroic singularity—as well as in the fact that Arnold does not so much argue for a universalism responding to the demands of difference and cultural specificity as rather suggest that universalism enacted simply *is* tact, that objectivity simply *is* impartiality. Both attracted and troubled by the conditions of freedom that attend disenchantment, Arnold thus risks attributing fixity to the very elements that promise to breathe life into his ideals of modernity.

[42] For a related discussion of Arnold's diffusion of political conflict between England and Ireland through a dialectical ideal of assimilation, see Lloyd, "Arnold, Ferguson, Schiller."

CHAPTER FOUR

The Cultivation of Partiality

GEORGE ELIOT AND THE JEWISH QUESTION

Insofar as Matthew Arnold's ideal of enacted disinterestedness risks fetishizing individual temperament or stance, it neglects to develop the discrete ways in which critical detachment might inform and indeed promote intersubjective and collective practices. It is this larger ethical and political potentiality of modern reason that John Stuart Mill's project of liberalism sought to advance, even as he too could not help but valorize the Victorian category of character. In this chapter I turn to what I regard as one of the most rigorous and complicated contributions to the Victorian literature of detachment: George Eliot's last completed novel, *Daniel Deronda*. As we saw through discussion of her early essay "The Natural History of German Life," Eliot believed that crucial distinctions must be made between different practices of detachment, and that the question of how best to cultivate critical distance was pertinent to the methodologies of art, social science, and politics. In *Daniel Deronda*, Eliot situates the problem of detachment in the context of a narrative about the instabilities and opportunities presented by modern cosmopolitan life. Through the story of a deracinated Jew who comes slowly to learn of, and affirm, his cultural heritage, Eliot articulates a complicated cosmopolitan ideal that promotes critical detachment not only as a means to self-fulfillment but also as the basis for an ever-expanding horizon of ethical and political engagement. This text ruminates powerfully on the relation between cosmopolitanism and nationalism, promoting an ideal of Jewish nationalism informed by cosmopolitan aspiration, and engaging in a profound reflection on how different forms of affiliation—to family, community, nation, and world—might best be practiced.

In general, Eliot's construction of Judaism in this novel has been faulted for its idealism. Terry Eagleton delivers a common verdict on *Daniel Deronda* when he argues that the utopianism of the Jewish plot, with its accompanying ideal of organic totality, disavows the unstable conditions of modernity so vividly depicted in the Gwendolen Harleth plot, with its countervailing emphasis on exchange value, amoralism, contingency, and sheer will to power.[1] In somewhat different terms, Christina Crosby has argued

---

[1] Terry Eagleton, *Criticism and Ideology: A Study in Marxist Literary Theory*

that Eliot's idealistic representation of Judaism ultimately negates the Jews themselves. As she puts it, in order for the Jews to "become the representative historical subjects, the specificity and materiality of the Jews and of Judaism must be radically disavowed."[2] In both readings, Eliot unreflectively reproduces troubling modern conceptions of Judaism. Because if Eagleton's assessment is accurate, Eliot's evasion of modernity ironically follows the fully modern tendency to relegate Judaism to the place of tradition. And by Crosby's account, of course, Eliot's attitude toward Judaism represents the worst tendencies of modernity's universalizing assimilationism.

A closer examination of Eliot's novel reveals that it is by and large the critiques, and not Eliot's own position, that reproduce the logic whereby Judaism's relation to modernity is too starkly drawn. Indeed, rather than simply offering up Judaism as a mystified organic ideal, Eliot seeks to elaborate through her ideal of cosmopolitan Judaism a critical and nondogmatic way of relating to one's cultural heritage. This is evident not only in the portrayal of Daniel's interactions with the representatives of his Jewish heritage, but also through Eliot's complex treatment of the ideals of Christianity

---

(London: Verso, 1978), 122–25. Also see Ann Cvetkovich, *Mixed Feelings: Feminism, Mass Culture, and Victorian Sensationalism* (New Brunswick: Rutgers University Press, 1992), 160; Deirdre David, *Fictions of Resolution in Three Victorian Novels: North and South, Our Mutual Friend, Daniel Deronda* (London: Macmillan Press, 1981), 142; Katherine Bailey Linehan, "Mixed Politics: The Critique of Imperialism in *Daniel Deronda*," *Texas Studies in Language and Literature* 34 (1992): 324–25; Catherine Gallagher, "George Eliot and *Daniel Deronda*: The Prostitute and the Jewish Question," in *Sex, Politics, and Science in the Nineteenth-Century Novel*, ed. Ruth Bernard Yeazell (Baltimore: Johns Hopkins University Press, 1986), 57.

[2] Christina Crosby, *The Ends of History: Victorians and "The Woman Question"* (New York: Routledge, 1991), 14. Crosby's argument joins with a group of recent essays arguing that the novel's Jewish plot is complicit with British imperialist and gender hierarchies. See Linehan, "Mixed Politics"; Susan Meyer, "'Safely to Their Own Borders': Proto-Zionism, Feminism, and Nationalism in *Daniel Deronda*," *ELH* 60 (1993): 733–58. Meyer claims that at the time *Daniel Deronda* was written, it was the British government, and not the Jewish community, that was promoting Jewish settlement in Palestine. Prior to the emergence of Zionism in England in the 1880s and 1890s, according to Meyer, Jews were more concerned with assimilation and civil rights, while the British gentile community sought to secure control of the Ottoman Empire and Middle Eastern interests, by encouraging British-sponsored settlements. Meyer's reading, however, suffers from imposing a parochialism on the highly cosmopolitan Eliot, who was deeply influenced by earlier continental, particularly German, debates on Judaism and nationalism. See William Baker, *George Eliot and Judaism* (Salzburg: Institut für Englishe Sprach und Literatur, 1975).

and cosmopolitanism that dominate Deronda's cultural horizon prior to his experiences with Mordecai and Kalonymos. Through the character of Deronda, Eliot advocates a form of cultural self-understanding that might best be called reflective dialogism: her model for one's relation to history, culture, and nationality becomes passionate argumentation, not simple embrace. To achieve reflective distance, one must be capable of disengagement from cultural norms and givens. But such achieved distance should in turn promote not a sustained or absolute disengagement—for Eliot a destructive delusion—but rather a cultivated partiality, a reflective return to the cultural origins that one can no longer inhabit in any unthinking manner.[3]

One might object that the deracinated Daniel cannot stand synecdochally for a Jewish ideal, due to his anomalous history as an adopted son brought up in ignorance of his cultural heritage. But Daniel's history functions more generally as an allegory about cosmopolitanism, which for Eliot is a condition of contemporary European life fully pertinent to any modern understanding of Judaism or Jewish nationalism. Put simply, the insistence that Judaism counters the negative portrayal of modern cosmopolitanism in *Daniel Deronda* occludes the significant ways in which modern cosmopolitanism informs both the Jewish condition and the ideal response to that condition as conceived by Eliot. Indeed, the discovery and subsequent affirmation of Jewish identity are best understood as expressions of Eliot's fundamentally mixed attitude toward the instabilities of modern cosmopolitan life, and not as her attempt to flee those instabilities by constructing Jewish identity as an absolute ideal or ground. Deronda finds a more stable cultural heritage to return to, but he does so only through a practice of moral questioning that issues out of the cosmopolitan forms of disengagement that are otherwise seen to compromise moral and cultural health. In a further paradox, that same disengagement promises to lend moral force to

---

[3] Alexander Welsh has argued that Mordecai's doctrines of Jewish nationalism, and Deronda's adoption of them, represent a form of ideology (as opposed to religious faith) insofar as they are the object of rational dialogue and debate for both characters. As I am attempting to show here, and will elaborate more fully later in the chapter, there is a crucial difference between Mordecai's and Daniel's conceptions of cultural transmission and exchange, as well as between Mordecai's conception of achieving race consciousness and Daniel's conception of the nationalist project. Welsh's reading nonetheless sensitively registers Eliot's studied approach to cultural ideals, something that more suspicious readings fail to do. Alexander Welsh, *George Eliot and Blackmail* (Cambridge: Harvard University Press, 1985), 309–10. For a similar argument about the "rationality" of Mordecai's visions, see Sara M. Putzell-Korab, "The Role of the Prophet: The Rationality of Daniel Deronda's Idealist Mission," *Nineteenth-Century Literature* 37 (1982): 170–87.

Deronda's own newly cultivated partiality, fostering an openness toward his own people as well as other races.[4]

In this chapter, I reconstruct Eliot's treatment of Judaism in light of the arguments that recur throughout the literature on the Jewish Question. Eliot herself had an extensive knowledge of many of the writings on the topic and had translated Feuerbach's *The Essence of Christianity*, which rehearses some of the foundational constructions of Judaism inherited from Hegel.[5] I begin with the assumption that Eliot's elaboration of a project of Jewish nationalism necessarily challenges the perception that Jews were unequal to the tasks of modernity. Contra Crosby, moreover, I suggest that in her portrayal of Daniel's cultural journey Eliot goes a long way toward balancing the claims of the particular against those of the universal; she does not merely subsume Judaism into the universal. It must be recognized nonetheless that *Daniel Deronda* generates two distinct understandings of the project of Jewish nationalism, represented respectively by Deronda and Mordecai. Deronda's nationalism persistently moves toward the universalist

---

[4] My understanding of *Daniel Deronda* has been influenced by Suzanne Graver's sensitive treatment of Eliot's ambivalences in *George Eliot and Community: A Study in Social Theory and Fictional Form* (Berkeley: University of California Press, 1984). Using the distinction between *Gemeinschaft* and *Gesellschaft* developed by the German social theorist Ferdinand Tönnies, Graver argues that Eliot was neither simply nostalgic for the forms of community represented by *Gemeinschaft* (with its emphasis on tradition, custom, and common interests) nor enthusiastic about the development of *Gesellschaft* (urban, heterogenous, industrial societies that foster individualism, cultural sophistication, and the rational pursuit of self-interest). Ultimately, Graver argues, Eliot sought to reconcile the two: "The end to be achieved was the reestablishment of common interests and shared feelings as the science and prose of Gesellschaft converged with a transformed poetry of Gemeinschaft to create the moral sanctions offered in the past by religion" (15). Graver traces in particular Eliot's promotion of choice and self-consciousness over the unreflective habit and custom associated with *Gemeinschaft*. This reading will pursue the implications of Eliot's ambivalence toward disengagement (as distinct from the broader concept of choice) as well as her more nuanced and dialogical treatment of cultural difference in *Daniel Deronda*; these two elements of the novel are left largely unexplored by Graver, who argues that the form of community promoted in the novel is merely imagined (243). Catherine Gallagher also discusses Eliot's ambivalences toward cosmopolitanism; ultimately, however, she reads Daniel's nationalist mission as an attempt to fully neutralize the threatening aspects of cosmopolitanism. Gallagher, "George Eliot and *Daniel Deronda*."

[5] For the influence of Hegel on Feuerbach's views of Judaism, see Emil L. Fackenheim, *Encounters Between Judaism and Modern Philosophy: A Preface to Future Jewish Thought* (New York: Schocken, 1980), 135–53.

civic model of nationality often associated with John Stuart Mill and built on the principles of critical reason and democratic debate, while Mordecai's follows the collectivist-romantic model issuing out of German idealism, and built on the more troubling model of a unified national will and a projected national destiny.[6] I trace the forms of Eliot's investment in each model and explore just how revisionist she is in her constructions of Judaism and modernity.

Recurringly, critiques of *Daniel Deronda*'s Jewish plot confine themselves to *Mordecai*'s rhetoric, focusing on his organicist views of the destiny of the Jewish race and his specific expectation that upon his impending death his soul and all his thoughts will be transmitted into Daniel, through the merger of souls as described in Kabbalistic doctrine. Taking Mordecai's word for it, many critics have felt comfortable conflating the views of two characters who appeared destined to merge anyway.[7] But Deronda actively resists Mor-

---

[6] For discussions of the variant nationalist theories arising in the modern era, and especially for the distinction between the German romantic doctrine and other forms, see Anthony D. Smith, *Theories of Nationalism* (New York: Holmes and Meier, 1983), esp. ch. 1; Liah Greenfeld, *Nationalism: Five Roads to Modernity* (Cambridge: Harvard University Press, 1992), esp. introduction. As my discussion of John Stuart Mill will show, it is not accurate to place him wholly within the camp of civic nationalism. Indeed, as Greenfeld stresses, these two forms of nationalism are ideal types, which never appear historically in pristine form.

[7] See Crosby, *The Ends of History*, 20–21; Linehan, "Mixed Politics," 335–36, 342; Cvetkovich, *Mixed Feelings*, 158–59; David, *Fictions of Resolution*, 147; William Myers, "George Eliot: Politics and Personality," in *Literature and Politics in the Nineteenth Century*, ed. John Lucas (London: Methuen, 1971), 123. Meyer acknowledges Daniel's resistance to Mordecai, but only to read it as Eliot's way of reconciling submission with self-fulfillment (assertiveness) in the case of male characters. Otherwise, she accords the text a unified view of Jewish nationalism and casts Deronda and Mordecai as the two central instances of Eliot's ideologically suspect use of "refined Jews" to articulate her ideal; see Meyer, "'Safely to Their Own Borders.'" Eagleton does not explicitly conflate the two characters, but neither does he distinguish their views from one another in his characterization of Eliot's mystifying organicist ideal; see Eagleton, *Criticism and Ideology*, 122–25. For a notable exception, see Nancy L. Paxton, *George Eliot and Herbert Spencer: Feminism, Evolutionism, and the Reconstruction of Gender* (Princeton: Princeton University Press, 1991), 223–24. Paxton argues, "While Mordecai articulates Eliot's reasons for insisting on the value of collective history, Daniel expresses her recognition of the individual's need for the freedom to interpret his or her own personal past and the obligations which arise from it." It is precisely this line of argument that I will be pursuing here. For a related approach, also see K. M. Newton, *George Eliot: Romantic Humanist* (Totowa, N.J.: Barnes and Noble, 1981), 187–200.

decai's vision of a complete mind-meld, precisely because it runs counter to his view of an open-ended dialogue, whether it be between individuals, between races, or between individuals and their own cultural heritage. In Mordecai's case, by contrast, a deluded ideal of intersubjective fusion accompanies a mystified nationalist ideal of organic destiny. The model for the relation to the other and the model for the relation to one's heritage are the same: absolute unity. As I will show, the text takes considerable pains to distance Daniel from Mordecai on both these counts.

The complexity of Eliot's approach to the gains and losses entailed by forms of modern rootlessness is also evident in this novel's portrayal of Leonora Halm-Eberstein, Daniel's mother, who has been predominantly read along the axis of gender rather than race, even when acknowledgment is made of her critique of a specifically Jewish patriarchy. As I shall show, Victorian ideals of femininity certainly inform Eliot's characterization of Leonora and lie behind Eliot's discomfort with Leonora's radical detachment from heritage and social convention. Yet this oft-discussed figure also reintroduces some fundamental questions about Judaism in her association with hypermodern cosmopolitanism, on the one hand, and extrinsic law, on the other. As in the case of Mordecai, she must be read against Daniel in order to draw out Eliot's complex attempt to construct an ideal modern relation between identity and cultural heritage. I will conclude by placing my discussion of Eliot in relation to contemporary Jewish cultural studies, which has itself pursued the fraught problem of particularism and universalism.

JUDAISM, MODERNITY, AND ELIOT'S DIALOGICAL IDEAL

The Jewish Question interrogates the limits of modernity. The tradition of debate on the topic, extending out of Enlightenment thought, left Hegelianism, and the varied itineraries of European nationalism, typically asks whether and how the particularity of the Jew might be assimilated to, or alternately accommodated by, a project conceived as modern in its pretensions to universality. Beginning with the era of the Enlightenment, the struggles for political emancipation of the Jews acutely raised the question of how desirable or possible it would be for Jewish communities and individuals to resist a fuller cultural assimilation into Christian states or predominantly Christian societies. For example, the Jewish Enlightenment thinker Moses Mendelsson, an early writer on the topic who also actively campaigned for Jewish rights, sought to reconcile Judaism to the project of universal reason, yet simultaneously resisted the common Enlightenment view that humanity in general should take precedence over any assertion of Jewish particularism or guarding of Jewish tradition. By contrast, many nineteenth- and twentieth-century socialist writings on the Jewish Question framed the issue in strongly assimilationist terms, rearticulating the universalist Enlightenment view within the radically emancipatory framework of international class struggle. Different still were the nationalist arguments for assimilation, as evidenced in the sociological theories of Max Weber, whose understanding of modernity entailed a commitment to unified national culture. Weber's position applies the rhetoric of assimilation to the level of the nation, arguing that recalcitrant Jewish traditionalism within Christian states will impede the modern nationalist project.[8]

One lesser known but important voice in the history of the Jewish Question was Leopold Zunz, a Jewish-German historian and co-founder in 1819 of the short-lived *Verein für die Kultur und Wissenschaft der Juden* in Berlin. This organization, which counted the later Christian convert Heinrich Heine among its members, rejected both the Enlightenment absorption of Jews into humanity in general and the nostalgic traditionalism that sought to divorce Judaism from the modern project. Zunz, whom Eliot read and admired, enacted a nineteenth-century version of the conflicted double gesture that characterized Mendelsson's important earlier contributions. An ardent believer in the possibility of a modern "science of Judaism," Zunz undertook a protracted study of Jewish history, literature, and tradition, zealous to convince his nineteenth-century European audience of the importance of Judaism to the history and progress of human culture as a whole. Zunz aimed to reconstruct Judaism's distinctive contribution to the project of modernity, thereby exposing the category of assimilation as distorting Judaism's internal relation to modern Western culture. While his ultimate position may be unclear, as Emil L. Fackenheim contends, his research, like Mendelsson's, testifies to a genuine tension shaping many non-anti-Semitic[9] responses to the debate, which exhibit a profound devotion to

---

[8] For discussion of both Weber and the socialists, see Gary A. Abraham, *Max Weber and the Jewish Question: A Study of the Social Outlook of His Sociology* (Urbana: University of Illinois Press, 1992).

[9] I use this somewhat cumbersome term to avoid the misleading term *philosemitic*, which occludes the conflicted positions harbored within all Semitic discourse, no matter which way its sympathies tend. On this issue of terminology, also see Bryan Cheyette, *Constructions of 'the Jew' in English Literature and Society: Racial Representation, 1875–1945* (Cambridge: Cambridge University Press, 1993), 8.

the preservation of Judaism as a culture as well as a desire to incorporate that tradition into a broader, universal project.[10]

Zunz's approach is less incoherent than plangeantly symptomatic of the constraints built into the very structure of the Jewish Question, which always already poses Judaism as a problem for modernity. In the Hegelian tradition, the Jewish people were construed as a problem for modernity because they were incapable of themselves becoming modern. From this perspective, the Jewish race manifested a recalcitrant separatist character that rendered it unequal to the tasks of modern citizenship, which required identifying oneself with humanity in general and the interests of the state in particular. Even where acknowledgment was made of the oppressions that promoted and often enforced separatism, the judgment that Jews were particularistic rather than universal, tradition-bound rather than modern, effectively wrote them out of the modern project. Being modern meant having a self-active or reflective relation to one's cultural heritage; Jewish culture, by contrast, was construed as a form of legalism (extrinsic law) that one followed unblinkingly.[11] The Jews thus are fundamentally unfree insofar as they fail to develop the dimension of interiority that characterizes Protestant Christianity and the capacity for self-authorization of beliefs that forms the core of the Enlightenment conception of autonomy.

Among the left Hegelians and others, however, a strange inversion of the above characterization of the Jew also begins to develop, one that constructs the Jew as *too* autonomous. Nation-forming was at the heart of the modern agenda, but so was the ideal of cosmopolitanism, which promoted detachment from parochial interests, broad understanding of cultures beyond one's own, and a universalism that saw all peoples as belonging to humanity over and above any individual nation. The civic model of nationalism, with its democratic, humanistic principles, had certain affinities with cosmopolitanism. The German romantic model, however, existed in tension with it, generating debate on whether the Jewish cultural heritage could be accommodated by a project of nation-building reliant on homogeneous culture. But even for those who emphasized civic principles, radical disidentification from national culture was seen as threatening. In his essay on Coleridge, as I noted in the introduction, John Stuart Mill emphasizes the importance of "national cohesion," deriving from specific historical tradition, as a necessary component for the maintenance of a stable society; this principle of cohesion, and the idea of homogeneous "national character" that animates it,

---

[10] Fackenheim, *Encounters Between Judaism and Modern Philosophy*, 127. On Zunz, see Luitpold Wallach, *Liberty and Letters: The Thoughts of Leopold Zunz* (London: East and West Library, 1959).

[11] Fackenheim, *Encounters Between Judaism and Modern Philosophy*, ch. 3.

conflicts with the liberal democratic principles he simultaneously espouses as a political ideal. For Mill, in other words, the ability to view one's own culture from a reflective distance, or to extend the reach of freedom and equality, was ethically desirable, but such activities should not be taken so far as to threaten national cohesion within a particular state.[12]

In turning to Coleridge, of course, Mill draws on the German romantic tradition to offset what are seen as the extremes of a modern liberal perspective; and his ideas on nationalism reveal how the two strains—civic and ethnic-romantic—frequently shared an uneasy cohabitation. Within debates on the Jewish Question, what we might call the internally exiled European Jew consistently raised the specter of radical disidentification. Lacking the grounding provided by national allegiance, yet often fully participating in the practices associated with cosmopolitanism, the Jews become culturally untethered, dangerously modern. As such, they may easily self-servingly ally themselves with transnational forces (capitalism, particularly). This is the conception of the Jews that underwrites Marx's representations in "On the Jewish Question"; it also pervades many popular conceptions of Jews as grasping moneylenders.[13]

Matthew Arnold's *Culture and Anarchy* interestingly reflects Judaism's association with both traditionalism and cosmopolitanism. In the preface, Arnold allies Judaism with cosmopolitanism. Pairing the Roman Catholic and Jewish religions, he cites them as exceptions to "the law which seems to forbid the rearing, outside of national establishments, of men of the highest spiritual significance." Arnold then goes on to claim, however, that "perhaps here, what the individual man does not lose by the conditions of his rearing, the citizen, and the State of which he is a citizen, loses."[14] Given that Arnold will uphold the state as that which guarantees culture over and against anarchy—largely associated with individualism and sectarianism—this "loss"

[12] John Stuart Mill, "Coleridge," in John Stuart Mill and Jeremy Bentham, *Utilitarianism and Other Essays*, ed. Alan Ryan (Harmondsworth: Penguin, 1987), 195–96.

[13] For a discussion of the association among Jews, cosmopolitanism, and "a realm of exchange divorced from production," see Gallagher, "George Eliot and *Daniel Deronda*," 43; on the centrality of a perceived Jewish threat to the cohesion of England's national identity in the nineteenth century, see Michael Ragussis, *Figures of Conversion: "The Jewish Question" and English National Identity* (Durham: Duke University Press, 1995). For an elaboration of the double view of the Jew, see Cheyette, *Constructions of 'the Jew' in English Literature and Society*, 9.

[14] Matthew Arnold, *Culture and Anarchy*, in *The Complete Prose Works of Matthew Arnold*, vol. 5: *Culture and Anarchy with Friendship's Garland and Some Literary Essays*, ed. R. H. Super (Ann Arbor: University of Michigan Press, 1965), 238. The preface was composed for the 1869 edition of *Culture and Anarchy*. Subsequent page number references will be cited parenthetically in the text.

places the Jew as well as the state at the mercy of the forces of anarchy, if it does not align the Jew with those forces themselves. Thus, the initially admirable cosmopolitanism of the Jew reappears all too readily as a form of dangerous detachment, one that weakens the binding power of the state. The main body of Arnold's text then goes on to heavily associate Judaism with traditionalism. The chapter "Hebraism and Hellenism" attributes to Hebraism a search for perfection that differs from Hellenism's search in that it relies on conduct and obedience, rather than disinterested contemplation. Arnold does not fully oppose Christianity to Judaism, construing the emphasis as common to both, if originating in Judaism. But he does argue that Christianity crucially "transformed and renewed Hebraism by criticising a fixed rule, which had become mechanical, and had thus lost its vital motive-power" (187–88). As a Hellenized Hebraism, Christianity "[let] the thought play freely around this old rule," thereby transcending Hebraism's "obedience to the letter of a law" (188, 169). For Arnold, Hellenism provides a contemplative relation to perfection, a self-reflective desire to "see things as they really are," undistorted by the dictates of duty or instrumental thinking. In this regard it is superior, and though originating in the classical premodern world, hailed by Arnold as particularly suited to the challenges of modernity.

Arnold's narrative acknowledges the importance and influence of the Hebraic ethos while simultaneously tracing its absorption into a broader English culture, thereby updating and re-elaborating the idea of the supersession of Judaism by a more universalist culture (an idea with roots extending back to early Christianity). In this sense, Arnold's theory marks its distance from those more rigid ethnological conceptions of racial determinism and hierarchy that stressed the atavism and unmodernizability of the Jew. Such strong racialist arguments were exemplified in John Knox's widely read *The Races of Man* (1850), which not only attributed unchanging characteristics to Jews, but specifically denied them the capacity for cultural and intellectual advancement, thereby associating them with unchangeability itself.[15] The idea of inevitable absorption or supersession of course performed various kinds of cultural work: it countered the threat to homogeneous national culture posed by a Jewish particularity perceived as unassimilable; it also became a self-congratulatory way to cast the very real drift toward secularization and away from communal cohesion among many Jews in nineteenth-century English culture.[16]

[15] Ragussis, *Figures of Conversion*, 26, 211.

[16] Todd M. Endelman, *Radical Assimilation in English Jewish History, 1656–1945* (Bloomington: Indiana University Press, 1990).

On a number of fronts, then, the figure of the Jew in Victorian culture became the charged site for underlying anxieties informing nationalist discourse, which is always trying to negotiate the challenges or disruptions caused by traditions or subcultures perceived to be particularist, alien, or, to adopt a recent term, transnational. As two extremes, the tradition-bound Jew and the cosmopolitan Jew figured threats to, and defined the limits of, modern national identity, which, however civic-minded, was never articulated wholly apart from a notion of shared ethnic or cultural heritage as well as strong forms of attachment. It is important to place Eliot within this broad context (which Mill and Arnold also share), rather than simply reading her in the context of a more insular set of British discourses or concerns, most critically because of her own highly self-conscious dialogue with continental and particularly German thought.[17] Eliot was certainly acutely affected by the movements toward assimilation and the gaining of civic and political liberties in England (punctuated dramatically in 1858 with the admittance of Jews to the House of Commons). As I will show, the strong civic traditions in England heavily inform her portrayal of Deronda's nationalist mission. But the complexities of Eliot's novel are best illuminated by placing her in the context of the longer-standing debates on Judaism's relation to modernity, whose outlines and permutations I have just sketched.

Like Mill and Arnold, Eliot wishes to steer a middle course between traditionalism and hypermodernism, but in *Daniel Deronda* she articulates that middle course precisely in terms of a Jewish ideal, thereby radically challenging the dominant cultural rhetoric, which associated the *extremes* with Judaism. Eliot's middle course emerges as a complex response to the conditions of modernity, expressing a sensitive and shifting assessment of modern forms of disengagement and detachment. To take a central example, Eliot displays a double attitude toward deracinated cosmopolitanism in her treatment of Deronda's highly attuned sympathetic imagination. Deronda's uncertain social position as an adopted and assumed illegitimate son of Sir Hugo is seen to promote his imaginative sympathy for all the disinherited and unprivileged, and especially for women in distress, whom he assimilates to the guiding image of an unknown mother presumed to have suffered the conventional torments of the abandoned or fallen woman. Yet the very cultivation of sympathy enabled by his unusual experience itself jeopardizes his own moral development:

His early-wakened sensibility and reflectiveness had developed into a many-sided sympathy, which threatened to hinder any persistent course of

[17] See note 2 above.

action: as soon as he took up any antagonism, though only in thought, he seemed to himself like the Sabine warriors in the memorable story—with nothing to meet his spear but flesh of his flesh, and objects that he loved. His imagination had so wrought itself to the habit of seeing things as they probably appeared to others, that a strong partisanship, unless it were against an immediate oppression, had become an insincerity for him. His plenteous, flexible sympathy had ended by falling into one current with that reflective analysis which tends to neutralise sympathy.[18]

Deronda himself experiences this condition as disabling and finds himself craving some event or influence that will "justify partiality" and make him "an organic part of social life, instead of roaming in it like a yearning disembodied spirit, stirred with vague social passion, but without fixed local habitation to render fellowship real" (413).

Yet Deronda also persistently acknowledges the benefits accrued by his own displacement. In his second interview with his mother, Deronda asserts that although he should have been brought up knowing he was a Jew, "it must always have been a good to me to have as wide an instruction and sympathy as possible" (725). Here Deronda explicitly links the "wide instruction" he received as a cosmopolitan Englishman with the wide sympathy that he developed through this experience. Somewhat misleading here is Daniel's assumption that Jewish identity would not have promoted such "wide" experience, for the diasporic European Jew was always living between cultures, in some sense already in the position that the cosmopolitan sought to cultivate. And what Daniel here implies as the more "narrow" activity, the Jewish devotion to tradition that many modern Gentile thinkers saw as anachronistic and insular, was, in the face of very real threats to cultural integrity and community, necessarily a self-conscious activity.

At bottom, however, Daniel's story plays on the similar predicaments of the cosmopolitan Englishman and the diasporic Jew. To the extent that Daniel's Jewish nationalism is valorized, it is because it provides an exemplary and considered response to the dangers of cosmopolitanism. That Judaism was particularly well poised to teach modern Europe about the importance of cultivated cultural memory and national identity is made clear in "The Modern Hep! Hep! Hep!" In this essay, the Jews become exemplary of a self-reflective affirmation of cultural community and heritage in the face of damaging dispersion and the disruptions of cosmopolitanism. In part Eliot is responding to the very real processes of radical Jewish secularization so

[18] George Eliot, *Daniel Deronda* (Harmondsworth: Penguin, 1967), 412. Subsequent page number references will be cited parenthetically in the text.

prevalent in England, and which Eliot wants the Jewish community to defend itself against. She worries that the greatest danger facing the Jews is that of "lapsing into cosmopolitan indifference equivalent to cynicism," which is of course the very mode of being which characterizes what we might call the thin and morally deficient forms of cosmopolitanism associated with the characters of the English plot.[19] But she gives far more weight to commonly held conceptions of the Jewish refusal to convert or assimilate, recasting Jewish cultural insularity as a sign of remarkable endurance predictive of the capacity for the noble condition of true nationhood. Likewise, "the feeling of separateness" ceases to be a reproach and is translated into "the organized memory of a national consciousness" (153). For Eliot, writing through the persona of Theophrastus Such, the best result of a lamentable diaspora is that it issues in a deliberate and chosen affirmation of those previously tacit communal and cultural bonds that have been subjected to such fragmenting and destructive forces. We may be struck by the potentially balkanizing effect of Eliot's discussions of Jewish nationalism in this essay, but she nonetheless poses a profound challenge to nineteenth-century understandings, in Britain and Europe, of Judaism as a threat to the very idea of national stability and cohesion.[20] Indeed, to drive home the relevance and value of Jewish experience, Eliot suggests that modern "migratory Englishmen" should themselves cultivate a sense of "special belonging" so as to preserve themselves "from the worst consequences of their voluntary dispersion" (147).

Despite Eliot's adherence to the importance of racial solidarity, moreover, Daniel Deronda's reflective and dialogical conception of nation-building in an international arena consistently works to transform the potentially atomizing effect of a static nationalistic pluralism that preserves ethnic homogeneity. Principles of individual liberty and rational deliberation inform his understanding of national identity and political practice, and Deronda consistently attempts to enfold civic principles into a fundamentally ethnic nationalism. When asked by Joseph Kalonymos if he will profess the faith of his fathers, Deronda responds, "I shall call myself a Jew. But I will not say that I shall profess to believe exactly as my fathers have believed. Our fathers themselves changed the horizon of their belief and learned of other

---

[19] George Eliot, "The Modern Hep! Hep! Hep!" in *The Impressions of Theophrastus Such* (London: Everyman, 1995), 146. Subsequent page number references will be cited parenthetically in the text.

[20] On the challenge posed by Eliot's insistence on the viability of Jewish nationalism, and its relevance to *Daniel Deronda*, see Ragussis, *Figures of Conversion*, 260–90.

races. But I think I can maintain my grandfather's notion of separateness with communication. I hold that my first duty is toward my own people, and if there is anything to be done towards restoring or perfecting their common life, I shall make that my vocation" (792). Significantly, Daniel's resistance to full submission in his dialogue with Kalonymos is directly paralleled by his conception of transformative dialogical interaction between races and nations, one that involves a delicate dialectic of detachment and engagement. Indeed, Eliot portrays Deronda's initial affirmation of an open-ended duty to his people as an act deriving from the specific quality of his conversation with Kalonymos: "It happened to Deronda at that moment, as it has often happened to others, that the need for speech made an epoch in resolve. His respect for the questioner would not let him decline to answer, and by the necessity to answer he found out the truth for himself" (792).[21]

The revelation of Deronda's birth may appear to underwrite his affirmation of Jewishness, but it is crucial that the identity he affirms, his political/cultural identity as a Jew, is itself in need of construction. In an influential essay, Cynthia Chase has argued that despite Daniel's emphasis on the act of choice or affirmation, his identity as a Jew is fully determined by narrative logic long before it is confirmed.[22] But Chase's deconstructive reading fails to acknowledge the complex dialectical process through which Deronda forges an identity from out of hybrid traditions. In an extension of Chase's argument, Crosby entirely conflates the monological aspects of Mordecai's rhetoric with Deronda's affirmation of identity, arguing,

> To "be" a Jew in Daniel Deronda, to claim that identity, is to submit to the law and the history incarnated in the corporate entity of Judaism, and to do so even at the sacrifice of personal gratification and advancement. . . . [W]hen Mordecai hails Deronda as the embodiment of his prophetic vision, the one who will be wholly devoted to the transmission of the law and the restoration of Israel, Deronda willingly responds to his call, and although he points out to Mordecai, "What my birth was does not lie in my will," the confirmation of his Jewishness is but a formality of the plot.[23]

[21] Patrick Brantlinger has made the related argument that Judaism in *Daniel Deronda* must be seen as "an *international* nationalism." See Patrick Brantlinger, "Nations and Novels: Disraeli, George Eliot, and Orientalism," *Victorian Studies* 35 (1992): 272.

[22] Cynthia Chase, "The Decomposition of the Elephants: Double-Reading *Daniel Deronda*," *PMLA* 93 (1978): 215–25.

[23] Crosby, *The Ends of History*, 20–21.

Ironically, Crosby, a vehement critic of Hegelianism, in fact recapitulates the Hegelian reduction of Judaism to a "positive" religion and misses Eliot's more reflective characterization of cultural identification. In the conversation with Kalonymos, Deronda exhibits a distinctly unanxious relation to the mutability of ethnic identity: he understands that the self-appellation "Jew" does not reify his cultural identity, but rather situates him in a Jewish "tradition" of dialogical transformation through intercultural encounters.[24]

If Deronda affirms the racial identity he discovers, in other words, he affirms it in no simple way: the precise form of his cultural identification will grow out of reflective judgment, selective appropriation, and a process of dialogue between himself and others, and between Judaism and other cultural traditions. As he says to Gwendolen, "The idea that I am possessed with is that of restoring a political existence to my people, making them a nation again, giving them a national centre, such as the English have, though they too are scattered over the face of the globe. . . . At the least, I may awaken a movement in other minds, such as has been awakened in my own" (875). This last sentence, presumed to have been added in proof by Eliot, has been adduced by Barbara Hardy as evidence of Eliot's desire "to make Daniel's statement and his political destiny sound more tentative and realistic."[25] But it is merely one instance of Eliot's larger strategy to make Daniel's aims sound appropriately tentative, based as they are on the contingency of his dialogical encounters with tradition. His mind has not been fixed by his identity, but rather "a movement has been awakened" within it; he in turn wishes to promote such movement in the minds of others, a movement toward political restoration, but one that will be enacted through an open-ended process of argumentation.

This is not to deny that Eliot's conception of cultural identity is ultimately race-based (after all, Gwendolen can't join the movement), but simply to establish that there are significant tensions within her own conception of Jewish nationalism. Commonly, the Jewish plot is cast as romance and the English as realism, but through Daniel's encounter with Judaism a complex tension between romance and realism is generated within the Jewish plot itself. Indeed, only after reconstructing Daniel's reflective and dialogical relation to his cultural heritage can we see the stark contrast between his form of nationalism and Mordecai's. Mordecai's descriptions of a restored Israel do partake of powerfully mystifying organicist rhetoric, as when he

[24] On the anti-essentialism of Eliot's approach to Jewish identity, see Brantlinger, "Nations and Novels," 269; Newton, *George Eliot*, 93.

[25] See Barbara Hardy's note in the Penguin edition, 903.

says at the "The Philosophers" discussion club, "I believe in a growth, a passage, and a new unfolding of life whereof the seed is more perfect, more charged with the elements that are pregnant with diviner form" (585). He is fully convinced of what Daniel wishes to explore and test through practice, and his attempts to raise his fellow Jews to a higher cultural and national self-consciousness are not cast in terms of the more open-ended dialogue that Deronda invokes. For Mordecai, becoming self-conscious as a Jew means simply recognizing an identity that is fully underwritten by the bonds of the past and fully determined by a scenario of future nationalistic self-actualization: "Let the torch of visible community be lit!" (596). In this regard, Mordecai reflects German romantic social doctrine, which reifies national community into a collective will modeled on the single individual. Moreover, this form of organicist nationalistic doctrine, deriving from Herder and exemplified most dramatically in Adam Müller, not only demands the total subsumption of the individual into the state, but also favors precisely that authoritarianism through charismatic leadership that Mordecai himself represents.[26]

Thus, although both Deronda and Mordecai employ the term *choice*, their uses are dissimilar. For Mordecai, choice is the unified collective acceptance and enactment of racial destiny; consequently, Mordecai tells his listeners, "Let us . . . choose our full heritage, claim the brotherhood of our nation, and carry into it a new brotherhood with the nations of the Gentiles" (598). Mordecai's account of his own early self-understanding as a Jew recapitulates this key distinction between the forms of choice represented by the two characters. Mordecai directly admonishes Deronda for imagining that his is "the story of a spiritual destiny embraced willingly, and embraced in youth," emphatically deleting the central element of reflective affirmation: "It was the soul fully born within me, and it came in my boyhood" (555). As a prophetic speaker, moreover, Mordecai's speech is monologic and circular: he exhorts his audience to enact what his prophecies project as already fated to occur: "The vision is there; it will be fulfilled" (598). Within the terms of this prophetic mode, the act of prophecy ultimately does not appear to require the external affirmation of its listener or audience, though it nonetheless seems intent on enjoining that affirmation. Prophetic speech thus can appear utterly self-contained and self-sufficient. Eliot herself registers this by the fact that Mordecai's impassioned speech at "The Philosophers" club ultimately quells all argument and dialogue. As the self-appointed interpreter of the collective will, Mordecai's vision is not open to dispute.

[26] Greenfeld, *Nationalism*, 344–52.

At no point, crucially, does Deronda explicitly embrace Mordecai's conception of guaranteed cultural transmission, or his vision of an ignited race consciousness that will automatically enact Israel's destiny. Indeed, he engages in the same even-tempered resistance that marks his encounters with Kalonymos, with whom he of course has a more attenuated relationship. At the moment of revelation, Deronda does avow to Mordecai that his "whole being is a consent to the fact" of his being a Jew, but he adds, "it has been the gradual accord between your mind and mine which has brought about that full consent" (819). The concept of "gradual accord," though seen by Daniel as an expression that will meet the long deferred desires of his companion, has no real place in Mordecai's rhetoric of destiny and pure transmission. Indeed, later in the same conversation, Deronda feels compelled to deny Mordecai's reassertion of his Kabbalistic desires. Mordecai claims:

> "It has begun already—the marriage of our souls. It waits but the passing away of this body, and then they who are betrothed shall unite in a stricter bond, and what is mine shall be thine. Call nothing mine that I have written, Daniel. . . . For I have judged what I have written, and I desire the body that I gave my thought to pass away as this fleshly body will pass; but let the thought be born again from the fuller soul which shall be called yours."
>
> "You must not ask me to promise that," said Deronda, smiling. "I must be convinced first of special reasons for it in the writings themselves. And I am too backward a pupil yet. That blent transmission must go on without any choice of ours; but what we can't hinder must not make our rule for what we ought to choose." (820–21)

Despite the appearance of conciliation, Daniel and Mordecai here occupy radically different philosophical universes, and Daniel attempts to perform a gentle but firm correction. Most importantly, Daniel's refusal to promise lights up the fact that Mordecai has not requested him to. Mordecai does not believe that the merging of souls depends upon reciprocal consent, as revealed by his use of the prophetic performative ("let the thought be born again"). Deronda avoids a direct clash by minimizing the ramifications of his refusal, but his equanimity masks a profound rejection of Mordecai's disregard for his informed consent. In order for a reflective return to cultural heritage to be authentic, Deronda insists, it must be predicated on the possibility for reflective refusal, a possibility Mordecai cannot entertain.[27]

---

[27] Critics such as Peter Garrett and John Kucich emphasize just such moments of failed understanding between Mordecai and Daniel, yet their aim is to undermine what they take to be Eliot's unsustained ideal of intersubjective fusion or sympathy.

The larger question concerns just how comfortable Eliot is with this possibility. The portrayal of Leonora Halm-Eberstein will help us to answer this question, but Daniel's own equivocation here ("what we can't hinder must not make our rule for what we ought to choose") already betrays a certain need for guarantees on Eliot's part. It also forces us to confront the interpretive difficulty posed by Eliot's dissonant portrayals of Daniel and Mordecai. What do we make of this structuring tension in the representation of Jewish nationalism? For, on the one hand, the careful distancing of Daniel from Mordecai reveals an alternative to Mordecai's subsuming organicism while, on the other hand, the cultural heritage that Daniel returns to, however reflectively and open-endedly, is a heritage represented in the novel primarily through Mordecai's doctrines. Put somewhat differently, although Deronda distances himself from Mordecai and quietly insists on modifying his claims, Mordecai is portrayed with profound sympathy.[28] Thus we cannot

---

I am arguing that Eliot's ideal, as articulated through Daniel's resistance to Mordecai, is a dialogical one. Indeed, a reconstructive reading of Eliot's use of reflective dialogism has implications not only for critiques of her treatment of Jewish nationalism, but also for more general critiques of her ideals of intersubjective experience. It has been argued that Eliot evades politics by focusing on ethics, promoting ideals of personal moral transformation through tutelary exercises in sympathy, solidarity, and mutual understanding. A number of critics have extended this critique by arguing that these ideals, already evasions of more complex social and political problems, simply do not hold, that the positive versions of intersubjective reciprocity or redemptive sympathy are radically undercut by a more primary egotism or inwardness, or by power, or by the indeterminacy of language itself. Yet such critiques themselves often assume Eliot's absolute belief in the ideals of fusion or selflessness that mark Mordecai's views. Eliot's use of a more complex dialogical ideal to figure a wider politics casts into doubt, at least for a reading of this novel, the idea that Eliot relinquishes a broader social perspective in favor of cozy intersubjectivity. For the argument that Eliot evades politics by focusing on ethics, see Raymond Williams, *The Country and the City* (New York: Oxford University Press, 1973), 180; Myers, "George Eliot"; Eagleton, *Criticism and Ideology*, 121. For more extended arguments exposing the forms of egotism, power, or indeterminacy undermining Eliot's ethical ideals, see John Kucich, *Repression in Victorian Fiction: Charlotte Brontë, George Eliot, and Charles Dickens* (Berkeley: University of California Press, 1987), 114–200; Peter Garrett, *The Victorian Multiplot Novel: Studies in Dialogical Form* (New Haven: Yale University Press, 1980), 167–79; Daniel Cottom, *Social Figures: George Eliot, Social History, and Literary Representation* (Minneapolis: University of Minnesota Press, 1987); Cvetkovich, *Mixed Feelings*, 128–64; D. A. Miller, *Narrative and Its Discontents: Problems of Closure in the Traditional Novel* (Princeton: Princeton University Press, 1981), 107–94.

[28] Evidence from letters by Eliot and George Henry Lewes indicates that Eliot certainly wanted to inspire sympathy and interest through her characterization of

say that Eliot unambiguously prompts us to reject Mordecai's views in favor of Daniel's: there is a genuine tension between their views.[29]

Within the terms of Eliot's cultural horizon, the double discourse of nationalism represented by Daniel and Mordecai represents a kind of split response to the challenges of modernity. Daniel's reflective return to his cultural heritage bespeaks an even-handed appraisal of cosmopolitanism and, more importantly, acknowledges the profound way in which what Habermas calls "postconventionality," or the denaturalization of cultural givens, characterizes the self-conscious subject of modern cultural and ethical life. For Eliot, the modern European Jew more than perhaps any other subject is poised to recognize and respond to these dramatic cultural conditions. Mordecai of course represents something different. It is tempting, in light of Deronda's trajectory, to relegate Mordecai to the position of a traditional and powerful text that the modern Deronda encounters and adapts. But the fact that Mordecai is giving voice to a nascent and influential form of nationalism makes this more than a little difficult. Like Daniel, Mordecai is engaged in a distinctly modern project of nation-building. For this reason, although Mordecai's rhetoric stresses submission to racial destiny, it should not be read as merely rehearsing the established association of Judaism with a tradition-bound emphasis on the Law.

Ultimately, what Mordecai seems to represent is Eliot's not fully relinquished dream of a reflective return to a kind of *prereflective* cultural embeddedness. Throughout her work, embeddedness—familial, communal, and cultural—is both a fact of human existence and a value that must be cultivated in the face of modernity's damaging dispersions. Persistently Eliot invokes the need for early rootedness, a deep attachment to the site and inhabitants of one's childhood home. As we see in the famous passage treating the morally stunted Gwendolen, her lack of such a home precluded the natural development of a prereflective partiality (what Eliot envisions as a "sweet habit of the blood") that would ideally serve as the affective founda-

---

Mordecai, and that she saw him as a noble and ideal figure. Gordon Haight, *George Eliot: A Biography* (New York: Penguin, 1968, 1985), 483; Carol A. Martin, "Contemporary Critics and Judaism in *Daniel Deronda*," *Victorian Periodicals Review* 21 (1988): 91–92.

[29] The same tension appears in "The Modern Hep! Hep! Hep!" The essay makes appeal, as I have shown, to a reflective affirmation of cultural memory in the face of diaspora and cosmopolitanism. Yet it too invokes the idea of collective will that marks the German romantic doctrine of nationalism, by construing national nobility as dependent upon "a great feeling that animates the collective body as with one soul" (138).

tion for the reflectiveness that allows one to become a "citizen of the world" (50). Early rootedness matters not only because it lends stability to character but also because it ultimately serves as the basis for a higher-order self-conscious affirmation of what had been merely taken for granted: the norms of affection and solidarity that characterize familial and communal bonds. For Deronda, in contrast to Gwendolen and despite his unknown origins, a partial rootedness is effected by his strongly grounded filial affection toward Sir Hugo and his deep connection to his boyhood home. Ironically, this foundation helps Daniel to affirm his Jewish identity and the new familial and communal bonds that attend it, despite his long limbo period of "social neutrality" (220).

The romanticized nationalist rhetoric attempts to bypass the recognition that cultivated partiality, like civic nationalism, fundamentally alters one's relation to the forces of tradition that define identity. Mordecai's doctrines promote the dangerous illusion that "brotherhood" is something that can be simply "claimed" and requires no safeguarding of the complementary republican principles of liberty and equality. Mordecai thus represents Eliot's strong pull away from the cosmopolitan and civic principles that otherwise inform her ethico-political vision. Where Eliot's reservations about cosmopolitanism translate into the refusal of false universalism or illusory detachment, as in the case of Deronda, they become the basis for a profound meditation on both the possibility and need for self-reflective and dialogical affirmations of cultural heritage. Where those reservations translate into the attempt to circumvent reflective dialogism and project a prior unity as a future actuality, as in the case of Mordecai, they play into the most dangerous doctrines of modern times.

ETHICS, AESTHETICS, AND THE LIMITS OF ELIOT'S DIALOGISM

Through a reflective return to a national mission, Deronda evades a too-great disengagement from cultural norms, which Eliot associates with the more threatening aspects of the modern world. The negative aspects of modern life are generally recognized to inhere in the Gwendolen plot, but the most striking displacement and refiguration of the dangers of cosmopolitanism are played out through the character of Leonora Halm-Eberstein. Others have written on the importance of this figure for an understanding of Eliot's conception of gender, her sensitivity to the constraints imposed on women who pursue unconventional paths, and her unwillingness ultimately to abandon conventional ideals of femininity.[30] What I wish to do is to interpret this character not only through the lens of sexuality and gender but also in light of debates over Judaism and modernity. For in the portrayal of Leonora's fraught encounter with Jewish patriarchy, we see brought to the fore the same defining poles of the Jewish Question more generally: rigid law and traditionalism on the one hand, deracinated cosmopolitanism on the other.

As a willfully cosmopolitan woman who has renounced her cultural heritage, Leonora represents for Eliot the more extreme dangers of modern detachment. Leonora's gender is crucial in heightening the threat that she represents, because for Eliot, femininity in its ideal form enacts and transmits the affective bonds of the community, from the level of the family to that of the nation. Mirah, drawn in contrast to both Gwendolen and Leonora, represents just such ideal femininity. Unable to achieve the higher-order, mediated cultural affirmation associated with Deronda, Mirah nonetheless represents what Deronda comes to recognize and avow: the importance of a deeply felt connection to family and culture. The ground of Mirah's goodness is her own loving mother, no longer living but memorialized through the "lisping" song that Mirah recalls her singing (423). This distinctively unreflective bond to the mother issues in spontaneous devotion to the spiritual mission of Mordecai and Daniel: "Mirah's religion was of one fiber with her affections, and had never presented itself to her as a set of propositions" (410).

The feminine ideal here represents a naturalized and entirely prereflective relation to community and cultural heritage, and it is defined against "perverse" forms of feminine detachment. This ideal participates in the same dream of intersubjective and communal immediacy that informs the portrayal of Mordecai, although in the case of Mordecai there is a higher-order reflective affirmation of that immediacy. Both Deronda and Mordecai are feminized so as to interfuse their intellectual quests with dimensions of romantic and familial love, but they are both allowed some form of distance from the affective ideal that animates their life projects.[31] The "lapsed" Leonora, however, demonstrates the threat of absolute detachment from the

---

[30] See Paxton, *George Eliot and Herbert Spencer*, 213–20; Alison Booth, *Greatness Engendered: George Eliot and Virginia Woolf* (Ithaca: Cornell University Press, 1992), 236–84.

[31] In feminizing her Jewish heroes, Eliot is positively inflecting the dominantly negative construction of the Jew as feminized. For an analysis of the cultural conflation of Judaism and femininity, see Daniel Boyarin, "Épater L' embourgeoisement: Freud, Gender, and the (De)Colonized Psyche," *Diacritics* 24 (1994): 17–41.

affective ground of community that she, as Jewish daughter, wife, and mother, ideally should represent.[32]

Interestingly, Leonora's own account of Judaism accords with those thinkers and philosophers who construed Judaism in terms of an extrinsic, constraining Law that forecloses the development of the modern, autonomous subject. To a certain extent her critique of Judaism is a critique specifically of Jewish patriarchy: she eloquently conveys to Daniel how painful it was to "have a man's force of genius within you, and yet to suffer the slavery of being a girl," to be expected to conform to a pattern and serve cheerfully as a "makeshift link" to the next generation of sons (694). Yet she speaks more generally of Jewish religion and culture as thwarting individuality through its emphasis on rigid conformity. In justifying her conversion to Christianity upon her second marriage, she claims, "I had a right to do it; I was not like a brute, obliged to go with my own herd" (698). She even appropriates and reverses the organic imagery that is otherwise reserved for the privileged male characters of the Jewish plot, arguing that her oppressive Jewish culture consisted of "things that were thrust on my mind that I might feel them like a wall around my life—my life that was growing like a tree" (700).[33]

In adopting this organic imagery, Leonora paradoxically naturalizes her own desire for rootless cosmopolitanism, which she pursues in the less constraining world of the European theater. As a hypermodern subject, Leonora aligns herself with the transnational force of art and seeks to divorce herself entirely from the stifling confinement of a tradition-bound cultural heritage. Indeed, it is precisely her hypermodern perspective that construes Judaism, as it would any form of determined cultural identity, as fundamentally extrinsic or positive in Hegel's sense. Eliot seeks of course to elaborate the project of Jewish nationalism as a middle course between traditionalism and untethered modernity. Leonora does not acknowledge a middle ground, and thereby enacts what Eliot saw as a dangerous alternative to cultivated partiality: a life of alienation, detached from those forms of "special belonging" that counter the centrifugal forces of modernity. She plays a similar role to that played by Miss Wade in *Little Dorrit*, whose embrace of alienation is contrasted sharply with Amy Dorrit's cultivation of attachment, duty, and purposive feminine vocation. Indeed, reflecting the novel's larger insistence on the link between familial, communal, and national bonds, Leonora ac-

[32] For a discussion of the broader literary tradition that places the threat of a daughter's conversion at the heart of England's nationalist rhetoric, see Ragussis, *Figures of Conversion*.

[33] Also see Graver, *George Eliot and Community*, 241.

tively repudiates elemental human attachments precisely because they underwrite submission to cultural constraint. As she says bluntly to Deronda, "I did not wish you to be born. I parted with you willingly. When your father died, I resolved that I would have no more ties, but such as I could free myself from" (697). All her devotion is to the freedom from fixed identity that acting enables: as she puts it, "I was to care for ever about what Israel had been; and I did not care at all. I cared for the wide world, and all that I could represent in it" (693). Leonora thereby also redefines a central term in Eliot's ethic of sympathy and duty, introducing a form of *care* that, eschewing community, takes the widest possible personal freedom, and the least circumscribed world, for its object.

Leonora's rejection of conventional existence and pursuit of a higher life devoted to the theater partly align her with the novel's own positive valuations of cosmopolitanism and art, as represented prominently by Herr Klesmer, who is, significantly, German, Slavic, and Semitic. But her radicalization of cosmopolitan values, her outright disidentification from her cultural heritage, stands in stark opposition to the notion of reflective return that undergirds Daniel's journey. As a form of cosmopolitanism associated with avant-garde aesthetics and hyperindividualism, moreover, Leonora's detachment is not characterized by the same kind of sympathetic imagination that distinguishes the deracinated Daniel prior to his cultivation of partiality. Where Daniel cultivates the habit of "[seeing] things as they probably appeared to others," Leonora cares only to "represent" dramatically, and for herself, all that she can. Daniel brings his detachment to the service of an ethics, Leonora to the service of an aesthetics. It is this fact, as well as Leonora's grave repudiation of feminine and maternal devotion, that dictates the limits of Eliot's sympathy for her.

In controlling the threat represented by Leonora, moreover, Eliot has recourse to the very forms of extrinsic law and destiny that her portrayal of Jewish cultural identification otherwise seeks to repudiate. Despite her reasoned rejection of patriarchal constraints, and her deliberate choice of the artistic life, Leonora's attempt to dissociate entirely from her Jewish past ultimately cannot sustain itself, and issues in torment and disease. In flagrant opposition to her own conscious will, her past compels acknowledgment. Thus it becomes clear that Eliot's model of reflective dialogism, as represented by Daniel, cannot remain open to the transgressive possibilities of a life defined against the project of an ethnically based cultural transmission. Moreover, in "correcting" the misguided Leonora through the figure of Deronda himself, Eliot reveals the limits of her commitment to the model of reflective dialogism. Deronda admonishes Leonora for continuing to struggle against her past even as she submits to the will of her dead father by summoning Deronda:

> The effects prepared by generations are likely to triumph over a contrivance which would bend them all to the satisfaction of self. Your will was strong, but my grandfather's trust which you accepted and did not fulfil— what you call his yoke—is the expression of something stronger, with deeper, farther-spreading roots, knit into the foundations of sacredness for all men. (727)

On one level, this statement appears to reject Leonora's extrinsic conception of cultural constraint, refusing the term "yoke" and elaborating an organic metaphor of the cultural family tree. Yet the notion of previous generations "triumphing" over the individual, and the irrelevance of Leonora's own evolving relation to her grandfather's trust—her initial "acceptance" of it as moot as her later rejection—reveals that "yoke" is precisely the right word here, and that Daniel is himself engaged in mystification. His earlier statement to Mordecai—"what we can't hinder must not make our rule for what we ought to choose"—undergoes a troubling transformation here, as he instructs his mother that she can't help but choose what she can't hinder.

In a crucial way, and despite his own struggle to sympathize, Leonora's story fails to reach Daniel, fails to result in the kind of transformative cultural dialogue that Deronda earlier envisioned occurring between himself and other Jews, or between Judaism and other nations. His resistance to her is overdetermined, of course: after all, she abandoned him and masked his heritage from him. But his resistance is symptomatic of the novel's failure to accommodate her. Revealingly, Deronda cannot imagine that perhaps his mother's experience of tradition was in fact profoundly alienating and could not accommodate her individuality, her art, or her gender; his more capacious dialogical model narrows and hardens in the face of a direct challenge to its underlying investments in family and nation. In chastising his mother, Deronda ironically recapitulates the rigid traditionalism that he ostensibly rejects in Leonora's characterization of Jewish life, and that Eliot generally refuses in her own recasting of the Jewish Question.

A larger question is raised here, one with ramifications for the ethico-political investments of contemporary theory. Leonora's individualist and aesthetic form of self-fashioning, yoked as it is to a highly conscious disaffiliation from her cultural past, resonates with the forms of detachment often valorized in recent literary and cultural studies, where an oppositional stance toward conventionality is accompanied by an insistence on the theatrical and plastic nature of identity. Theorists and critics who valorize this mode of detachment, moreover, often tend to look suspiciously upon the kinds of modernist ideals that animate Deronda's reflective dialogism, associating them with Enlightenment thought and a too-stabilizing approach to cultural identity. I have tried to show that Deronda's practices of detachment and reaffiliation are never marked by fixity or complacency, largely in response to those forms of criticism that would elevate a Leonora over a Daniel. But it is also the case, as I am stressing here, that a recuperation of Daniel's character should not be made at the expense of Leonora, who represents a viable and deeply felt response to her own cultural context and personal past. If raised to a higher level of consistency, one consonant with the critical pluralism I outlined in the introduction, Eliot's project should be better able to accommodate Leonora's enactment of postconventionality.

THE ILLUMINATIONS OF EXILE

Eliot's multivalent approach to the Jewish Question testifies to the complexity of her response to the challenges of modernity. At the most basic level, it is clear that she sought to insert the nineteenth-century European Jew fully into the modern project of nation-building. Yet this is not a simple assimilationism whereby Judaism adopts, or is seen as worthy of admittance into, the dominant nationalist practices of Western Europe. Rather, through the figure of Deronda, a nascent Jewish nationalism is projected as exemplary, along with the future state it heralds. By this reading, Judaism does not obediently subordinate itself to the dictates of modernity, but rather makes good on modernity's most important and defensible ideals: self-reflective affirmation of cultural heritage, individual and political self-determination, democratic will-formation, and recognition of cultural differences. And as Eliot's portrayal of Deronda persistently implies, all of these ideals are only made possible through the careful cultivation of dialogical openness—to the individual other, to one's own cultural heritage(s), and to other cultures.

What the story of Deronda suggests is the somewhat paradoxical proposition that the project of universalism will only become and remain viable if its terms are set by the excluded particular. That is, as a people afflicted by exclusion, dispersion, and profound suffering, the Jews are prepared to enact and extend the forms of redemptive dialogism that will serve as a modern covenant between peoples and nations. In this, Eliot's thinking displays affinities with some of the most suggestive ethico-political claims in Jewish studies. According to Fackenheim, for example, Hegel and his followers mistakenly read the concept of "chosenness" as failed universalism and remain blind to the complexities of a tradition in which "universalism is implicit in an original particularism." "What if," Fackenheim asks, "according to the biblical self-understanding God chooses Israel for purposes transcending Israel from the start?"[34] This premise requires a radical recontextualization of "chosenness" and a far more nuanced understanding of the relation between particularism and universalism. More recently, from within the significantly different horizon of contemporary cultural studies, Daniel Boyarin has argued that the patterns of male Jewish subjectivity generated by the political conditions of nineteenth-century Europe should be read not simply as "a reactive artifact of the 'unnatural' situation of Diaspora Jews but a positive cultural product." By this reading, the modern European Jew is a form of "postcolonial subject," one who "has come into contact with the dominating society and is partly free to act out a mediation of one sort or another between the 'native' and Metropolitan cultures."[35] Boyarin is not using the term "postcolonial" in its strictest sense here, but rather asserting a significant analogy between post-Emancipation Jews (whom he contrasts with the "colonized" Jews of premodern Europe) and other persons who have undergone the politically illuminating experiences of decolonization, hybridity, and diaspora.

These disparate articulations invite the possibility, also present in Eliot, that Judaism's ongoing resistance to universalism's assimilationism itself might serve as a basis for a reconstructed universalism committed to dialogical openness in the face of cultural and ethnic multiplicity. This reconstructed universalism must of course be rigorously distinguished from the form of idealism that Crosby, based on a privileging of Mordecai's rhetoric, attributes to Eliot wholesale. But the question remains whether Eliot's devotion, even in Deronda's story and discourse, to the linked concepts of race, homeland, and state fundamentally undermines the possibilities for dialogical openness. In an important essay informed by the history of the Jews and Israel in the twentieth century, Daniel Boyarin and Jonathan Boyarin have argued for a conception of Jewish identity that is based not on achieved nationhood but rather on unending diaspora. For Boyarin and Boyarin, a "particular discourse of ethnocentricity is ethically appropriate only when the cultural identity is an embattled (or, at any rate, nonhegemonic) identity."[36] Favoring a notion of cultural belonging based on generational con-

---

[34] Fackenheim, *Encounters Between Judaism and Modern Philosophy*, 98.

[35] Boyarin, "Épater L' embourgeoisement," 39, 33.

[36] Daniel Boyarin and Jonathan Boyarin, "Diaspora: Generation and the Ground of Jewish Identity," *Critical Inquiry* 19 (1993): 718.

nection rather than autochthony, the Boyarins see Zionism as a betrayal of the Jewish culture rather than its culmination.

Deeply suspicious of European models of nationhood and cultural identity, the Boyarins seek to define Judaism against what they construe as a somewhat monolithic Western Europe. But as Eliot's double discourse reveals, there are different voices of nationalism within Western Europe itself. Moreover, as Daniel Boyarin has himself stressed, in the tradition of Leopold Zunz, Jews have participated in the debates over modernity throughout the history of Europe.[37] Thus it becomes possible, as in the case of Deronda, to incorporate models of democratic civic nationalism into one's idea of domestic as well as international relations. Openness to otherness and radical particularity need not be seen as fatally compromised in any formalized political state. It may be that the rhetoric of autochthony surrounding Zionism works against civic nationalism, but this does not mean that we must jettison completely the model of national self-determination, as the Boyarins advise in their promotion of a "notion of identity in which there are only slaves but no masters."[38]

I have been stressing the possibilities held out by Deronda's reflective and dialogical discourse, but in many ways the Boyarins' essay might be read as reminding us never to lose sight of the destructive capabilities of the romantic doctrine of nationalism that influences Eliot's portrayal of Mordecai. And of course we must also do justice to the fact that the plight of Leonora bears witness to the limits of Deronda's own dialogism. In the story of Deronda's return to his cultural heritage, Eliot intervenes in the debate on the Jewish Question, refusing simple oppositions between Jewish tradition and European modernity, and drawing out the ways in which radical Jewish cosmopolitanism might become, to borrow Boyarin's phrase, a "positive cultural product."[39] But the negative effects of such radical dislocation threaten Eliot profoundly, and she has recourse, as we have seen, to a dangerous romantic nationalism in her portrayal of Mordecai and to atavistic conceptions of cultural fate in her disciplining of the transgressive individuality of Leonora. Thus the fault lines in Eliot's narrative teach us that even the most reflective dialogical models of cultivated detachment can harbor violent

[37] Boyarin, "Épater L'embourgeoisement," 26 n. 16.

[38] Boyarin and Boyarin, "Diaspora," 711.

[39] For a discussion of contemporary reconstructions of cosmopolitanism as an ethico-political ideal, see Amanda Anderson, "Cosmopolitanism, Universalism, and the Divided Legacies of Modernity," in *Cosmopolitics: Thinking and Feeling Beyond the Nation*, ed. Pheng Cheah and Bruce Robbins (Minneapolis: University of Minnesota Press, 1998).

blindnesses and exclusions. Ironically, Eliot's own focus on the illuminating position of the modern European Jew grew out of that very insight, and out of the belief, which I would like to close this chapter by endorsing, that such negative potentialities are best guarded against not by rejecting the ideals of modernity, but by continuously testing them against the articulated experience of the excluded particular.

CHAPTER FIVE

"Manners Before Morals"

OSCAR WILDE
AND EPIGRAMMATIC DETACHMENT

Unlike the Victorian writers that I have been treating thus far, the proponents of the late-century Aesthetic Movement directly and flagrantly espoused the cultivation of radical detachment. Oscar Wilde, the most prominent practitioner of this movement in England, may therefore seem like the natural telos for this study. In many ways he looks to be either the reversal or transcendence of what we have previously encountered, especially in his valorization of those forms of detachment (the amoral, the aesthetic, the ironic) that formed the negative pole of other authors' ambivalence toward the cultivated distances of modern intellectual, artistic, and ethical practices. Indeed, the most radical critical and philosophical claims associated with Wilde—his sharp divisions between art and ethics, thought and action, truth and beauty—reversed the studied attempt by other authors to integrate the ethical and aesthetic spheres of life, or to secure the primacy of ethical value in the face of modern relativity, the indifference of objective method, or the celebration of the aesthetic. This element of Wilde's thought has been seen as closely allied with his transgressive attitude toward Victorian convention and Victorian morality and has contributed to the establishment of his heroic status within contemporary queer and postmodern studies.[1]

But if Wilde seems by one reading to contest the values of Victorian culture, largely by challenging conceptual hierarchies, he also repeats the fundamental ambivalence we have noted in other authors. In this sense he fully belongs with the group of authors I have studied in previous chapters, and reveals the continuities between mid- and late-Victorian approaches to detachment, which differ from each other more in emphasis than in essentials. Wilde displays the characteristic ambivalence toward detachment in his

---

[1] See, for example, Jonathan Dollimore, *Sexual Dissidence: Augustine to Wilde, Freud to Foucault* (Oxford: Oxford University Press, 1991); Lee Edelman, *Homographesis: Essays in Gay Literary and Cultural Theory* (New York: Routledge, 1994); Christopher Craft, *Another Kind of Love: Male Homosexual Desire in English Discourse, 1850–1920* (Berkeley: University of California Press, 1994).

rather well-known oscillations, particularly in the society comedies and *The Picture of Dorian Gray*, between irony and melodrama, between dandyism and sentimentality, and between aestheticism and moralism. Those who wish to downplay this aspect of Wilde's writings tend to valorize *The Importance of Being Earnest*, with its flawless irony, dismissing the previous society comedies as abortive attempts still entangled in melodrama or unproductively torn between the perspective of the dandy and a more conventional morality.[2] By this reckoning, *De Profundis* is mere bathos, a falling away, an embarrassment. Such a reaction to Wilde's complexity is not simply postmodern willfulness or wish-fulfillment, I would contend. Rather, it registers a fundamental torsion in Wilde's work, one wrought by the force of the epigram, which seems always to pull away from the text, and from the context of the action, announcing itself as quotable, transferable, and indifferent. Just as the epigrams seem persistently to comment upon the action of the narrative or drama, which serves as straight man to their endless generative capacity and self-conscious artificiality, they also simultaneously announce their easy exit from the text, their extractability. Wilde is careful to denude many of the epigrams of any remnant of their original context, constructing the dialogue so that no phatic or transitional indices mar their perfect quotability. The fact that many of Wilde's epigrams float intertextually among his works, and the way in which Wilde's own studied public performances placed him in alliance with the mode of the epigrammatic dandy, only enforces the impulse which wants to subordinate the forces of melodrama, poetic justice, and sentimentality to the free play of the epigram.

In this chapter, I examine the Wildean epigram as a way of further elaborating Wilde's approach to forms of detachment, and specifically in order to advance our understanding of the relation between aesthetics and ethics in his work. My analysis will ultimately displace the opposition between melodrama and irony, taking into account an alternative movement in Wilde's art, one that belongs neither to the side of conventional morality nor to the side of willful aestheticism. This alternative movement may be defined as a certain punctuation of the aesthetic mode: it is not so much living for every moment, as Pater would have us do, but rather seizing the moment which

---

[2] My phraseology is borrowed from Anthony Lane, who refers to *An Ideal Husband* as Wilde's "last entanglement with melodrama (in the theatre, at any rate)." This is a sentiment expressed widely by those invested in a true Wilde somehow betrayed by his lamentable lapses into sentimentality or melodrama. See Anthony Lane, "An Ideal Husband," *The New Yorker*, July 5, 1999, 90.

the drama of life only occasionally or intermittently presents to us. To seize the moment requires simultaneously an ethical finesse and an artful capacity; it is entirely outside of the sphere of conventional morality or virtue and in fact often flies in the face of such morality. A mode of self-realization that is at once pragmatic, self-conscious, and unconventional, seizing the moment significantly alters the mode of detached irony that is frequently seen to define the Wildean dandy. I will explore this feature of Wilde's philosophy of life, and particularly its relation to the force of the epigram, in Wilde's society comedies prior to *The Importance of Being Earnest*, which I would personally demote for its lack of complexity in relation to this very important aspect of Wilde's work.

In part, my approach shares affinities with those analyses that seek to reconcile the aesthetic and the ethical in Wilde, or rather, that seek to demonstrate that Wilde himself reconciled them, despite his many programmatic utterances to the contrary. Certainly such movements of reconciliation are visible in Wilde's own critical works, which display what Julia Prewitt Brown calls "the main contradiction of aestheticism—that is, the paradoxical separation yet interdependence of art and life."[3] Richard Ellmann has cogently synthesized the ways in which that interdependence is formulated, showing that Wilde conceives of art as variously reproaching, outraging, or seducing the world from which it is ostensibly separate. Through these actions, art and life become interpenetrated, and art takes on an ethical purpose.[4]

However, such approaches tend to falter when confronted by the more intractable formal problems presented by Wilde's plays or *The Picture of Dorian Gray*. Ellmann himself introduces the more sharply divergent trajec-

[3] Julia Prewitt Brown, *Cosmopolitan Criticism: Oscar Wilde's Philosophy of Art* (Charlottesville: University Press of Virginia, 1997), 72.

[4] "In his criticism and in his work generally, Wilde balanced two ideas which, we have observed, look contradictory. One is that art is disengaged from actual life, the other that it is deeply incriminated with it. . . . That art is sterile, and that it is infectious, are attitudes not beyond reconciliation. Wilde never formulated their union, but he implied something like this: by its creation of beauty art reproaches the world, calling attention to the world's faults through their very omission; so the sterility of art is an affront or parable. Art may also outrage the world by flouting its laws or by picturing indulgently their violation. Or art may seduce the world by making it follow any example which seems bad but is discovered to be better than it seems. In these various ways the artist forces the world toward self-recognition, with at least a tinge of self-redemption." Richard Ellmann, "Introduction," in *The Artist as Critic: Critical Writings of Oscar Wilde*, ed. Richard Ellmann (Chicago: University of Chicago Press, 1982; originally published 1968), xxvi–xxvii.

tories of the literature after his analysis of Wilde's critical views.[5] Brown, who has advanced a highly developed reconciliation of Wilde's aesthetic and ethical views, tellingly places most of her emphasis on *De Profundis*, which she argues not only makes the case for the ethical power of artistic distance but also enacts it, taking the artist's troubled existence for its object. Brown in fact claims that Wilde's reconciliation of ethics and aesthetics is best described as a form of cosmopolitanism, hinging her argument on Wilde's few key uses of the term in "The Critic as Artist." Toward the end of that critical dialogue, Wilde employs the term *cosmopolitanism* as both synonym for and effect of the critical temper. The appearance of this word is not surprising, since Wilde's text is insistently in dialogue with Arnold, who also gives prominence to cosmopolitanism at crucial points in his critical writing.[6] Wilde introduces the term largely to argue that criticism, rather than appeals to emotions or abstract ethics, will conduce most to peace and understanding among nations and races. It is a term that allows him to move away from any sentimental or moral rhetoric without ceding the ethical sphere entirely to those social and political reformers who employ such rhetoric. For Wilde, criticism "will annihilate race-prejudices, by insisting on the unity of the human mind in the variety of its forms."[7] The habits of intellectual rigor associated with criticism will extinguish precisely those forms of untutored emotion that lead to violence, destruction, and rage. Thus while

[5] In a passage directly following the one I quote in note 4, Ellmann adds, "Yet this ethical or almost ethical view of art coexists in Wilde with its own cancellation. He could write *Salomé* with one hand, dwelling upon incest and necrophilia, and show them as self-defeated, punished by execution and remorse. With the other hand, he could dissolve by the critical intellect all notions of sin and guilt. He does so in *The Importance of Being Earnest*, which is all insouciance where *Salomé* is all recrimination." Ibid., xxxii.

[6] In its first published form, "The Critic as Artist" announced its dialogue with Arnold in its title, which was "The True Function and Value of Criticism: With Some Remarks on the Importance of Doing Nothing." For discussion of Wilde's debt to Arnold in this essay, see William E. Buckler, "Building a Bulwark against Despair: 'The Critic as Artist,'" *English Literature in Transition* 32 (1989): 284. As Buckler points out, "Indeed, except for the disproportionately celebrated reversal of one of Arnold's basic critical precepts, all the major thrusts of 'The Critic as Artist' are profoundly indebted to Arnold—from 'the importance of the critical element in all creative work' to criticism as the catalyst of culture, the arbiter of the future, the annihilator of race-prejudice, the intellectual unifier of Europe, and the modern focus of the 'World Spirit.'" For a fuller discussion of Arnold's use of the term *cosmopolitanism*, see chapter 3.

[7] Oscar Wilde, "The Critic as Artist," in *The Artist as Critic*, ed. Ellmann, 405. Subsequent page number references will be cited parenthetically in the text as CA.

cosmopolitanism promotes a fuller understanding of other national traditions, especially as they are manifested in their cultural achievements, it
remains fairly abstract in its universalism and does not take the "layered"
form that we saw in Arnold, where especially fortuitous hybrid formations
become the sites of privileged modernity.[8] Yet Wilde does share with Arnold
the tendency to make interracial or international expansiveness, rather than
interclass understanding, the site of ethical development. This allows him to
speak disparagingly of philanthropy, reform, and realism, without entirely
abandoning the ethical sphere.

My own analysis will begin with a discussion of Wilde's critical views, in
particular his arguments in favor of key analytical and practical divisions
between spheres of life, and the multiple ways in which he makes and modifies the case for detachment. I will be especially concerned to demonstrate
Wilde's revisions of the Arnoldian conception of criticism, which, along with
Pater's views, exercised a powerful influence upon him. My aim is first to
contextualize my analysis of Wilde's most pervasive formal device—the epigram—and second to set the stage for a reconsideration of formal tensions in
the dramas, where the epigram serves a key role in Wilde's conceptualization of the dramatic moment, and where the category of gender becomes
primary in the conceptualization of the epigrammatic mode of the dandy, in
the understanding of dramatic self-realization, and in the playing out of tensions between melodrama and irony. It is my view that Wilde's concern with
the ethics of detachment is played out most extensively and tellingly
through his literary use of the epigram and through his delineation of the
dandy, rather than through his more gestural remarks about cosmopolitanism, which remains a minor form of detachment in his oeuvre, one that
moreover does not capture the most significant form that Wildean detachment takes: an irony leveled persistently at the conventions of English mid-
dle- and upper-class society.[9] Insofar as this particular form of late-Victorian

[8] In general, Wilde's aestheticism stressed universalist or transracial commonality,
as is evident in the passages espousing cosmopolitan criticism. However, in keeping
with his strategy of reversing hierarchies, Wilde at certain points valorizes the Celt
over the Saxon, aligning Celtism with the values of aestheticism and, more generally,
with antimoralism. This emphasis in his writings of course vies somewhat with his
declared cosmopolitanism, or his alliance with the transcendence of racial antipathies or separatism. For a discussion of Wilde's treatment of Celtism, see David
Alderson, "Momentary Pleasures: Wilde and English Virtue," in Sex, Nation, and
Dissent in Irish Writing, ed. Eibhear Walshe (New York: St. Martin's Press, 1997),
43–59.

[9] In this I am in fundamental disagreement with Brown, who wishes to redirect
Wildean criticism toward the concept of cosmopolitanism: "Wilde's cosmopolitan

detachment has had such a long-lived effect on both the modern and post-modern sensibility, my aim here is to explore its form and limits in one of its most influential practitioners.

By way of conclusion, I will more directly consider some of the ways in which the contemporary critical fascination with Wilde reveals key features of our disciplinary approach to the topic of detachment, which, as a constitutive problem of the modern era, continues to provoke ambivalent responses among theorists and critics. Most basically, the fascination with Wilde indicates the predilection among postmodern and literary theorists for the mode of irony, a form of detachment that can claim the insights of critical distance without carrying the onus of earnest enlightenment. By showing the concrete difficulties Wilde faces in his attempt to pursue a mode of portable epigrammatic irony, I hope in this chapter to suggest the limits of any general valorization of irony.

MAKING THE CASE FOR DETACHMENT: THE CRITICAL WILDE

In many ways, Wilde's conception of criticism, as elaborated in "The Critic as Artist," can be seen as a radicalization of Arnold's ideal of disinterestedness. While from one perspective Wilde seems to follow Pater's subjective turn, valorizing criticism as the creative expression of the practitioner's unique individuality, he is at the same time interested in defining criticism as a stance of cultivated detachment, one that comprises both reflective distance—what Wilde generally means by "self-consciousness"—and freedom from constraints or limits. Reflective distance is the condition of all art and the condition of all criticism. Through Gilbert's rejection of Ernest's romantic conception of unconscious artistic inspiration, Wilde is voicing his own rejection of any aesthetic or cultural ideal that seeks to overcome or diminish the condition of heightened self-consciousness. This places him firmly not only against Carlyle, who saw self-consciousness as a negative condition of modern life, but also against Ruskin and Morris, who promoted a synthetic unity of thought and action, art and labor. On the one hand, heightened self-consciousness simply means self-awareness; it is a cognitive practice

---

aestheticism is a much weightier achievement than has been recognized by those who take the view that late nineteenth-century aestheticism is no more than an anti-bourgeois—that is, superlatively bourgeois—reaction against a utilitarian culture." Brown, *Cosmopolitan Criticism*, 28.

that translates prereflective conditions such as instinct or taste into forms of critical discernment. On the other hand, however, Wilde seeks to protect the process of thinking that he associates with self-consciousness or criticism from any constraint, limit, or determination: it must be entirely free in order to perform its creative and life-enhancing function. In this sense, critical thought is defined not only as the becoming self-conscious of the prereflective but also as that which is fundamentally cut off from all aspects of embodied life: action, intersubjective entanglement, pain, sorrow, necessity, heredity. In being so freed, thought is also released from the limitations of any given viewpoint and ascends to the realm of disinterestedness, which is also, paradoxically, the realm of unfettered self-realization, or individuality. Wilde's position constitutes a radicalization of Arnold's position, then, insofar as criticism's condition of radical freedom means that it is simultaneously disinterested and, necessarily, "the purest form of personal impression" (CA 365). Where Arnold's ideal of disinterestedness leads to a characterological ideal of enacted objectivity, Wilde's ideal of disinterestedness leads instead to an aggrandizement of an entirely "pure" subjectivity, purged of all embodiment, constraint, or reference to "any standard external to itself" (CA 365).

To understand Wilde's conception of detachment as both reflective distance and radical freedom permits us to reconcile a wide range of potentially conflicting positions that appear across his critical writings. The desire for freedom from constraint or from the limitations of any given viewpoint can result in statements that clearly evoke Arnold: "It is Criticism that, recognizing no position as final, and refusing to bind itself by the shallow shibboleths of any sect or school, creates that serene philosophic temper which loves truth for its own sake, and loves it not the less because it knows it to be unattainable" (CA 405). Only at the end of the statement does Wilde begin to alter the terms of the Arnoldian position, refusing the notion of attainable truth, emphasizing instead the contemplative act, cut free not only from any ground of interest but also from any knowable objective standard. This final turn appears in extreme form as "The Decay of Lying," which elevates willful artificiality above truth. From there we do not have to travel far to get to the notion of radical individualism, which is suddenly free to express any temper whatsoever in the pursuit of self-realization.

Indeed, the subversive force of the analytical divisions that Wilde pursues—the severance of thought from action, or art from ethics, for example—is sometimes transferred to the self-realizing individual who is otherwise imagined to benefit from the existence of a realm of weightless freedom. Sometimes, that is, self-realization involves the flouting of convention, setting oneself directly against the customs or laws of society—in a word, sin: "What is termed Sin is an essential element of progress. Without it the world would stagnate, or grow old, or become colourless. By its curiosity, Sin increases the experience of the race. Through its intensified assertion of individualism, it saves us from monotony of type" (CA 360). Both in his reversal of hierarchy, and in his appeal to transgression as self-realization, Wilde here places emphasis on the act of rebellion, on the coincidence of negation and self-actualization: "Art is Individualism, and Individualism is a disturbing and disintegrating force. Therein lies its immense value. For what it seeks to disturb is monotony of type, slavery of custom, tyranny of habit, and the reduction of man to the level of the machine";[10] or, as he writes self-referentially in *De Profundis*: "I am one of those who are made for exceptions, not for laws."[11] This rebellious position always exists in some tension with the desire for a purer realm of freedom where such negations would become meaningless.[12]

"Socialism" in Wilde's conception is largely the utopian expression of this desire. "What I mean by a perfect man is one who develops under perfect conditions; one who is not wounded, or worried, or maimed, or in danger. *Most personalities have been obliged to be rebels. Half their strength has been wasted in friction*" (SMS 262: Wilde's emphasis). The "true personality of man," impossible under existing conditions, is imagined as something that in a future utopia would "grow naturally and simply, flower-like, or as a tree grows" (SMS 263). Yet what appears in "The Soul of Man under Socialism" as a self-consciously utopian conception appears throughout the critical essays as an assertion of an already existing realm of freedom, whether it be conceived as artistic autonomy, spiritual detachment, or the purer air of the intellect. Wilde is thus near the truth of self-description when he speaks of

[10] Oscar Wilde, "The Soul of Man under Socialism," in *The Artist as Critic*, ed. Ellman, 272. Subsequent page number references will be cited parenthetically in the text as SMS.

[11] Oscar Wilde, *De Profundis and Other Writings* (Harmondsworth: Penguin, 1986), 154. Subsequent page number references will be cited parenthetically in the text as *DP*.

[12] Another version of this tension, as manifested in "The Critic as Artist," is that between a realm of pure contemplation and a conception of thinking as destruction. As Gilbert says to Ernest, thought is actively dangerous insofar as "the security of society lies in custom and unconscious instinct" (CA 388). Or, as Lord Illingworth says in *A Woman of No Importance*, "All thought is immoral. It's the very essence of destruction. If you think of anything, you kill it. Nothing survives being thought of." Oscar Wilde, *A Woman of No Importance*, in *The Importance of Being Earnest and Other Plays*, ed. Peter Raby (Oxford: Clarendon Press, 1995), 137.

powerful personalities losing half their strength in friction, since he himself seems torn between embattled refusals and claims to Olympian detachment.

This tension is also reflected in Wilde's treatment of literary form, specifically, through his critique of realism and persistent privileging of the epigram as well as those particular genres that most conduce to epigrammatic display and prominence: the society comedy, the critical dialogue, the essay. Wilde faults what he refers to as "realism" on several counts. Most fundamentally, by attempting merely to imitate life, the realist does not produce genuine art, which should always stand free from life.[13] Wilde aligns realism with the inferior practices of social science and social reform, as well as their vulgar forms of knowledge (statistics, facts, science) and their informing morals (sympathy, charity, improvement of character). He shares with Arnold the tendency to see the objective scientific standpoint, which he faults realism for overvaluing, as something which serves only to disclose and hence reinforce a certain determinism. At best, by showing us the severe limitations on all action, it prompts our recognition of the unlimited freedom of thought.

Wilde's insistence on a realm free of determinations is everywhere matched by his severe apprehension of forms of constraint, which he acknowledges yet also seeks to disavow through a repudiation of those intellectual, social, and artistic practices which seem to reproduce or rely upon any form of determinism.[14] Thus realism, and more particularly naturalism, is faulted for its formal commitment to the intractability of social determinations. This explains, as Lawrence Danson points out, why Wilde so vehemently opposed Zola, whose naturalist doctrine was in many ways in alliance with Wilde's antimoralism.[15] When Wilde writes in the preface to *The Picture of Dorian Gray*, "The nineteenth century dislike of Realism is the rage

[13] When Wilde elevates criticism above art in "The Critic as Artist," as that which is "never trammelled by any shackles of verisimilitude," he synecdochally extends realism's deficiency to all art, though this is not of course a position he holds across his writings (CA 365).

[14] For a discussion of tensions between voluntarism and fatality in Wilde, specifically with regard to category of desire, see Jeff Nunokawa, *Desire Lite* (forthcoming). My analysis of Wilde's attraction to weightlessness and his countervailing fatalism is indebted to ongoing conversations with Nunokawa, as well as the inspiration of his work on Wilde. See, in particular, Jeff Nunokawa, "The Importance of Being Bored: The Dividends of Ennui in *The Picture of Dorian Gray*," in *Novel Gazing: Queer Readings in Fiction*, ed. Eve Kosofsky Sedgwick (Durham: Duke University Press, 1997), 151–66. Also see Lawrence Danson, *Wilde's Intentions: The Artist in His Criticism* (Oxford: Clarendon Press, 1997), 18–19.

[15] Danson, *Wilde's Intentions*, 49.

of Caliban seeing his own face in the glass," he is thus largely displacing outward his own ambivalence. Wilde wanted to shock his readers, yet he was also repelled by the idea of countering moral pieties with naked truth or the deep delineation of character, which for him meant running aground on the shoals of human nature:

> Where we differ from each other is purely in accidentals: in dress, manner, tone of voice, religious opinions, personal appearance, tricks of habit, and the like. The more one analyses people, the more all reasons for analysis disappear. Sooner or later one comes to that dreadful universal thing called human nature. Indeed, as anyone who has ever worked among the poor knows only too well, the brotherhood of man is no mere poet's dream, it is a most depressing and humiliating reality.[16]

While in "The Soul of Man under Socialism" Wilde could contend that human nature was fundamentally changeable, here he emphasizes that there is an underlying essence that only Art, the true enactment of Individualism, can transcend. That Wilde's work can house such a contradiction stems in large part from the very tension I have been analyzing. On the one hand, art is appealed to as a force that can transform reality, of which human nature forms a part. On the other hand, art must exist at a remove from life and its intractable nature in order to freely express its individuality. According to the first view, human nature is infinitely malleable, because it is not "nature" at all; according to the second view, by contrast, the bedrock of human nature is unchanging, and the entirely separate realm of art is the site of freedom. In expressing the second view, Wilde positions himself against the moral claims of realists like George Eliot or Elizabeth Gaskell, who believed that careful delineation of their fellow humans would prompt feelings of understanding, sympathy, and fellowship.[17]

Wilde makes a similar double move when he considers scientific theories of racial determination. In this his thought parallels Arnold, whose apprehensions of racial determination, as disclosed by science, led to a compensatory investment in the idea that specific racial elements in the life of a people could be augmented, suppressed, or brought into harmonious balance by the cultivated and self-aware individual. In a similar manner, Wilde on the

[16] Oscar Wilde, "The Decay of Lying," in *The Critic as Artist*, ed. Ellmann, 297.

[17] Wilde of course appeals to such moral claims himself when he writes *De Profundis*; likewise, *The Picture of Dorian Gray* certainly draws, however transformed by Gothic, on a realist conception of character analysis and development. But I am interested here in the implications of Wilde's critique of realism for an understanding of his views on detachment.

one hand cedes the potency of racial determination—what he calls "the scientific principle of Heredity"—yet restricts its force to the realm of embodied action, leaving the realm of contemplation as the site of freedom (CA 382–83). But rather than simply imagining a controlling force of reason that can selectively foster or curtail specific racial elements, Wilde defeats the logic of racial determinism in a more complex manner, by attributing to the power of the imagination a productively receptive capacity, a capacity to realize modernity by reliving the multiple experiences of the race: "It seems to me that with the development of the critical spirit we shall be able to realize, not merely our own lives, but the collective life of the race, and so to make ourselves absolutely modern, in the true meaning of the word modernity. For he to whom the present is the only thing that is present, knows nothing of the age in which he lives" (CA 382).

While Wilde's view of the critical spirit here imagines a culminating ability to comprehend the whole of history, the critique of realism implies that cultivating a distanced view of the social totality is not good for the individual, for art, or for society. Wilde recapitulates Arnold's apprehensions of the limits disclosed by the project of scientific objectivity, which he explicitly associates with realism. Realism, and the correlative project of social science, is accordingly cast as the negative form of detachment against which the refined aims of art and criticism are defined. It is also illuminating to compare Wilde with Dickens on this score. For Dickens, as we saw, the cultivation of omniscient detachment threatened purposive, embedded character, insofar as it inevitably nourished suspicion and a corrupting awareness of systemic corruption. For Wilde, by contrast, scientific forms of social knowledge, whether in the guise of statistics or realist narrative, conduce to replicate the status quo through the force of their formal presentation, and thereby stifle individuality, reducing it to common human nature. Mimesis becomes sheer replication, repetition of the conventions that only artful transformation can alter. The question of form is paramount. It is not merely the practice of objectivity or the aspiration to the systemic view that threatens the more positively conceived project of cultivated detachment—it is also crucially the forms through which such practices find expression, and by means of which conventionality, custom, and nature become entrenched.

It is therefore not surprising that Wilde emphasizes an alternative form when he attempts to elaborate the artful existence that will disrupt and transform solidified habits and customs. The primary aim was to conceive of an art that would maximize its distance from conventional life. In "The Soul of Man under Socialism," Wilde attempts to define art *tout court* precisely in these terms; there he argues that it is fallacious to call writers "morbid" whose subject matter is morbid: every artist, Wilde contends, necessarily takes distance from that which he represents (SMS 274).[18] It is the premise of this chapter, however, that the epigram serves in keys ways as the solution to Wilde's quest for an appropriate form in which to express the project of detachment, a project that cannot be adequately specified through the generalized assertion that distanced treatment is constitutive of all art, especially in light of Wilde's negative assessment of realism and social science, both of which rely, of course, upon distanced treatment. Wilde's eclectic experimentation with a range of genres—among them the fairy tale, the critical dialogue, the essay, comedic drama, epistolary memoir—foregrounds alternatives to strict mimesis and certainly to conventional literary forms. But the formal signature most associated with Wilde, evident in all the genres he adopted, is the epigram. Most fundamentally, the epigram enacts an *ironic* detachment—it pulls back and comments upon a topic, a prior response, a set of conditions. In Wilde's hands, moreover, it also characteristically pulls back and comments upon the more conventional epigram or moral maxim, reversing terms, refusing niceties, using the traditional form of moral observation to thwart moral piety: "Moderation is a fatal thing." "Life is far too important a thing ever to talk seriously about it." "Scandal is gossip made tedious by morality."[19]

The epigram also takes the form of generalization. In that regard alone it takes distance from the specific context of its utterance, positioning the speaker at a certain vantage point. The human face of the epigram is dandyism, of course. Wilde's dandies are the participant spectators of otherwise embedded experience. They have done something that seems counterintuitive, and threatening, to the cultural ethos of Victorian society: they have made a habit of the nonhabitual, paradoxically naturalizing the practice of denaturalization. Insofar as the epigram is associated with the figure of the dandy, whose unconventional subjectivity is very much "in your face," both sartorially and linguistically, it also serves to express the radically indi-

[18] For an illuminating discussion of Wilde's arguments about morbidity in "The Soul of Man under Socialism," see Danson, *Wilde's Intentions*, 148–67. Danson attributes Wilde's arguments against the public in this essay to his obsessive concern with recent negative reviews of *The Picture of Dorian Gray*.

[19] The first epigram appears in Wilde, *A Woman of No Importance*, 138. The other two epigrams appear in Oscar Wilde, *Lady Windermere's Fan*, in *The Importance of Being Earnest and Other Plays*, ed. Raby, 12, 43. Subsequent page number references will be cited parenthetically in the text.

vidual, and so perfectly embodies the coincidence of detachment and self-realization, the two elements that Wilde's criticism sought persistently to hold together.[20]

DANDYISM AND THE FORM OF WILDE'S ETHICS

The typical movement of reversal in the epigrams, the mode of ironic detachment represented by the dandy, and the transgressive frisson associated with Wilde's notion of self-actualization through sin: all of these might be taken to suggest that Wilde has not himself escaped a certain negative logic. He cannot transvalue: caught in a stance of rebellion, he can only gesture toward a frictionless realm of freedom, all the while remaining vulnerable to the sudden undertow of melodrama, sentimentality, or a purely conventional virtue. From this perspective, the syntheses suggested by Ellman and especially by Brown seem undermined by the evidence of a dominant tendency toward negation, evasion, and frustrated idealism.

Yet I want to suggest that there is an alternative movement in Wilde, a subspecies of dandified action, that permits a somewhat different light to fall upon Wilde's thinking and Wilde's art. Indeed, I suggest that this alternative movement grows out of Wilde's own apprehension, explored in the comedies, of the specifically ethical limits of epigrammatic detachment. For Wilde, the dandy ideally represents the function of criticism in the modern era, which seeks to further self-consciousness by subverting custom, habit, and the oppressive social stability that they work to secure. In this conception, the dandy is participant critic: self-conscious, artful, and committed to demystification, at the center of the conversation yet to the side of cultural norms, drawing both gasps and admiration, intervening by forcing a mode of detached irony to subvert the "natural" assumptions of his interlocutors. Others have written about the class-marked nature of dandyism in Wilde, the ways in which it itself is situated within a leisure-class, aristocratic ethos. There are gendered elements to Wilde's dandyism as well, which I will be especially focusing on in my reading of the comedies. These lines of argument both show that Wilde's ideal of detachment may pretend to be the view from nowhere but is clearly invested in specific social sites nonethe-

[20] There are of course variations on the primary structure of a single dandy dominating the action. The most interesting variation, which I will discuss later, might be called the epigrammatic duet, enacted in a mode of ironic flirtation, between the dandy and the dandified woman.

less. What I want to draw out here, however, is a self-conscious movement within Wilde to limit the free-floating detachment of the dandy. For in key instances in the Wildean oeuvre, this purely critical and seemingly endlessly transferable practice is supplemented or punctuated by a crucially different form of dandiacal action that is self-consciously local, pragmatically driven, and specifically intended as a constructive intervention into the action of the drama. Such moments are typically represented as both ethical interventions that will benefit others and heightened instances of self-realization on the part of the dandy. The most striking example of this type of action can be found in *An Ideal Husband*, where Wilde underscores it by providing an explicit and somewhat unusual stage-direction. This is the moment in the play where Lord Goring vehemently and successfully challenges Lady Chiltern's conviction that her chastened husband, just rescued from the brink of exposure for a serious though isolated moral error committed long ago, should refuse a position of high honor in the Cabinet and retire altogether from public life. The stage direction to Goring's rather lengthy speech reads, *"pulling himself together for a great effort, and showing the philosophy that underlies the dandy,"* and Goring emphasizes his sense of timing: "Now is the moment when you really want my help, now is the time when you have got to trust me, to trust in my counsel and judgment."[21]

Rather than the ongoing application of a heightened aesthetic sense to every moment that passes and every opportunity that conversation presents, this is rather a timely intervention, a moment requiring extra focus and energy, entirely defined by a careful reading of particulars and context. It is at once aesthetic and ethical, responding to the fine mesh of claims and counterclaims, giving voice to an imperative yet reliant upon tact, form, and timing for its successful articulation. Wilde's lexicon often stretched, or recuperated denigrated terms, when he was imagining this kind of ethical action, as for example in the strange conjunction of the terms *conscience* and *instinct* in the following passage from "The Critic as Artist," which starts out on familiar territory but then becomes more elusive: "The mere existence of

[21] Oscar Wilde, *An Ideal Husband*, in *The Importance of Being Earnest and Other Plays*, ed. Raby, 241. Subsequent page number references will be cited parenthetically in the text. For discussion of the class dimensions of Wilde's dandyism, see Alan Sinfield, *The Wilde Century: Effeminacy, Oscar Wilde, and the Queer Moment* (New York: Columbia University Press, 1994), 74–75; Richard Dellamora, *Masculine Desire: The Sexual Politics of Victorian Aestheticism* (Chapel Hill: University of North Carolina Press, 1990), 198–99; Regenia Gagnier, *Idylls of the Marketplace: Oscar Wilde and the Victorian Public* (Stanford: Stanford University Press, 1986). On the gendered aspects of Wilde's dandyism, see Rita Felski, *The Gender of Modernity* (Cambridge: Harvard University Press, 1995), 91–114.

conscience, that faculty of which people prate so much nowadays, and are so ignorantly proud, is a sign of our imperfect development. It must be merged in instinct before we become fine" (CA 360). Wilde is here insisting that conduct must not be reduced to duty; the intermediate conception here is similar to the "cultivated instinct" that defines taste and serves as the precursor to the self-conscious art of criticism (CA 395). A movement toward an art of ethics is consonant with Wilde's general conviction, which he shared with Pater, that there can be no generalities in the realm of ethics. As Lord Illingworth says in *A Woman of No Importance*, "intellectual generalities are always interesting, but generalities in morals mean absolutely nothing" (127). It is no accident that one of the two main topics that Wilde assigned himself for the future, while he was still in prison, was "the artistic life considered in its relation to conduct" (*DP* 175).

The challenge for Wilde, in the realm of ethics, was to imagine conduct in a way that did not subordinate it to rule or custom. Because he generally found it so difficult to conceive of ethics outside of conventional morality, he was prompted to the more extreme utterances of "The Critic as Artist": "The first condition of criticism is that the critic should be able to recognize that the sphere of Art and the sphere of Ethics are absolutely distinct and separate" (CA 393). "All art is immoral" (CA 380). "Aesthetics are higher than Ethics" (CA 406). When he does employ a language more suffused with moral rhetoric, as in the passage in *De Profundis* where he embraces a newfound humility, he is careful to assert a mode of action and self-scrutiny that does not make appeal to extrinsic law, and that draws on all the terms that he formerly associated more directly with aesthetics:

> Now I have realized that [humility] is in me, I see quite clearly what I ought to do; in fact, must do. And when I use such a phrase as that, I need not say that I am not alluding to any external sanction or command. I admit none. I am far more of an individualist than I ever was. Nothing seems to me of the smallest value except what one gets out of oneself. My nature is seeking a fresh mode of self-realization. That is all I am concerned with. And the first thing that I have got to do is free myself from any possible bitterness of feeling against the world. (*DP* 153)

Focusing on the society comedies, I will consider the vicissitudes of this aspect of Wilde's ethics, especially as it relates to the more prominent and ubiquitous mode of epigrammatic detachment represented by dandyism. While epigrammatic detachment allows for a persistent practice of negative critique that Wilde wanted to ally not only with criticism but with self-realization, the action of the dramas repeatedly reveals Wilde's apprehension that the very transferability of the epigram, its status as a generality, rendered it inflexible as a distinctly ethical form. In what follows I will explore the symptoms of this apprehension, and the ways in which it informs the famous tensions of the plays.

THE EPIGRAM AND THE ETHICAL MOMENT

Wilde's treatment of the relation between detachment and ethical life in the society comedies does not manifest any clear line of development, and I will not be structuring my own discussion according to strict chronology. Indeed, *Lady Windermere's Fan*, Wilde's earlier play, expresses with a kind of bold clarity the dual impulses at play in Wilde's subsequent portrayals of dandyism. In many ways, most prominently in its portrayal of a female dandy, it represents a more complex vision than either *A Woman of No Importance* or *An Ideal Husband*. For that reason, I will reserve discussion of *Lady Windermere's Fan* until after I have considered the representation of dandyism and epigrammatic detachment in the other two plays. This approach better illuminates the impasses generated by Wilde's vying impulses toward the negative critique of ironic detachment, and various versions of ethical heroism, the latter of which Wilde cannot always sufficiently distinguish from the conventional morality his epigrammatic sallies repeatedly repudiate.

A Woman of No Importance presents an interesting case, insofar as the dandy in this play attempts a timely intervention that bears some similarity to Goring's celebrated moment in *An Ideal Husband* yet fails to achieve its aim. The character of that failure discloses a particularly stark and embattled relation between the two modes of the dandy, for once Lord Illingworth fails, he entrenches himself more firmly in the mode of persistent epigrammatic detachment. The action of the play centers around Lord Illingworth's unwitting encounter with his own illegitimate son (Gerald Arbuthnot), to whom he takes a strong liking and offers the job of secretary. He shortly thereafter discovers Gerald's identity through a meeting with the boy's mother, an ex-lover whom twenty years back he had seduced, refused to marry, and eventually abandoned. The mother insists that the boy decline the job and, with the aid of a young American girl who is in love with Gerald, successfully turns the boy against the Lord and all that he represents. While the outcome of the action does not favor Illingworth, he animates the play with a torrent of Wildean epigrams, even in the midst of dramatic crises that affect him deeply.

The key dramatic and ethical tension in the play surrounds the question of whether Gerald should take the rare opportunity offered him or not. It is made clear that this is a chance of a lifetime for him, given his otherwise dim prospects as "an underpaid clerk in a small provincial bank in a third-rate English town" (128). His mother is unwavering in her conviction that he should not go with his father, though she vainly imagines that she will be able to persuade him without revealing the secret of his identity, and her own fallen past. This proves to be impossible, the secret is revealed, and the son affirms loyalty to the mother. Lord Illingworth, however, takes an entirely different view of the matter, and couches his dissent in distinctly moral terms. In his first conversation with Mrs. Arbuthnot, they clash on the question of whether their past relationship should determine Gerald's future:

MRS. ARBUTHNOT:	Do you think I would allow my son—
LORD ILLINGWORTH:	*Our* son.
MRS. ARBUTHNOT:	My son (*Lord Illingworth shrugs his shoulders*)—to go away with the man who spoiled my youth, who ruined my life, who has tainted every moment of my days? You don't realise what my past has been in suffering and in shame.
LORD ILLINGWORTH:	My dear Rachel, I must candidly say that I think Gerald's future considerably more important than your past.
MRS. ARBUTHNOT:	Gerald cannot separate his future from my past.
LORD ILLINGWORTH:	That is exactly what he should do. That is exactly what you should help him to do. What a typical woman you are! You talk sentimentally, and you are thoroughly selfish the whole time. (127–28).

Seemingly aligned with conventional morality, Mrs. Arbuthnot employs the language of stage melodrama, which simultaneously bores and provokes Lord Illingworth. Lord Illingworth wishes to free Gerald from the moral logic that Mrs. Arbuthnot employs, appealing to the superior good of unfettered self-realization even as he engages in the persistent irony that more consistently defines the Wildean dandy. Yet he fails, and the play's outcome favors the efforts of Mrs. Arbuthnot, through whose portrayal Wilde simultaneously seeks to challenge the normative view that would uniformly condemn the fallen woman and expel her from society. This normative view is represented early in the play's action by the American Hester Worsley, who is eventually moved to abandon her rigid moral stand and to acknowledge that a sexual lapse does not obliterate the possibility for goodness. She does not abandon, however, her persistent judgment against the levity and amorality flaunted by English society, most strikingly in the conversation of Lord Illingworth and the dandified Mrs. Allonby.

Both Mrs. Arbuthnot and Hester Worsley judge Lord Illingworth according to a conception of identifiable moral character; the former bases her judgment primarily on a defining past action, while the latter adduces his persistently cynical and faithless mode of social presentation and interaction. But the play does not exactly invite us to connect and equally weight these two forms of moral judgment, or the objects of their disapprobation. For Hester's moralizing reaction to the ironic epigrammatic repartee of Lord Illingworth and Mrs. Allonby is as excessive as her initial declaration that everyone must pay for their sins, without reprieve, a position she later modifies. In other words, it is not the epigrammatic mode per se that the play condemns as immoral; nor are we justified in reading the epigrammatic mode as an indication of fundamentally compromised moral character. Not only is epigrammatic repartee at the heart of the play's formal energy and forward movement, but here, as elsewhere in Wilde, the dandy is a significant and charismatic social critic, challenging moral pieties, disrupting the smooth surface of unthinking custom, inducing reflective distance and the heightened self-consciousness that it engenders.

The play does invite distinctions, however, between different uses and effects attaching to the epigrammatic mode. There is a disparity, that is, between the flirtatious ironic pas de deux between Mrs. Allonby and Lord Illingworth, calculated to set them apart from conventional social norms, and the way in which Lord Illingworth employs stinging epigrams in his encounters with his ex-lover and the mother of his son. Epigrammatic irony fulfills the aims of Wildean criticism in a relatively uncomplicated way when it is part of a general conversation between people whose own histories or opportunities have not been mutually determined to any significant degree. This is why the weightlessness of the flirtatious mode is so important to Wilde: it allows the freedom for epigrammatic circulation without immediate consequences. As *The Picture of Dorian Gray* attests, Wilde also holds a notion of seduction as sinister, surreptitious influence, especially of one personality by a powerful other; but there is a zone of freedom associated with the nonnormative interactions of flirtation and repartee. Once lives have become entangled through extended relationships that have generated expectations, obligations, or shared suffering, then the epigram becomes a freighted speech act that necessarily does more than announce the heightened postconventionality of the ironic critic.

In a reading of *A Woman of No Importance*, David Alderson argues that the realm of same-sex relations, as represented by Lord Illingworth and Gerald, shares the privileged values that Wilde assigns to art and dandiacal self-realization and is defined against the constraining shackles of normative relations, just as art and dandyism are defined against bourgeois culture. "[M]ale same-sex acts are coded as preserving the pristine intensity of the moment divorced from any moral implications. On the other hand normative prescriptions on sexuality lead to familial claims and the consequent limitations on subjective experience and racial diversity which Wilde believed this entailed."[22] Such a reading registers the appeal that less institutionally constraining relations had for Wilde, but it diminishes his own vexed and considered relation to ethical issues revolving around mutual obligation and responsibility, not to mention loyalty and devotion. Wilde was fundamentally divided on this score. This can be seen with particular clarity in *De Profundis*, where Wilde attempts to shame Douglas into recognition of his ethical failings, appealing to principles of loyalty and care, yet at the same time reveals his own sense of developed relations as constraint: "My habit—due to indifference chiefly at first—of giving up to you in everything had become insensibly a real part of my nature. Without my knowing it, it had stereotyped my temperament to one permanent and fatal mood" (*DP* 105).

In the plays, this internal division is legible as well, however much Wilde's fans may wish to discount or explain away this aspect of his work. In tense moments between people who share complicated histories, or whose lives have become deeply embedded in one another's, the epigram suddenly loses its easy portability and transferability. And the dandy can appear at once violent and ineffectual, as Lord Illingworth does when he accuses Mrs. Arbuthnot of a selfishness that typifies her sex. Lord Illingworth is angered that Mrs. Arbuthnot does not meet what he sees as the demands of the moment, which in his eyes will enable a future self-realization for Gerald, yet his efforts at persuasion are repeatedly interrupted by what now appear as epigrammatic tics, whose flights toward greater generality jar with the delicate moral situation at hand. "Discontent is the first step in the progress of a man or a nation." "Children begin by loving their parents. After a time they judge them. Rarely, if ever, do they forgive them" (128). And in the second scene between him and Mrs. Arbuthnot, he is driven to even sharper attacks, especially when Mrs. Arbuthnot refuses his explicitly strategic offer

---

[22] Alderson, "Momentary Pleasures," 54.

of marriage: "I suppose [your reasons are] intensely sentimental. . . . You women live by your emotions and for them. You have no philosophy of life" (155).

The shifting weight and force of the epigrammatic mode, from an artful critical irony in the service of social criticism to forms of sadism or indifference toward the distinct feelings, individuality, and personal histories of others, contributes to the wild swings from irony to melodrama. Through the heavy hand of melodrama, and most prominently through the plaint of beleaguered virtue, the plays awkwardly assert the ethical limits of an epigrammatic style that cannot sufficiently recognize and respond to suffering. Inconsistent in his attitudes toward human suffering, which he saw variously as both expressive and repressive of individuality, Wilde does not subject his thought to any rigorous self-examination on this score; it remains at the level of formal symptom. But the crucial thing to realize is that the moral reaction to certain excesses of ironic detachment is itself consonant with Wilde's insistence on the relativity of ethics, even if the predictability of the melodramatic form seems to reproduce the same failure to move beyond generality that the epigrams display. It is because these moments seem so utterly lacking in taste and aesthetic refinement that they cause reactions among readers who would like fundamentally to discount them, insofar as they think that something like an aesthetic taste or refined irony must govern any ethical view Wilde might espouse.

It is thus true that Mrs. Arbuthnot, Hester, and Gerald are still locked in traditional moral categories in their reaction to Lord Illingworth. If Lord Illingworth falls short of the challenge presented by the situation and reverts to epigrammatic maneuvers of attack and disengagement, then the other principal characters fail to provide an alternative that in any way supersedes the mode of overgeneralization. There is no transvaluation of values in this play, in other words. Feminine virtue is erected as a ground, and masculine detachment is aligned with old-fashioned villainy. *A Woman of No Importance* thus represents in a particularly legible way how melodrama both signals and fails sufficiently to resolve the tension between the aesthetic mode of the dandy—aligned with irony, criticism, and self-consciousness—and a thwarted ethical impulse. But this impasse also carries with it the revelation that ironic detachment and unfettered self-realization are always situated. If the melodramatic scenes represent an overly compensatory notion of constraint or fate, the ironic dialogue of the dandified figures lights up the fact that Wilde must work to create contexts in which the repartee can appear weightless.

An Ideal Husband and *Lady Windermere's Fan* significantly modify, even if they do not fully abandon, the Wildean opposition between melodrama and irony, and they do so precisely through the staging of successful instances of seizing the moment, or what we might call heroic dandyism. In these plays, characters who tend toward an idealized conception of virtue, and a stark notion of good and bad character, come to learn that the world is more mixed than they had imagined. But unlike Hester Worsley, who comes to a similar realization through the example of Mrs. Arbuthnot's noble suffering, the characters in these plays are schooled by the example of the dandy in a moment of critical intervention.

I have already made brief mention of Lord Goring's intervention in *An Ideal Husband*, a moment whose significance is announced through the stentorian stage direction that is meant to highlight the entire passage for us. It is worthwhile to look a little more closely at this passage to see precisely what philosophy Wilde means to ascribe to this privileged dandy, who, to quote another loud stage direction, "stands in immediate relation to modern life, makes it indeed, and so masters it" (212). When Lord Goring delivers his speech to Lady Chiltern, the crisis of blackmail, exposure, and ruin has just been averted, largely through the stratagems of Goring himself, who has managed a successful act of counterblackmail against Mrs. Cheveley. Lady Chiltern, originally devastated by the knowledge of her idealized husband's tainted past, has come to forgive him, though she feels that resignation from public life is morally obligatory. It is this attempt to force Lord Chiltern to withdraw from the world, his head bowed by the sense of the justness of exile, that provokes Lord Goring to redraw Lady Chiltern's ethical universe:

> Now is the moment when you really want my help, now is the time when you have got to trust me, to trust in my counsel and judgement. You love Robert. Do you want to kill his love for you? What sort of existence will he have if you rob him of the fruits of his ambition, if you take him from the splendour of a great political career, if you close the doors of public life against him, if you condemn him to sterile failure, he who was made for triumph and success? Women are not meant to judge us, but to forgive us when we need forgiveness. Pardon, not punishment, is their mission. Why should you scourge him with rods for a sin done in his youth, before he knew you, before he knew himself? A man's life is of more value than a woman's. It has larger issues, wider scope, greater ambitions. A woman's life revolves in curves of emotions. It is upon lines of intellect that a man's

life progresses. Don't make any terrible mistake, Lady Chiltern. A woman who can keep a man's love, and love him in return, has done all the world wants of women, or should want of them. (241–42)

When Lady Chiltern continues to protest, saying that Robert himself feels retirement from public life is his duty, Goring claims that he is only trying to please her and save the marriage, continuing,

If he has fallen from his altar, do not thrust him into the mire. Failure to Robert would be the very mire of shame. Power is his passion. He would lose everything, even his power to feel love. Your husband's life is at this moment in your hands, your husband's love is in your hands. Don't mar both for him. (242)

The form of heroism called for here is one in which Lady Chiltern would entirely subordinate her principles, needs, and desires to those of her husband. Lord Goring does not imagine her as capable of the kind of self-realization that he accords to Lord Chiltern, though he does imagine her as capable of understanding and supporting that form of self-realization. The demarcation of separate spheres here is undeniable, as is the reliance on women to underwrite and stabilize the moral vicissitudes of masculine public life. But what also appears is a transvaluation of values in the case of the masculine sphere. Replacing the moral terms of purity and fallenness (which in this case had been applied too starkly to Lord Chiltern) are the terms power and passion. While Chiltern sees himself as publically representing principle and integrity, he also has a deeply pragmatic approach to the gaining and wielding of power in a corrupt world. When Goring asks Chiltern earlier in the play whether he has any regrets for his past action, the selling of a state secret to Baron Arnheim so that he could secure the fortune necessary to his own political rise, Chiltern replies, "No, I felt that I had fought the century with its own weapons, and won" (194). Goring replies that he feels sorry for Chiltern, but this ambiguous response is consonant with the notion that Chiltern has had to engage in necessary evils in order to better the world that demanded the compromised behavior from him in the first place. In order to accommodate such worldliness, Lady Chiltern is not asked to serve as a beacon of suffering virtue, in the manner of Lady Arbuthnot, but rather to bring a form of expansive moral judgment to supplement her limited nature, with its defining curves of emotion.

The demarcation of a properly pragmatic practice of making and mastering modern life is articulated by contrast to the forms of life that are assigned to the women: for most of the play, Lady Chiltern represents a conventional moral order, along with its deluded and constricting idealism, and Mrs. Cheveley represents unprincipled villainy. There is a question, in light of this gender atavism, whether the play itself stands in a sufficiently immediate relation to modern life. In a conversation with Mrs. Cheveley, Lord Goring tries to convince her that Lord Chiltern's isolated youthful transgression does not give sufficient indication of who he really is.

> MRS. CHEVELEY: ...You seem to forget that I know his real character.
> LORD GORING: What you know about him is not his real character. It was an act of folly done in his youth, dishonourable, I admit, shameful, I admit, unworthy of him, I admit, and therefore ... not his true character. (225–26)

Goring here seems to appeal to traditional moral categories in speaking of Chiltern's past action and of his character. How do we square this with the transvaluation of values, the more profoundly pragmatic stance, that seems to animate his final speeches to Lady Chiltern and even his muted response to Lord Chiltern's claim that he does not regret his past action? I would contend that here, facing the villainness Lady Cheveley, who is drawn according to a model of true, essential, underlying character, Goring is himself suddenly speaking in the terms that govern Wilde's delineation of her, and her delineation of Lord Chiltern. That is, Wilde is truly entangled by his own atavism—given the reliance on villainy in the portrayal of Chiltern's persecutor, Wilde is constrained to appeal to underlying virtue in this scene. An appeal to pragmatism would threaten the very ground upon which Mrs. Cheveley stands condemned and Chiltern remains protected.[23]

Drawn according to a model of essential character, Mrs. Cheveley is thus a character who can be, and who is, unmasked. When Goring confronts her with his own knowledge of one of her prior crimes, effectively thwarting her plan of blackmail, she reveals herself. Once again, Wilde reverts to explicit stage directions in order to drive home his point: we are told that Mrs Cheveley *"is now in an agony of physical terror. Her face is distorted. Her mouth awry. A mask has fallen from her. She is, for the moment, dreadful to*

---

[23] Though he speaks predominantly in the ironic mode, Goring intermittently speaks in morally resonant terms throughout the play, most notably in his conversation with Lord Chiltern about Mrs. Cheveley's act of blackmail and also in his direct excoriation of Mrs. Cheveley. While these moments often carry with them a certain ambiguity (in this case, via the ellipsis before the phrase "not his true character"), they also typically support the moralism that insists on a key distinction between Mrs. Cheveley's ruthless self-interest and the appropriately chastened pragmatism of Lord Chiltern.

look at" (228). Mrs. Cheveley does not belong to the modern universe, pro-pounded by Wilde as much as anyone, in which there is nothing behind the masks, and where artificiality and fiction are genuine modes of self-realiza-tion. Her self-presentation to the world covers an essentially malicious na-ture, intent upon securing its own gain at whatever cost to others.

Goring of course generates epigrams in his moment of heroic intervention in the name of pragmatic worldliness, and I would like to conclude my dis-cussion of this play by considering the role that these epigrams play, and how their function contrasts with the use of epigrams in Lord Illingworth's ineffectual reactions to his own compromised past actions. Although Goring makes appeal to a pragmatic understanding of power that moves beyond Lord Illingworth's arrested appeal to self-realization, his delineation of gen-der relations reverts to the same type of generality that marked Lord Illing-worth's epigrammatic responses to Mrs. Arbuthnot, although he implores rather than excoriates his interlocutor. *An Ideal Husband*'s move to a prag-matic understanding of power, and the refusal of purism in the conception of action for good in the world, is thus promoted alongside and by means of a traditional conception of female subordination, adapted to underwrite its pragmatically inflected ethics. Rather than serving as a symbol of moral pu-rity protected from the compromises of worldly power, an angel in the house who will serve as inspiration and influence for masculine subjects who must resignedly perform in the tainted public sphere, the woman is called upon to act as knowing supporter of that behavior. Lady Chiltern took her princi-ples too seriously and attempted to impose her ideals upon her husband; she must accept the fallen world and its mixed nature, forgive and support her husband. She conforms to this duty, and simultaneously reveals her own inability to accede to the level of the self-conscious dandy, by simply repeat-ing verbatim the words about a woman's place that Goring has just said to her. Unlike the epigrammatic duets in which dandified men and women exchange aphorisms, or complete them for one another ("Mrs. Allonby: Moods don't last. Lord Illingworth: It is their chief charm" [109]), the final scene in *An Ideal Husband* presents a woman who simply repeats a cate-chism, dictated to her. As in the unmasking scene with Mrs. Cheveley, Gor-ing uses the forms of the very conventional morality he ostensibly seeks to combat in order to secure the acquiescence of a female character. Still, the philosophy of masculine action in the world moves beyond the simply nega-tive stance of paradox and irony that has otherwise defined the dandy in Wilde.

By way of conclusion, I return to Wilde's earlier play, *Lady Windermere's Fan*, which more fully compresses Wilde's ambivalence toward detachment by creating an anomalous hybrid in the character of Mrs. Erlynne, a dandi-fied fallen woman who performs a heroic act which on one level presents itself as the simple action of putting "manners before morals." In no other play will the relation between gender and dandyism be more complicated, or more fully challenged. At the beginning of the play, in the exchanges between Lady Windermere and Lord Darlington, Lady Windermere repre-sents conventional moral judgment and Lord Darlington represents the ironic stance of the dandy, who very clearly replaces moral categories with aesthetic ones: "It is absurd to divide people into good and bad," he tells Lady Windermere. "People are either charming or tedious" (10). By the end of the play, this opposition will be displaced. The naïve and idealistic Lady Windermere will have learned that the world is mixed morally, a lesson she will attempt to teach her husband, who reverts to classing women as pure and impure. And the position of Lord Darlington will have been eclipsed by the force of Mrs. Erlynne's character, a fallen woman who combines the several modes of the dandy: epigrammatic irony, pragmatic transvaluation, and heroic intervention.

Mrs. Erlynne first appears as a dandified woman who puts her own social standing above all, who is pragmatically using the little power she has in order to gain entrance into the kind of society from which, as a fallen woman, she has for so long been exiled. The play invites a mixed judgment in its initial presentation of her. Before she appears, reasons are suggested why one should not view her social and personal aspirations negatively. Indeed, Lord Windermere's support, falsely assumed by those in his circle to be-speak an illicit interest in the woman, is shown to be prompted by sympathy toward her desire to reintegrate. Although his sympathy is of course at least partly motivated by his knowledge that she is his wife's (unknown) mother, Lord Windermere speaks of Mrs. Erlynne's past in the same capacious way that Lord Goring speaks of Lord Chiltern's youthful error. And, as in the case of *An Ideal Husband*, it is the personal connection and inside knowl-edge that prompts the wider view, that thwarts the easy act of moral judg-ment, on the one hand, and the ironic distance, on the other.

When we first meet Mrs. Erlynne, she speaks in the voice of the Wildean dandy, demystifying the pretenses of those around her, approaching her own project of reintegration not with humility but with élan. Indeed, her behavior seems not to comport with the expectations set up by Lord Win-dermere's previous defense of her to his wife, suggesting that she may have adopted a false attitude of atonement or humility with him in order to secure his support. And she displays an oddly detached indifference toward seeing her lost daughter when she enters the party. Her behavior thus seems to place her within the morally bracketed world of dandyism, where she along with Lord Darlington performs an ongoing act of ironic critique in the manner of a Lord Goring or a Lord Illingworth. But the prospect of her own daughter's incipient fall, a fall prompted by the seductions of Darlington, causes her to falter and reveal another side: "What can I do? What can I do? I feel a passion awakening within me that I never felt before. What can it mean? The daughter must not be like the mother—that would be terrible. How can I save her? How can I save my child? A moment may ruin a life. Who knows that better than I?" (34).

It is as though Lord Illingworth and Mrs. Arbuthnot are mixed in a single character. Mrs. Erlynne shows great feeling for her child, and acute pain at the prospect of her disgrace, yet at the same time she only partly capitulates to the rhetoric of fallenness as it is traditionally conceived: "You—why, you are a mere girl, you would be lost. You haven't got the kind of brains that enables a woman to get back" (40). Or, upon seeing a picture of herself in girlhood: "Ah yes, I remember. How long ago that seems. It was done before I was married. Dark hair and an innocent expression were the fashion then" (53). The callous irony displayed in these statements does not guide her actions, however. To shield Lady Windermere, Mrs. Erlynne compromises her own reputation further by allowing suspicion to fall upon her instead of her daughter and then decides not to reveal her true identity, a decision that draws admiration from Lord Windermere. She thus displays the ethical finesse of the dandy and enacts the pragmatic use of power that Goring both draws upon and defends in his speech to Lady Chiltern.

Wilde displays profound ambivalence in his portrayal of Mrs. Erlynne: he cannot fully allow this feminine figure to transcend the shackles of fallenness; the capacity to denaturalize and ironize meets its limit in maternal feeling and feminine fallenness. Stage directions invite us to infer that Mrs. Erlynne is herself wearing a mask of ironic detachment, a mask that covers over great pain. In her final visit to her daughter, when Lord Windermere asks her challengingly how she could dare to come, Mrs. Erlynne's response is accompanied by the following direction: *In her accents as she talks there is a note of deep tragedy. For a moment she reveals herself* (53). In Goring's great moment of intervention, he is not revealing a deep self that has been otherwise covered over by the act of the dandy; he is instead the *consummate* dandy, one who can artfully finesse a complicated ethical situation. Mrs. Erlynne is herself shown to be capable of such artful enactment, though it issues out of struggle, with a structure of repression suggested— hence the appearance of a split in her character. This is close to the Wilde of *De Profundis* and reflects the tension between the sense of constrained selfhood and the impulse to free self-actualization that animates many of Wilde's doctrines. What underlies the dandy, in other words, may not be so much Goring's "philosophy" as Mrs. Erylnne's haunting sense of tragic determination, and the heroic irony that seeks to face it down. The end of *Lady Windermere's Fan* indicates as much, insofar as Mrs. Erlynne's morally weighty exit, and expressed intention to undergo self-imposed exile outside of England, is suddenly offset by Lord Augustus's revelation, in a description of a subsequent scene that Wilde places offstage, that Mrs. Erlynne has fully explained her behavior of the previous night and has consented to marry him. The implication here is that Mrs. Erlynne will not languish in exile, and that she has no intention of relinquishing the passionate pursuit of power in a fully public arena.

Widely seen as a great celebrant of irony and epigrammatic wit, Wilde grapples throughout the society comedies with what he apprehends as the ethical limits of detachment. In their strained formal tensions, Wilde's dramas register a half-lit awareness that epigrammatic irony, while dependent upon the situated, conventional claims of social actors in order to perform its reversals and assert its paradoxes, remains in large part a purely negative and reactive practice. It aids in the project of heightened self-consciousness, social critique, and artfully subversive living, yet it lacks a positive normative dimension that can sufficiently respond to the specific needs of others, or genuinely travel beyond good and evil. Wilde responds to this lack in two ways: first, and most conservatively, by reasserting conventional virtue, often in the guise of a feminine purity that is not susceptible to the forms of detachment that define the (male) dandy; second, and more radically, by a transvaluation of values in the name of power, passion, and ethical finesse. In *An Ideal Husband*, this potentially vertiginous transvaluation appears only to yoke its fortunes to a subordinated femininity that will somehow provide it with necessary emotional support. In *Lady Windermere's Fan*, which is the most complicated of Wilde's plays with respect to these issues, a single woman character is allowed to house the dual impulse toward a pragmatically heroic dandyism and a traditional morality based on the maternal impulse to protect. While from one perspective she may thus appear as a character marred by incoherence, or as a rather more compressed instance of a tension usually distributed between characters, from another perspective her intrasubjective duality allows for a potent insistence on the relativity of ethics.

When they hear from Lord Augustus at the end of the play's action that Mrs. Erlynne has fully explained herself and engaged herself to marry him, Lord Windermere remarks that she is clever, and Lady Windermere remarks that she is good. Neither claim captures Mrs. Erylnne. Lord Windermere is appalled at what he takes to be her immorality; his assumption is that all her actions can be explained as forms of self-interested manipulation. When she announces that she is going into exile, then, she is performing a part to impress Lord and Lady Windermere; as soon as she walks out the door, she adapts her performance so as to secure her marriage to Lord Augustus. But Lord Windermere's view of Mrs. Erlynne is based on the assumption that her tragic regret over her own lapse should provide the bass note of all her actions, that she is immoral whenever she imagines a context for action that is free of that haunting determination. By contrast, Wilde suggests that general principles, whether they express or deconstruct traditional morality, gain half their meaning from the concrete context in which they are situated. Lord Illingworth's epigrams become something other than general social critique when they are aimed at his ex-lover, but this does not taint their uses in other, less freighted contexts. Likewise, Mrs. Erlynne is moved by her daughter's danger, moved even to compromise herself, but this does not mean that she will wear sackcloth the rest of her days. Indeed, Wilde's attempt to curtail Mrs. Erlynne's freedom by showing her as constrained by her past and her maternity is offset by his refusal to make this constraint definitive of all her action, present and future. Interestingly, Wilde's earlier version of this play, which opened to somewhat bewildered audiences, kept Mrs. Erlynne's identity as the mother of Lady Windermere hidden until the close of Act IV, thereby formally thwarting the notion that a fallen woman is irrevocably defined by a past that remains legible through any situation or context that the present or future offers.[24] Under considerable pressure, Wilde revised it. The history of this play's versions is a parable: it shows how fully the pressure of disavowed constraint, or the dream of detachment, "underlies" the dandy.

The gendered pattern of this disavowal should not be unfamiliar, both within this study and as a more general finding within criticism of modern literature. There is a developed line of feminist criticism arguing that the freedom and self-consciousness of the aesthete is often constructed as a privilege of gender and also, typically, of class. For example, Rita Felski argues in *The Gender of Modernity* that women are frequently defined as lacking the self-reflexivity that defines the modern male aesthetic subject.[25] This

[24] See Joseph Bristow, "Dowdies and Dandies: Oscar Wilde's Refashioning of Society Comedy," *Modern Drama* 37 (1994): 53–70.

[25] See Felski, *The Gender of Modernity*. A similar argument about the emergence of modernism in France appears in Charles Bernheimer, *Figures of Ill-Repute: Representing Prostitution in Nineteenth-Century France* (Cambridge: Harvard University Press, 1989).

feminist argument by no means promotes a celebration of aestheticism, but rather questions those economies that structure the valorization of modernist aesthetic freedom. The example of *Lady Windermere's Fan* shows an ambivalence and even hesitancy written into that very gesture, disclosing yet another facet of Wilde's complex and fraught relation to the detachment he is often assumed to practice with such insouciance. It is the specific character of his engagement with this problem that this chapter has sought to reconstruct, focusing especially on the ways in which Wilde himself apprehends the limits of irony's portability. Those studies that too easily celebrate or critique Wilde's relation to detachment obscure the potential legacy of his contribution to this distinctive debate of Victorian modernity.

Ironic Outcomes

Wilde's own flamboyant practices of detachment have received significant attention among queer and postmodern critics precisely because, as I have remarked previously, the mode of irony is not currently subjected to the critique of detachment that has been waged against Enlightenment reason. Indeed, there is a tendency among postmodern critics to valorize detachment only if it is fully ironized or otherwise defined against reflective reason. As I argued in the introduction to this study, the embrace of irony paradoxically exists alongside a disparagement of critical reason as the disavowal of situatedness, embodiedness, and particularity. Here is where I think we can learn something from Wilde's own vexed relation to the cultivation of a specifically ironic detachment. It is not the form of irony itself that is good or bad: detachment, whatever form it takes or predominantly allies itself with, is always situated—it is always a detachment from a particular mode of experience, a social situation, or a form of identity.

The arc of Judith Butler's thinking on this topic is illuminating here. Her book *Gender Trouble*, published in 1990, argued that parodic relations to social identity performed the crucial work of exposing and destabilizing normative conventions, thereby forwarding the larger desirable project of reimagining and pluralizing our conceptions of gendered identity. This powerful book, which had a profound influence on contemporary theory and criticism, thus made an argument about the general efficacy of deconstructive, ironic, and parodic ways of relating to established social forms. This general argument, however, was subsequently revised by Butler. Partly in response to critics who claimed that Butler did not take the situatedness of all ironic practices fully enough into account, Butler reformulated her position in *Bodies That Matter*, particularly through her reading of *Paris Is*

Burning, where she insisted on drag's dual capacity both to subvert and renaturalize: "I want to underscore that there is no necessary relation between drag and subversion, and that drag may well be used in the service of both the denaturalization and reidealization of hyberbolic heterosexual norms."[26]

Yet such admissions tend to be accompanied, both in Butler and elsewhere, by a residual belief in deconstruction's special powers to subvert the normative, and by a valorization of the negative modes of irony and parody above critical reason and philosophy, which are in turn subjected to vehement forms of denigration. This is a misleading and unproductive tendency. To get beyond some of the most recalcitrant impasses in contemporary debate, particularly those between postmodernism and critical theory, we need to recognize that the valorized form of ironic detachment in queer and postmodern theory is ultimately continuous with—and hence should not be opposed to—the postconventional critical reflection appealed to as the basis for critical social theory. It involves the same cultivated distance from conventions, norms, and habits that characterizes critical reason. And it typically involves similar utopian or universalist aspirations, however encrypted or explicitly disavowed.

Wilde's own dual conception of criticism as reflective distance and radical freedom houses both these forms of detachment and reveals the impulse toward radical detachment that a critical perspective on conventional life often produces. A critical pluralism of the type I discussed in the introduction capaciously recognizes the potency of both forms of detachment, while refusing to insist that one form be schooled by the other.

[26] Judith Butler, *Bodies That Matter: On the Discursive Limits of "Sex"* (New York: Routledge, 1993), 125.

The Character of Theory

The reading of Oscar Wilde's society comedies that I have offered draws attention to a common structure in the literature of detachment, whereby the freedom of the aesthete or the self-making hero is defined against forms of unfreedom assigned to less privileged figures: the atavism or constraint associated with specific races and religions or the inability of particular social actors to transcend or transform their assigned social scripts. Wilde's works both reflect and resist this structure, as is most dramatically evident in the portrayal of Mrs. Erlynne in *Lady Windermere's Fan*. The critique of detachment within contemporary theory typically isolates the moments of negative definition and misses such internal divisions, insisting that forms of exclusion and violence necessarily attend the valorization of critical reason or the distanced view. Throughout the study, I have drawn out moments of exclusion or invidious distinction when they occur, as should be evident not only in the chapter on Wilde but also in my readings of Eliot's treatment of the transgressive Jewess, Dickens's portrayal of pathologized worldly figures, or Arnold's representation of Celtism. But my overriding goal has been to redirect our approach to the question of detachment by giving a fuller picture of the various aspirations and ambivalences that motivate Victorian ideals of critical distance, and by reconstructing the multiple forms through which these ideals were expressed. The current critique of detachment, which identifies and dismisses appeals to such practices as disinterestedness and objectivity, too swiftly delivers its verdict with respect to this complicated human aspiration and fails sufficiently to recognize its own debt to the tradition of detached critique.

By contrast, my argument is in the service of a larger defense of the critical, dialogical, and even emancipatory potential of cultivated detachment— a potential that can be expressed in aesthetic modes like irony and parody as well as through the more serious mode of critical social theory. Attempts to pit such forms against one another have obscured our ability to construct a genealogy of detachment and have produced regrettable internal divisions among those who share progressive goals. Thus it is important not simply to criticize the postmodern tendency to elevate irony over reflective reason— as I do in the previous chapter—but also to fault critical theory for trying to defend against and even sometimes denigrate ironic and aesthetic modes of detachment. Only a more capacious understanding of critique, one that includes ironic, aesthetic, and more elusive forms of detachment, will be able to acknowledge the force of Brontë's vertiginous phenomenology, Dickens's critical cosmopolitanism, or the radical stance of Eliot's Alcharisi.

Beyond that, I have tried to recreate the cultivation of detachment as a structure of feeling, as a lived relation to what were in many ways conceived as estranging, impersonal practices. I have done so in large measure because the Victorians themselves seemed intent upon imagining forms of detachment as intimately connected to the moral project of self-cultivation. Such attempts to bring impersonal practices—such as science, reason, disinterestedness, or systemic critique—within the orbit of the personal are evident in the Arnoldian ideal of perfection, Mill's ideal of benevolent spectatorship, or the reflective dialogism of Eliot's Deronda. There are also negative versions of the characterology of detachment within Victorian culture. Arnold is critical of the moral consequences of persistent irony, as is Eliot, who also opposes certain forms of scientific abstraction, especially as applied to social life. Dickens is haunted by the possibility that a systemic awareness of power relations will breed pathologies of bitterness, resentment, and pride—that awareness of power is always necessarily a form of wariness that vitiates the needful myopia of innocence, duty, and vocations of appropriately limited scope. In many ways, this particular Victorian cultural formation—which yokes the impersonal to the personal—may sound foreign to contemporary critical approaches, where "character" is a seeming anachronism and where the negative consequences of detachment are often conceived in transpersonal terms: as effects of power that exclude others or thwart sociality, rather than as practices that might advance or harm one's moral standing. Yet it would be wrong to say that the impulse or tendency to imagine an ideal subjectivity in terms of its cultivated relations to impersonal stances has passed away. The new cosmopolitanisms are perhaps the most striking example, especially insofar as they conceive, in both an echo and a refinement of Arnold, a universalism modified by tact, phronesis, and cultivated stances. But theories of performativity, as discordant as they may sound in relation to a project of disinterestedness, in keys ways simply reverse the values of Victorian ambivalence, as did modernists and late Victorians like Oscar Wilde. In such theories it is the previously denigrated modes of irony and radical disaffiliation that constitute the privileged forms of detachment, while formerly prestigious ideals—disinterestedness, scientific objectivity, reason—find themselves discredited. While advocates of parodic performativity would certainly not see themselves as cultivating character, it is nonetheless the case that they, like the Victorian writers I have been discussing, conceive the practice of detachment as an attempt to enact and own the impersonal.

Part of the project of imagining detachment not only as method but also as ethos involves moving beyond a restrictively individualized notion of cultivated distance. In both the Victorian and contemporary contexts, the emphasis on individual enactment serves to breathe life into what may seem lifeless and inhuman ideals, divorced from embodied existence and the dense particularities of any given situation. The attempt to embody subjective detachment within narrative or formal practices is evident in very different forms across the writers I have analyzed—from the phenomenological method of Brontë's first-person narration to the dramatization of heroic dandyism in Wilde. A similar movement appears within the horizon of contemporary theory: parodic performativity's emphasis on enactment is explicitly promoted as an alternative to more mechanistic or deterministic understandings of social constructionism; cosmopolitanism is an attempt to both particularize and pluralize the practice of universalism; Foucault's practices of the self are embraced by critics frustrated by his own earlier emphases on the monolithic nature of modern disciplinary power. Yet this move toward a more fluid and situated understanding of the individual's relation to impersonal modes and forces has at times precluded a fuller conception of detachment as a dialogical or collective ideal. Among the writers I examine here, George Eliot can be singled out for her well-developed conception of the ethical and political potentialities of cosmopolitan detachment, and for her studied, if incomplete, attempt to enfold the principles of intercultural dialogue and deliberative democracy into her project of nation-building. Many of the more politically minded of the new cosmopolitanisms, as well as the ongoing refinements of critical theory and discourse ethics, aim to combine the ethical insights and characterological dimensions of cultivated detachment with the aspirations of deliberative democracy and internationalist politics.[1] It is these projects that currently seek to make good on the promise of modernity that the Victorians apprehended, and rightfully so, with such mixed feelings.

[1] I particularly have in mind here Bruce Robbins, *Feeling Global: Internationalism in Distress* (New York: New York University Press, 1999); Pheng Cheah and Bruce Robbins, eds., *Cosmopolitics: Thinking and Feeling Beyond the Nation* (Minneapolis: University of Minnesota Press, 1998); Seyla Benhabib, *Situating the Self: Gender, Community, and Postmodernism in Contemporary Politics* (New York: Routledge, 1992); Seyla Benhabib, ed., *Democracy and Difference: Contesting the Boundaries of the Political* (Princeton: Princeton University Press, 1996).

As I stated at the outset, the primary goal of this study has been both to pluralize and to defend the ideal of cultivated distance, and thereby to defend much of the modern project. But as I hope is clear from the forms of argument manifest in each chapter, this does not mean relinquishing judgment. The limitation of many critiques of detachment lies in their rush to judgment, and in their reductive understandings of the claims of critical reflection. An alternative project, one to which this book hopes to contribute, would seek to give fuller characterization to modern practices of detachment—their concrete aims, forms, and effects—all of which remain, in a fundamental sense, open to debate. For if no one single form or mode of detachment can be held up as inherently violent or exclusionary, neither can any single form or mode of detachment be held up as uniformly or exclusively progressive. Yet there is always at least a progressive potentiality in the very commitment to ongoing self-reflexivity expressed by the most rigorous ideals of postconventional critique. The cultivation of detachment—which in some sense is only another name for the examined life—is always an ongoing, partial project, whose interrelated ethical and epistemological dimensions ideally promote the reflexive interrogation of its own practices and thereby further the possibility for individual and collective self-determination.

❖ Bibliography ❖

Abraham, Gary A. *Max Weber and the Jewish Question: A Study of the Social Outlook of His Sociology.* Urbana: University of Illinois Press, 1992.

Adams, James Eli. *Dandies and Desert Saints: Styles of Victorian Manhood.* Ithaca: Cornell University Press, 1995.

Alcoff, Linda, and Elizabeth Potter, eds. *Feminist Epistemologies.* New York: Routledge, 1993.

Alderson, David. "Momentary Pleasures: Wilde and English Virtue." *Sex, Nation, and Dissent in Irish Writing.* Edited by Eibhear Walshe. New York: St. Martin's Press, 1997. 43–59.

Anderson, Amanda. "Cosmopolitanism, Universalism, and the Divided Legacies of Modernity." In *Cosmopolitics: Thinking and Feeling beyond the Nation.* Edited by Pheng Cheah and Bruce Robbins. Minneapolis: University of Minnesota Press, 1998. 265–89.

———. "Debatable Performances: Restaging Contentious Feminisms." *Social Text* 54 (1998): 1–24.

———. *Tainted Souls and Painted Faces: The Rhetoric of Fallenness in Victorian Culture.* Ithaca: Cornell University Press, 1993.

———. "The Temptations of Aggrandized Agency: Feminist Histories and the Horizon of Modernity." *Victorian Studies* 43 (2000): 43–65.

Antony, Louise M., and Charlotte Witt. *A Mind of One's Own: Feminist Essays on Reason and Objectivity.* Boulder: Westview Press, 1993.

Armstrong, Nancy. *Desire and Domestic Fiction: A Political History of the Novel.* New York: Oxford University Press, 1987.

Arnold, Matthew. *The Complete Prose Works of Matthew Arnold.* Edited by R. H. Super. 11 vols. Ann Arbor: University of Michigan Press, 1960–1977.

———. *Culture and Anarchy.* In *The Complete Prose Works of Matthew Arnold.* Vol. 5: *Culture and Anarchy with Friendship's Garland and Some Literary Essays.* Edited by R. H. Super.

———. "Democracy." In *Culture and Anarchy and Other Writings.* Edited by Stefan Collini. Cambridge: Cambridge University Press, 1993. 1–25.

———. "A French Critic on Milton." In *The Complete Prose Works of Matthew Arnold.* Vol. 8: *Essays Religious and Mixed.* Edited by R. H. Super. 1972. 165–87.

———. "The Function of Criticism at the Present Time." In *The Complete Prose Works of Matthew Arnold.* Vol. 3: *Lectures and Essays in Criticism.* Edited by R. H. Super. 1962. 258–85.

———. "Heinrich Heine." In *The Complete Prose Works of Matthew*

Arnold. Vol. 3: *Lectures and Essays in Criticism*. Edited by R. H. Super. 1962. 107–32.

Arnold, Matthew. "Literature and Science." In *The Complete Prose Works of Matthew Arnold*. Vol. 10: *Philistinism in England and America*. Edited by R. H. Super. 1974. 53–73.

———. "Marcus Aurelius." In *The Complete Prose Works of Matthew Arnold*. Vol. 3: *Lectures and Essays in Criticism*. Edited by R. H. Super. 1962. 133–57.

———. "Numbers; or The Majority and the Remnant." In *The Complete Prose Works of Matthew Arnold*. Vol. 10: *Philistinism in England and America*. Edited by R. H. Super. 1974. 143–64.

———. "On the Modern Element in Literature." In *The Complete Prose Works of Matthew Arnold*. Vol. 1: *On the Classical Tradition*. Edited by R. H. Super. 1960. 18–37.

———. *On the Study of Celtic Literature*. In *The Complete Prose Works of Matthew Arnold*. Vol. 3: *Lectures and Essays in Criticism*. Edited by R. H. Super. 1962. 291–398.

———. "Preface to the First Edition of Poems." In *The Complete Prose Works of Matthew Arnold*. Vol. 1: *On the Classical Tradition*. Edited by R. H. Super. 1960. 1–18.

———. "Spinoza and the Bible." In *The Complete Prose Works of Matthew Arnold*. Vol. 3: *Lectures and Essays in Criticism*. Edited by R. H. Super. 1962. 158–82.

Auerbach, Nina. *Communities of Women: An Idea in Fiction*. Cambridge: Harvard University Press, 1978.

Baker, William. *George Eliot and Judaism*. Salzburg: Institut für Englishe Sprach und Literatur, 1975.

Benhabib, Seyla. "Feminism and Postmodernism." In Seyla Benhabib et al., *Feminist Contentions: A Philosophical Exchange*. With an introduction by Linda Nicholson. New York: Routledge, 1995. 17–34.

———. *Situating the Self: Gender, Community, and Postmodernism in Contemporary Politics*. New York: Routledge, 1992.

Benhabib, Seyla, ed. *Democracy and Difference: Contesting the Boundaries of the Political*. Princeton: Princeton University Press, 1996.

Bernheimer, Charles. *Figures of Ill-Repute: Representing Prostitution in Nineteenth-Century France*. Cambridge: Harvard University Press, 1989.

Boone, Joseph Allan. *Libidinal Currents: Sexuality and the Shaping of Modernism*. Chicago: University of Chicago Press, 1998.

Booth, Alison. *Greatness Engendered: George Eliot and Virginia Woolf*. Ithaca: Cornell University Press, 1992.

Bourdieu, Pierre. *Pascalian Meditations*. Translated by Richard Nice. Stanford: Stanford University Press, 2000.

Bordo, Susan. *The Flight to Objectivity: Essays on Cartesianism and Culture*. Albany: State University of New York Press, 1987.

Boyarin, Daniel. "Épater L' embourgeoisement: Freud, Gender, and the (De)Colonized Psyche." *Diacritics* 24 (1994): 17–41.

Boyarin, Daniel, and Jonathan Boyarin. "Diaspora: Generation and the Ground of Jewish Identity." *Critical Inquiry* 19 (1993): 693–725.

Brantlinger, Patrick. "Nations and Novels: Disraeli, George Eliot, and Orientalism." *Victorian Studies* 35 (1992): 255–75.

Brennan, Tim. *At Home in the World: Cosmopolitanism Now*. Cambridge: Harvard University Press, 1997.

Bristow, Joseph. "Dowdies and Dandies: Oscar Wilde's Refashioning of Society Comedy." *Modern Drama* 37 (1994): 53–70.

Brody, Jennifer. *Impossible Purities: Blackness, Femininity, and Victorian Culture*. Durham: Duke University Press, 1998.

Bromwich, David. "The Genealogy of Disinterestedness." *Raritan* 1 (1982): 62–92.

Brontë, Charlotte. *Villette*. Harmondsworth: Penguin, 1979.

Brown, Julia Prewitt. *Cosmopolitan Criticism: Oscar Wilde's Philosophy of Art*. Charlottesville: University Press of Virginia, 1997.

Buckler, William E. "Building a Bulwark against Despair: 'The Critic as Artist.'" *English Literature in Transition* 32 (1989): 279–89.

Burgan, William M. "Little Dorrit in Italy." *Nineteenth-Century Fiction* 29 (1975): 393–411.

Butler, Judith. *Bodies That Matter: On the Discursive Limits of "Sex."* New York: Routledge, 1993.

———. "For a Careful Reading." In Seyla Benhabib et al., *Feminist Contentions: A Philosophical Exchange*. With an introduction by Linda Nicholson. New York: Routledge, 1995. 127–44.

———. *Gender Trouble: Feminism and the Subversion of Identity*. New York: Routledge, 1990.

Buzard, James. "'Anywhere's Nowhere': Bleak House as Autoethnography." *The Yale Journal of Criticism* 12 (1999): 7–39.

———. "Anywhere's Nowhere": Fictions of Autoethnography in the United Kingdom*. Princeton: Princeton University Press, forthcoming.

———. *The Beaten Track: European Tourism, Literature, and the Ways to "Culture," 1800–1918*. Oxford: Clarendon Press, 1993.

———. "Translation and Tourism: Scott's *Waverley* and the Rendering of Culture." *The Yale Journal of Criticism* 8 (1995): 31–59.

Calhoun, Craig, ed. *Habermas and the Public Sphere*. Cambridge: MIT Press, 1992.

Carlisle, Janice M. "The Face in the Mirror: *Villette* and the Conventions of Autobiography." *ELH* 46 (1979): 262–89.

Carlisle, Janice M. "*Little Dorrit*: Necessary Fictions." *Studies in the Novel* 7 (1975): 195–214.

Chase, Cynthia. "The Decomposition of the Elephants: Double-Reading *Daniel Deronda.*" *PMLA* 93 (1978): 215–25.

Cheah, Pheng. "Introduction Part II: The Cosmopolitical—Today." In *Cosmopolitics: Thinking and Feeling Beyond the Nation*. Edited by Pheng Cheah and Bruce Robbins. Minneapolis: University of Minnesota Press, 1998. 20–41.

Cheah, Pheng, and Bruce Robbins, eds. *Cosmopolitics: Thinking and Feeling Beyond the Nation*. Minneapolis: University of Minnesota Press, 1998.

Cheyette, Bryan. *Constructions of "the Jew" in English Literature and Society: Racial Representation, 1875–1945*. Cambridge: Cambridge University Press, 1993.

Clark-Beattie, Rosemary. "Fables of Rebellion: Anti-Catholicism and the Structure of *Villette.*" *ELH* 53 (1986): 821–47.

Cohen, Monica F. *Professional Domesticity in the Victorian Novel: Women, Work, and Home*. Cambridge: Cambridge University Press, 1998.

Cottom, Daniel. *Social Figures: George Eliot, Social History, and Literary Representation*. Minneapolis: University of Minnesota Press, 1987.

Craft, Christopher. *Another Kind of Love: Male Homosexual Desire in English Discourse, 1850–1920*. Berkeley: University of California Press, 1994.

Crosby, Christina. *The Ends of History: Victorians and "The Woman Question."* New York: Routledge, 1991.

Cvetkovich, Ann. *Mixed Feelings: Feminism, Mass Culture, and Victorian Sensationalism*. New Brunswick: Rutgers University Press, 1992.

Danson, Lawrence. *Wilde's Intentions: The Artist in His Criticism*. Oxford: Clarendon Press, 1997.

Daston, Lorraine. "The Moral Economy of Science." *Osiris* 10 (1995): 3–24.

———. "Objectivity and the Escape from Perspective." *Social Studies of Science* 22 (1992): 597–618.

Daston, Lorraine, and Peter Galison. "The Image of Objectivity." *Representations* 40 (1992): 81–128.

David, Deirdre. *Fictions of Resolution in Three Victorian Novels:* North and South, Our Mutual Friend, Daniel Deronda. London: Macmillan Press, 1981.

———. *Rule Britannia: Women, Empire, and Victorian Writing*. Ithaca: Cornell University Press, 1995.

Davidoff, Leonore, and Catherine Hall. *Family Fortunes: Men and Women of the English Middle Class, 1780–1850*. Chicago: University of Chicago Press, 1987.

DeLaura, David J. *Hebrew and Hellene in Victorian England: Newman, Arnold, and Pater.* Austin: University of Texas Press, 1969.

de Lauretis, Teresa. *Technologies of Gender: Essays on Theory, Film, and Fiction.* Bloomington: Indiana University Press, 1987.

Dellamora, Richard. *Masculine Desire: The Sexual Politics of Victorian Aestheticism.* Chapel Hill: University of North Carolina Press, 1990.

Derrida, Jacques. *The Other Heading: Reflections on Today's Europe.* Translated by Pascale-Anne Brault and Michael B. Naas. Bloomington: Indiana University Press, 1992.

Dickens, Charles. "The Chinese Junk." In *Miscellaneous Papers.* London: Chapman and Hall, 1908. 102–5.

———. "Insularities." *Household Words*, January 19, 1856.

———. *Little Dorrit.* Harmondsworth: Penguin, 1967, 1985.

Dickstein, Morris. *Double Agent: The Critic and Society.* New York: Oxford University Press, 1992.

Dollimore, Jonathan. *Sexual Dissidence: Augustine to Wilde, Freud to Foucault.* Oxford: Oxford University Press, 1991.

Dudley, Fred A. "Matthew Arnold and Science." *PMLA* 57 (1942): 276–86.

Eagleton, Terry. *Criticism and Ideology: A Study in Marxist Literary Theory.* London: Verso, 1978.

Edelman, Lee. *Homographesis: Essays in Gay Literary and Cultural Theory.* New York: Routledge, 1994.

Eliot, George. *Daniel Deronda.* Harmondsworth: Penguin, 1967.

———. "The Modern Hep! Hep! Hep!" In *The Essays of Theophrastus Such.* London: Everyman, 1995. 135–55.

———. "The Natural History of German Life." In *Selected Essays, Poems and Other Writings.* Edited by A. S. Byatt and Nicholas Warren. Harmondsworth: Penguin, 1990. 107–39.

Ellmann, Richard. "Introduction." In *The Artist as Critic: Critical Writings of Oscar Wilde.* Edited by Richard Ellmann. Chicago: University of Chicago Press, 1982; originally published 1968. ix–xxviii.

Endelman, Todd M. *Radical Assimilation in English Jewish History, 1656–1945.* Bloomington: Indiana University Press, 1990.

Fackenheim, Emil L. *Encounters Between Judaism and Modern Philosophy: A Preface to Future Jewish Thought.* New York: Schocken, 1980.

Faverty, Frederic E. *Matthew Arnold the Ethnologist.* Evanston: Northwestern University Press, 1951.

Felski, Rita. *The Gender of Modernity.* Cambridge: Harvard University Press, 1995.

Fish, Stanley. "Critical Self-Consciousness, or Can We Know What We're Doing?" In *Doing What Comes Naturally: Change, Rhetoric, and the Practice of Theory in Literary and Legal Studies.* Durham: Duke University Press, 1989.

Fish, Stanley. *Is There a Text in This Class? The Authority of Interpretive Communities*. Cambridge: Harvard University Press, 1980.

Forster, John. *The Life of Charles Dickens*. Edited by A. J. Hoppé. 2 vols. London: J. M. Dent & Sons, and New York: Dutton, 1966.

Foucault, Michel. *The History of Sexuality: An Introduction*. Vol. 1. Translated by Robert Hurley. New York: Random House, 1978.

―――. *Power/Knowledge: Selected Interviews and Other Writings, 1972–1977*. New York: Pantheon, 1980.

Fraser, Nancy. *Justice Interruptus: Critical Reflections on the "Postsocialist" Condition*. New York: Routledge, 1997.

Fuss, Diana, ed. *Inside/Out: Lesbian Theories, Gay Theories*. New York: Routledge, 1991.

Gadamer, Hans-Georg. "On the Scope and Function of Hermeneutical Reflection." In *Philosophical Hermeneutics*. Translated by David E. Linge. Berkeley: University of California Press, 1976. 18–43.

Gagnier, Regenia. *Idylls of the Marketplace: Oscar Wilde and the Victorian Public*. Stanford: Stanford University Press, 1986.

Gallagher, Catherine. "George Eliot and *Daniel Deronda*: The Prostitute and the Jewish Question." In *Sex, Politics, and Science in the Nineteenth-Century Novel*. Edited by Ruth Bernard Yeazell. Baltimore: Johns Hopkins University Press, 1986. 39–62.

Garrett, Peter. *The Grasp of Form* (forthcoming).

―――. *The Victorian Multiplot Novel: Studies in Dialogical Form*. New Haven: Yale University Press, 1980.

Gilbert, Sandra M., and Susan Gubar. *The Madwoman in the Attic: The Woman Writer and the Nineteenth-Century Literary Imagination*. New Haven: Yale University Press, 1979.

Gilroy, Paul. *Against Race: Imagining Political Culture Beyond the Color Line*. Cambridge: Harvard University Press, 2000.

Graver, Suzanne. *George Eliot and Community: A Study in Social Theory and Fictional Form*. Berkeley: University of California Press, 1984.

Greenfeld, Liah. *Nationalism: Five Roads to Modernity*. Cambridge: Harvard University Press, 1992.

Habermas, Jürgen. *The Inclusion of the Other: Studies in Political Theory*. Edited by Ciaran Cronin and Pablo De Greiff. Cambridge: MIT Press, 1998.

―――. *On the Logic of the Social Sciences*. Translated by Shierry Weber Nicholsen and Jerry A. Stark. Cambridge: MIT Press, 1988.

―――. *The Philosophical Discourse of Modernity*. Translated by Frederick Lawrence. Cambridge: MIT Press, 1987.

Haight, Gordon. *George Eliot: A Biography*. New York: Penguin, 1968, 1985.

Hall, Catherine. *White, Male, and Middle-Class: Explorations in Feminism and History*. Cambridge: Polity Press, 1992.

Harding, Sandra. *The Science Question in Feminism*. Ithaca: Cornell University Press, 1986.

Harman, Barbara Leah. *The Feminine Political Novel in Victorian England*. Charlottesville: University Press of Virginia, 1998.

Herbert, Christopher. *Culture and Anomie: Ethnographic Imagination in the Nineteenth Century*. Chicago: University of Chicago Press, 1991.

Herring, Paul D. "Dickens' Monthly Number Plans for *Little Dorrit*." *Modern Philology* 64 (1966): 22–63.

Hollinger, David A. *Postethnic America: Beyond Multiculturalism*. New York: Basic Books, 1995.

Huyssen, Andreas. *After the Great Divide: Modernism, Mass Culture, and Postmodernism*. Bloomington: Indiana University Press, 1986.

Jacobus, Mary, Evelyn Fox Keller, and Sally Shuttleworth, eds. *Body/Politics: Women and the Discourses of Science*. New York: Routledge, 1990.

Jaggar, Alison. *Feminist Politics and Human Nature*. Totowa, N.J.: Rowman and Allenheld, 1983.

Jordanova, L. J. *Sexual Visions: Images of Gender in Science and Medicine Between the Eighteenth and Twentieth Centuries*. Madison: University of Wisconsin Press, 1989.

Keller, Evelyn Fox. *Reflections on Gender and Science*. New Haven: Yale University Press, 1984.

Kucich, John. *The Power of Lies: Transgression in Victorian Fiction*. Ithaca: Cornell University Press, 1994.

————. *Repression in Victorian Fiction: Charlotte Brontë, George Eliot, and Charles Dickens*. Berkeley: University of California Press, 1987.

Lane, Anthony. "An Ideal Husband." *The New Yorker*, July 5, 1999. 89–90.

Langland, Elizabeth. *Nobody's Angels: Middle-Class Women and Domestic Ideology in Victorian Culture*. Ithaca: Cornell University Press, 1995.

Lanser, Susan Sniader. *Fictions of Authority: Women Writers and Narrative Voice*. Ithaca: Cornell University Press, 1992.

Larson, Janet. "The Arts in These Latter Days: Carlylean Prophecy in *Little Dorrit*." *Dickens Studies Annual* 8 (1980): 139–96.

Lawrence, Karen. "The Cypher: Disclosure and Reticence in *Villette*." *Nineteenth-Century Literature* 42 (1988): 448–66.

Lettis, Richard. *The Dickens Aesthetic*. New York: AMS Press, 1989.

Levine, George. "The Narrative of Scientific Epistemology." *Narrative* 5 (1997): 227–51.

————. *Dying to Know: Scientific Epistemology and Narrative in Nineteenth-Century England*. Chicago: University of Chicago Press. Forthcoming.

Lewis, Raina. *Gendering Orientalism: Race, Femininity, and Representation.* New York: Routledge, 1996.

Linehan, Katherine Bailey. "Mixed Politics: The Critique of Imperialism in *Daniel Deronda.*" *Texas Studies in Language and Literature* 34 (1992): 323–46.

Litvak, Joseph. "Charlotte Brontë and the Scene of Instruction: Authority and Subversion in *Villette.*" *Nineteenth-Century Literature* 42 (1988): 467–89.

Lloyd, David. "Arnold, Ferguson, Schiller: Aesthetic Culture and the Politics of Aesthetics." *Cultural Critique* 2 (1986): 137–69.

Lucas, John. *The Melancholy Man: A Study of Dickens's Novels.* Sussex: Harvester Press, 1970, 1980.

Lyotard, Jean-François. *The Postmodern Condition: A Report on Knowledge.* Translated by Geoff Bennington and Brian Massumi. Minneapolis: University of Minnesota Press, 1988.

McCarthy, Thomas. *The Critical Theory of Jürgen Habermas.* Cambridge: MIT Press, 1978.

———. *Ideals and Illusions: On Reconstruction and Deconstruction in Contemporary Critical Theory.* Cambridge: MIT Press, 1991.

McKillop, Alan D. "Local Attachment and Cosmopolitanism: The Eighteenth-Century Pattern." In *From Sensibility to Romanticism.* Edited by Frederick W. Hilles and Harold Bloom. New York: Oxford University Press, 1965. 191–218.

Marcus, Steven. "Culture and Anarchy Today." In *Culture and Anarchy.* Edited by Samuel Lipman. New Haven: Yale University Press, 1994. 165–85.

Martin, Carol A. "Contemporary Critics and Judaism in *Daniel Deronda.*" *Victorian Periodicals Review* 21 (1988): 90–107.

Metz, Nancy Aycock. "The Blighted Tree and the Book of Fate: Female Models of Storytelling in *Little Dorrit.*" *Dickens Studies Annual* 18 (1989): 221–41.

Meyer, Susan. "'Safely to Their Own Borders': Proto-Zionism, Feminism, and Nationalism in *Daniel Deronda.*" *ELH* 60 (1993): 733–58.

Mill, John Stuart. *Autobiography.* Edited by Jack Stillinger. Boston: Houghton Mifflin, 1969.

———. "Bentham." In John Stuart Mill and Jeremy Bentham, *Utilitarianism and Other Essays.* Edited by Alan Ryan. Harmondsworth: Penguin, 1987. 132–75.

———. "Coleridge." In John Stuart Mill and Jeremy Bentham, *Utilitarianism and Other Essays.* Edited by Alan Ryan. Harmondsworth: Penguin, 1987. 177–226.

———. "On Liberty." In *On Liberty and Other Essays.* Edited by John Gray. Oxford: Oxford University Press, 1991. 5–128.

―――――. "Utilitarianism." In John Stuart Mill and Jeremy Bentham, *Utilitarianism and Other Essays*. Edited by Alan Ryan. Harmondsworth: Penguin, 1987. 272–338.

Miller, D. A. *Narrative and Its Discontents: Problems of Closure in the Traditional Novel*. Princeton: Princeton University Press, 1981.

―――――. *The Novel and the Police*. Berkeley: University of California Press, 1988.

Myers, William. "George Eliot: Politics and Personality." In *Literature and Politics in the Nineteenth Century*. Edited by John Lucas. London: Methuen, 1971. 105–29.

―――――. "The Radicalism of *Little Dorrit*." In *Literature and Politics in the Nineteenth Century*. Edited by John Lucas. London: Methuen, 1971. 77–104.

Nadel, Ira Bruce. "'Wonderful Deception': Art and the Artist in *Little Dorrit*." *Criticism* 19 (1977): 17–33.

Nagel, Thomas. *The View from Nowhere*. New York: Oxford University Press, 1986.

Newton, Judith. "History as Usual?: Feminism and the 'New Historicism'." *Cultural Critique* 9 (1988): 87–121.

Newton, K. M. *George Eliot: Romantic Humanist*. Totowa, N.J.: Barnes and Noble, 1981.

Nord, Deborah Epstein. *Walking the Victorian Streets: Women, Representation, and the City*. Ithaca: Cornell University Press, 1995.

Nunokawa, Jeff. *The Afterlife of Property: Domestic Security and the Victorian Novel*. Princeton: Princeton University Press, 1994.

―――――. *Desire Lite*. Forthcoming.

―――――. "The Importance of Being Bored: The Dividends of Ennui in *The Picture of Dorian Gray*." In *Novel Gazing: Queer Readings in Fiction*. Edited by Eve Kosofsky Sedgwick. Durham: Duke University Press, 1997. 151–66.

Pateman, Carole. *The Disorder of Women: Democracy, Feminism, and Political Theory*. Stanford: Stanford University Press, 1989.

Pater, Walter. *The Renaissance: Studies in Art and Poetry*. Edited by Donald L. Hill. Berkeley: University of California Press, 1980.

Paxton, Nancy L. *George Eliot and Herbert Spencer: Feminism, Evolutionism, and the Reconstruction of Gender*. Princeton: Princeton University Press, 1991.

Perera, Suvendrini. *Reaches of Empire: The English Novel from Edgeworth to Dickens*. New York: Columbia University Press, 1991.

Pollock, Griselda. *Vision and Difference: Feminism, Femininity, and the Histories of Art*. London: Routledge, 1988.

Poovey, Mary. *Uneven Developments: The Ideological Work of Gender in Mid-Victorian England*. Chicago: University of Chicago Press, 1988.

Putzell-Korab, Sara M. "The Role of the Prophet: The Rationality of Daniel Deronda's Idealist Mission." *Nineteenth-Century Literature* 37 (1982): 170–87.

Ragussis, Michael. *Figures of Conversion: "The Jewish Question" and English National Identity*. Durham: Duke University Press, 1995.

Robbins, Bruce. *Feeling Global: Internationalism in Distress*. New York: New York University Press, 1999.

―――. *Secular Vocations: Intellectuals, Professionalism, Culture*. London: Verso, 1993.

―――. "Telescopic Philanthropy: Professionalism and Responsibility in *Bleak House*." In *Nation and Narration*. Edited by Homi K. Bhabha. New York: Routledge, 1990. 213–29.

Rorty, Richard. *Consequences of Pragmatism: Essays, 1972–1980*. Minneapolis: University of Minnesota Press, 1982.

Ruskin, John. "Of Queens' Gardens." In *Sesame and Lilies*. Edited by Robert Kilburn Root. New York: Henry Holt, 1901.

Schlereth, Thomas J. *The Cosmopolitan Ideal in Enlightenment Thought: Its Form and Function in the Ideas of Franklin, Hume, and Voltaire, 1694–1790*. South Bend: University of Notre Dame Press, 1977.

Scott, Joan Wallach. "Gender: A Useful Category of Historical Analysis." In *Gender and the Politics of History*. New York: Columbia University Press, 1988. 28–50. Originally published in 1986.

Sedgwick, Eve Kosofsky. "Paranoid Reading and Reparative Reading; or, You're So Paranoid, You Probably Think This Introduction is about You." In *Novel Gazing: Queer Readings in Fiction*. Edited by Eve Kosofsky Sedgwick. Durham: Duke University Press, 1997. 1–37.

Sharpe, Jenny. *Allegories of Empire: The Figure of the Woman in the Colonial Text*. Minneapolis: University of Minnesota Press, 1993.

Showalter, Elaine. *Sexual Anarchy: Gender and Culture at the Fin de Siècle*. New York: Viking, 1990.

Silver, Brenda R. "The Reflecting Reader in *Villette*." In *The Voyage In: Fictions of Female Development*. Edited by Elizabeth Abel et al. Hanover: University Press of New England, 1983. 90–111.

Sinfield, Alan. *The Wilde Century: Effeminacy, Oscar Wilde, and the Queer Moment*. New York: Columbia University Press, 1994.

Smith, Anthony D. *Theories of Nationalism*. New York: Holmes and Meier, 1983.

Smith, Barbara Herrnstein. *Contingencies of Value: Alternative Perspectives for Critical Theory*. Cambridge: Harvard University Press, 1988.

Snyder, Thomas S. "Matthew Arnold and the Irish Question." *The Arnoldian* 4 (1977): 12–20.

Steedman, Carolyn Kay. *Landscape for a Good Woman: A Story of Two Lives*. New Brunswick: Rutgers University Press, 1987.

Stocking Jr., George W. *Victorian Anthropology*. New York: The Free Press, 1987.

Stolnitz, Jerome. "On the Origins of 'Aesthetic Disinterestedness.'" *Journal of Aesthetics and Art Criticism* 20 (1961–62): 131–43.

Stone, Donald. *Communications with the Future: Matthew Arnold in Dialogue*. Ann Arbor: University of Michigan Press, 1997.

Suchoff, David. *Critical Theory and the Novel: Mass Society and Cultural Criticism in Dickens, Melville, and Kafka*. Madison: University of Wisconsin Press, 1994.

Taylor, Barbara. *Eve and the New Jerusalem: Socialism and Feminism in the Nineteenth Century*. London: Virago, 1983.

Taylor, Charles. *Sources of the Self: The Making of Modern Identity*. Cambridge: Harvard University Press, 1989.

Thompson, Dorothy. "Women and Nineteenth-Century Radical Politics: A Lost Dimension." In *The Rights and Wrongs of Women*. Edited by Juliet Mitchell and Ann Oakley. Harmondsworth: Penguin, 1976. 112–38.

Trilling, Lionel. *Matthew Arnold*. New York: Harcourt Brace Jovanovich, 1954. Originally published 1939.

———. *The Opposing Self*. New York: Viking Press, 1955.

Walkowitz, Judith R. *City of Dreadful Delight: Narratives of Sexual Danger in Late-Victorian London*. Chicago: University of Chicago Press, 1992.

———. *Prostitution and Victorian Society: Women, Class, and the State*. Cambridge: Cambridge University Press, 1980.

Wallach, Luitpold. *Liberty and Letters: The Thoughts of Leopold Zunz*. London: East and West Library, 1959.

Warner, Michael, ed. *Fear of a Queer Planet: Queer Politics and Social Theory*. Minneapolis: University of Minnesota Press, 1993.

Weber, Max. "Science as a Vocation." In *From Max Weber: Essays in Sociology*. Edited by H. H. Gerth and C. Wright Mills. New York: Oxford University Press, 1946. 129–56.

Welsh, Alexander. *George Eliot and Blackmail*. Cambridge: Harvard University Press, 1985.

Wilde, Oscar. "The Critic as Artist." In *The Artist as Critic*. Edited by Richard Ellmann. Chicago: University of Chicago Press, 1982. 341–408.

———. *De Profundis and Other Writings*. Harmondsworth: Penguin, 1986.

———. "The Decay of Lying." In *The Artist as Critic*. Edited by Richard Ellmann. Chicago: University of Chicago Press. 290–320.

———. *An Ideal Husband*. In *The Importance of Being Earnest and Other Plays*. Edited by Peter Raby. Oxford: Clarendon Press, 1995. 159–245.

———. *The Importance of Being Earnest and Other Plays*. Edited by Peter Raby. Oxford: Clarendon Press, 1995.

———. *Lady Windermere's Fan*. In *The Importance of Being Earnest and Other Plays*. Edited by Peter Raby. Oxford: Clarendon Press, 1995. 1–59.

Wilde, Oscar. "The Soul of Man Under Socialism." In *The Artist as Critic*. Edited by Richard Ellmann. Chicago: University of Chicago Press. 255–89.

―――. *A Woman of No Importance*. In *The Importance of Being Earnest and Other Plays*. Edited by Peter Raby. Oxford: Clarendon Press, 1995. 93–157.

Williams, Raymond. *The Country and the City*. New York: Oxford University Press, 1973.

―――. "Social Criticism in Dickens: Some Problems of Method and Approach." *Critical Quarterly* 6 (1964): 214–27.

Wolff, Janet. "The Invisible *Flâneuse*: Women and the Literature of Modernity." *Feminine Sentences: Essays on Women and Culture*. Berkeley: University of California Press, 1990. 34–50.

Wood, Mrs. Henry. *East Lynne*. New Brunswick: Rutgers University Press, 1984.

Yeazell, Ruth Bernard. *Fictions of Modesty: Women and Courtship in the English Novel*. Chicago: University of Chicago Press, 1991.

Young, Robert J. C. *Colonial Desire: Hybridity in Theory, Culture and Race*. New York: Routledge, 1995.

❖ Index ❖

Abraham, Gary A., 125n8
Adams, James Eli, 45n13
aesthetic disinterestedness, 92
Aesthetic Movement, 147
Alcoff, Linda, 24n17
Alderson, David, 151n8, 165
Anderson, Amanda, 44n11, 45n12, 71n19,
    82n30, 145n39
Antony, Louise M., 24n17
Armstrong, Nancy, 36–39, 42, 48, 50
Arnold, Matthew: abstract universalism,
    110–12; cosmopolitanism, 93–96, 108–12,
    116–18, 150–51; *Culture and Anarchy*, 93,
    103–4, 109, 111, 127–28; culture defined,
    64–65; disinterestedness, conception of,
    91–93; ethics, 116–18; Judaism, 127–28;
    modernity, 96–97, 101–2, 105–9, 112–15;
    moral character, 91, 97, 112–15; morality,
    96, 106–8; *On the Study of Celtic Litera-
    ture*, 98–101, 104–7, 118; race, 98–109,
    156–57; science, 102–8; state, role of the,
    115, 127–28
Auerbach, Nina, 49n18, 49n19, 51n21

Baker, William, 120n2
Benhabib, Seyla, 26–27
Bentham, Jeremy, 18
Bernard, Claude, 11
Bernheimer, Charles, 25n19, 174n25
Bhabha, Homi, 41n9
Bildung, 4, 6, 85, 114
Boone, Joseph Allan, 49n18, 49n19
Booth, Alison, 139n30
Bordo, Susan, 24n17
Bourdieu, Pierre, 30, 39
Boyarin, Daniel, 139n31, 144–45
Boyarin, Jonathan, 144–45
Brantlinger, Patrick, 132n21, 133n24
Brennan, Tim, 31n31, 65–66
Bristow, Joseph, 174n24
Brody, Jennifer, 40n9
Bromwich, David, 116n39

Brontë, Charlotte: cosmopolitanism, 51–52,
    63; femininity, 47–53, 55–59; moral charac-
    ter, 54–55; psychological detachment, 59–
    62; *Villette*, 46–62
Brown, Julia Prewitt, 149–50, 151–52n9,
    159
Buckler, William E., 150n6
Burgan, William M., 67n11, 68–69, 69n15,
    75n23
Butler, Judith, 26, 175–76
Buzard, James, 16, 65, 73n22

Calhoun, Craig, 25n20
Carlisle, Janice M., 49n17, 80n28
Carlyle, Thomas, 20
character, moral. *See* moral character
Chase, Cynthia, 132, 132n22
Cheah, Pheng, 31n30, 31n31, 64n2
Cheyette, Bryan, 125n9, 127n13
Clark-Beattie, Rosemary, 51n21, 51n22,
    52n23
Cohen, Monica F., 46n15
Collins, Wilkie, *Woman in White, The*, 46
cosmopolitanism: Arnold, 93–96, 108–12,
    116–18, 150–51; Brontë, 51–52, 63; con-
    ceptions of, 63–66; detachment, compared
    to, 30–32; Dickens, 66–71, 77–84, 88–90;
    Eliot, 29, 64, 66, 119–24, 129–33, 137–43,
    179; universalism and detachment, 31,
    178–79; Wilde, 150–51. *See also* travel
cosmopolitical, 31n31
Cottom, Daniel, 8n6, 136n27
Craft, Christopher, 147n1
critical reason, 7, 92–93, 115
critical theory, 25–28, 177–78
Crosby, Christina, 119–20, 120n1, 123n7,
    132–33, 132n23, 144
Cvetkovich, Ann, 120n1, 123n7, 136n27

dandyism, 7, 149, 158–62, 164–67, 170–73
Danson, Lawrence, 155, 155n14, 155n15,
    158n18